Consumption Intensified

Maureen O'Dougherty

CONSUMPTION INTENSIFIED

The Politics of Middle-Class Daily Life in Brazil

*Period covered in
book is 1980-1994*

DUKE UNIVERSITY PRESS

Durham & London

2002

© 2002 Duke University Press   All rights reserved

Printed in the United States of America on acid-free paper ∞

Designed by C. H. Westmoreland   Typeset in Bembo

with Gill Sans display by Keystone Typesetting, Inc.

Library of Congress Cataloging-in-Publication Data appear

on the last printed page of this book.

Some of the material in chapter 1 originally appeared as "Auto-Retratos da Classe
Média: Hierarquias de 'Cultura' e Consumo em São Paulo," in *DADOS—Revista de
Ciências Sociais* 41(2), 1998. Some of the material in chapter 5 originally appeared as
"Consumption and Middle Class Identity: Shopping during Brazil's Economic Crisis," in *Anthropology for a Small Planet: Culture and Community in a Global Environment,*
ed. Anthony Marcus. Ithaca: Brandywine Press, 1996. Some of the material in chapters 7 and 8 appeared as "The Devalued State and Nation: Neoliberalism and the
Moral Economy Discourse of the Brazilian Middle Class, 1986–1994" in *Latin American Perspectives* 26(1), 1999. All are cited here with permission.

to the memory of my father,

James Aquinas O'Dougherty

for my mother, Patricia Coyne,

and for Michel Ravaz

CONTENTS

ILLUSTRATIONS

ACKNOWLEDGMENTS

My debt to Brazilians who have educated me on the middle class stems from my first visit to the country to the present. I am ever grateful for the wonderful hospitality I enjoyed at the home of the family who hosted me in high school. Dr. Adherval, Dona Carminha, Malu, Carol, and Flávio Lins e Melo Torres made me one of the family, were my primary teachers of Portuguese, and opened up for me the unequal worlds of Recife and realities of the repression. During my next stay in Recife, Patrícia and Claudia Chaves taught me much about the political economic circumstances at work, gave advice on practicalities, and most of all, offered their unwavering friendship. My deepest gratitude goes to the Souto Silvas, the family of my former husband, Jorge, from Pão de Açúcar, Alagoas, Sr. Zequinha, and Tonho (may they rest in peace), Dona Haidea, Cira, Zélia, and their families; Zé, Rosele, Rosângela, and their families. Special thanks to Zé, reliable analyst of Brazilian economy, generous brother-in-law, adviser, and friend, and to Rosângela, for her understanding over the years. I am most indebted to Jorge. Besides benefiting from his rare intellectual sensibilities and erudition, I thank him for listening carefully to my commentaries on things I had seen and heard about class in Brazil. The concern all these friends have for Brazil and Brazilians gave me a sense of this middle class not often recognized.

Starting fieldwork in a city of more than 17 million in which I had one casual acquaintance was daunting. Paulinho "da Macedônia" and Claudia housed me during a prefieldtrip visit to São Paulo in 1991. Their open invitation thereafter, Paulinho's political commentary with a sharp Nordestino perspective, the music he fostered, and Claudia's empathy made this a second home for me. For hospitality and friendship during my return trip in 1996, I thank Adriana Monte.

Many colleagues in São Paulo gave invaluable support and critical commentary on my fieldwork. In the department of anthropology at the Universidade Estadual de Campinas (UNICAMP), Sueli Kofes de Almeida, Adriana Piscitelli, Célia Sakurai, and especially Mariza Corréia gave me ongoing support and ever relevant advice. I thank historian Leila Mezan Algranti of UNICAMP for providing crucial assistance in obtaining a school's consent to participate in the study; Clarice Herzog for allowing me to work with transcriptions from focus groups held by Standard, Ogilvy, and Mather; Guilherme Medina for his support and pertinent questions on the middle class; and Ceres de Arantes Leite Sassy and Lucy Ribeiro Frey for their excellent transcriptions. Sociologist Heitor Frúgoli arranged for me to give a seminar on middle classes and consumption at the Núcleo de Estudos de Consumo e de Cultura at the Fundação Getúlio Vargas. Historian Francisco Alembert's hilarious commentaries were pertinent for chapter 5. Chico's sister Paola Armelin housed me in Miami and made it possible for me to waste no time in becoming acquainted with the Brazilian outlets there. Above all, anthropologists Danielle Ardaillon and Esther Império Hamburger (of the Universidade de São Paulo) steered me through fieldwork. With Esther's invitation, I was able to participate in a forum at CEBRAP Centro Brasileiro de Análise e Planejamento, on the media, relevant for chapter 6. Esther lent her creative mind to my questions, offered friendship and hospitality, and was such a dynamic positive assistance at every moment of the fieldwork that I can hardly begin or end thanking her.

Trips to Rio were always welcome, reenergizing experiences. At the Museu Nacional, Gilberto Velho acquainted me with relevant ethnographies of Rio and made critical interjections, especially useful for chapter 1. For assistance obtaining news clippings of the Collor period helpful for chapter 6, and her enthusiasm, I thank Lys France Portella. It is hard to express in words my affection and gratitude to historian Fernanda Baptista Bicalho of the Universidade Federal Fluminense and Martha Bicalho, dear friends in Rio who provided much-needed respite from fieldwork, sisterly hospitality, and support, and were both confidantes and astute commentators on my research.

Brazilianist colleagues from the United States with whom contact has been enriching include Bert Barickman, Seth Garfield, Jerry Lombardi, and John Norvell. Special thanks to Robin Sheriff for her perspective "do morro," to Cristiana Bastos for her breadth of knowledge, and to Donna Goldstein for her good-humored debates and solidarity. Also doing research in São Paulo at the same time as I, historian Jeff Lesser was a delightful adviser-friend. His ironic wit on the ongoing state of affairs and his lovely family made life there much more sane and enjoyable for me. I owe so much to historian Sueann Caulfield, who has been generous in every imaginable way: offering me her fine analytical mind and feminist perspective, warm encouragement, and wonderful hospitality in Rio, where she opened up her life and friends to me. Beyond her dedicated scholarship, Sueann's vivaciousness and love for Brazil are forever an inspiration to me. I had the honor of taking a course in Brazilian history from Warren Dean, who then served on my dissertation committee. Like so many of his students, I mourn his tragic, untimely death. Professor Dean's combination of excellence in scholarship and commitment to Brazil is a model to us all.

At the City University of New York (CUNY), I benefited greatly from committee members Jane Schneider, Vincent Crapanzano, and my adviser, Shirley Lindenbaum. In particular, I thank Jane for her course on commoditization and discussions of class and consumption; Vincent for his ability to enter into one's thought and move it onto another level; and Shirley for her open-minded commentary, careful guidance through the proposal and thesis writing, and continuing support. Steve Topik's critical guidance strengthened my work on politics in chapter 7. Barbara S. Weinstein's good spirit in undertaking the task of external reader of my lengthy dissertation and her meticulous review of it helped turn that phase into a step forward.

I was fortunate in having classmate-friends at CUNY whose faith in me was continuously encouraging. Those who generously pored over drafts of proposals and dissertation chapters, returning them with copious analyses and suggestions, include the late Hélio Belik, Elizabeth Chin, Arlene Dávila, Molly Doane, Jonathan Hearn, Trenholme Junghans, Yvonne Lassalle, Kate McCaffrey, and Ara Wilson. Their own work as well as direct assistance to me have been immensely helpful. Elizabeth's innovative work on consumption and African American children constantly redirects one's attention to inequality. Arlene's interventions on ethnicity and popular culture, her analytical clarity, and her urgent encouragements have moved me ahead many times. Yvonne's uncanny ability to double the stakes, or better, to dislodge the train of thought and locate it on a whole new plane is always an unexpected, refreshing, and restabilizing experience. The setting many of us shared as graduate students in a Long Island City brownstone also made its mark on my work.

Knowing Betina Zolkower was upstairs avidly working on her dissertation was a positive inducement beyond the direct discussions we had on class theory. Many others in New York provided invaluable solidarity to me over these years of writing. Thanks to Lori Bohm, Kimberly Flynn, Mitu Hirshman, Carmen Medeiros, and, especially, Vinny Tirelli.

Research for this book was completed with a Fulbright-Hays fellowship. Grants from the Graduate School and University Center of CUNY and P.E.O. Sisterhood assisted in the preliminary and write-up phases, respectively.

The most incisive critical assistance that helped turn the manuscript into final form was given by the two anonymous readers for Duke University Press. I am as grateful to them for challenging me as for their generosity in envisioning the work. Crucial, strategic advice at the last phase of writing was also provided by several colleagues: Molly Doane, Yvonne Lassalle, Barbara Weinstein, Marisa Quaglia, Sueann Caulfield, Arlene Dávila, Murphy Halliburton, and Aisha Khan. Graphic assistance was provided by Claudia Chaves, Kimberly Kowal, Michel Ravaz, Chris Scruton, and Cathy Spengler. I greatly appreciate the ongoing support given by editor Valerie Millholland, associate editor Miriam Angress, and assistant managing editor Justin Faerber, particularly at difficult moments of revision and the copyeditor's meticulous and light touch.

The revising of the manuscript toward publication commenced in New Haven, where colleagues at Yale University provided a congenial and stimulating environment. Thanks to K. David and Beth Jackson, Marisa and Jordano Quaglia, Patricia Pessar, Gil Joseph, and Stuart Schwartz in Latin American Studies. In anthropology, I owe special thanks to Linda-Anne Rebhun, who delights with her wealth of knowledge on the *nordeste*, and to Bill Kelly, whose deadpan wit, erudition, and solid thinking helped steer me through these past years. Eric Worby and Kira Hall were delightful, solidary colleagues. The Department of Family Social Science at the University of Minnesota and Graduate Liberal Studies of Hamline University subsequently offered welcome institutional and collegial support. At Hamline and Yale, students in my courses on middle classes invigorated and deepened my comparative perspective on class.

Over the years, the support of family and friends has anchored me. My sister Peg gives me the wisdom of her experience in academia. My

sister Mary Ann also lived in Recife for a number of years. Her dedica-
tion to Brazilian music and culture always reminds me to counter stress
with purpose. With her, I thank Brazilian musicians for their art, which is
an inexhaustible resource. Special thanks to my mother, Patricia Coyne,
for her enthusiastic interest in and support of my academic endeavors. I
also benefit from her experience of class matters and the example she
gave to us through her work dedicated to counter social inequality. My
father, James Aquinas, who died before I started graduate school in
anthropology, gave me an inspiring example by abandoning work that
was not his and taking a risk to do work he loved as an attorney.
Longtime friend Mame Osteen and new friends Jeff Mittelmark, Fran
Lowell, Bryan Iwamoto, Marnie Larkin, Natalie Stoer, and Michael Garr
grounded me with their interest in my work, their creative titling, and
their excellent company.

For the most part, I wrote this book at home in Minneapolis, where
Michael Ravaz Mittelmark fills my life with "música, letra e dança," as
the song "Fullgás" goes. My efforts were bolstered by Michel's aesthetic
vision, startling quickness, and occasional visits to my study, which always brightened the atmosphere. Michel's love, buoyancy, and confidence in me created just the right balance to this solitary project.

I close with thanks to those who made my research possible. Special
thanks to school administrators who made the bridge between families of
their schools and me: Fernando José de Almeida, Thelma Ocdy, Helena
Yazbek, and Marília Ancona-Lopez (of the Universidade Paulista). I
thank the people who participated in the initial survey for their openness.
To those families who participated in the study from beginning to end, I
owe everything. All gave wonderful hospitality and generously shared
their time—so precious in the hectic city, especially during the crisis that
added such burden and stress. Additional thanks go to those parents and
their children who included me on special occasions and who maintained contact afterward. I thank the parents for their clarity of expression
and patience in working through the many issues. I was especially heartened by the seriousness with which they undertook involvement in the
project. I must ask them to *desculpar qualquer coisa*—forgive the inadequacies of my work—and to bear with me while I prepare Portuguese
versions of it. My best to all parents and children! *Que Deus lhes abençoe.*

INTRODUCTION

Middle-class Brazilian homes are graceful and gracious. Welcomed in from the hot sun into the cool, soothingly uncluttered interior, the visitor is offered refreshment, and later enjoined to dine with the family. If the stay is an extended one, the guest returns after a morning out to smells rising from this and neighboring kitchens of beans cooking and of fresh fruit being squeezed for the midday meal. The solicitous hostess has arranged for the cook to prepare three main dishes: a beef in tomato sauce, a pasta dish, and garlic chicken, or on a special day, seafood in palm oil and coconut sauce. The hostess's arrival, after her morning's work as volunteer director of an orphanage school, and a quick stop downtown to deliver fabric to the tailor, coincides with that of her husband, a doctor, whose light honk summons the maid to open the back gate. The two daughters arrive from their law- and medical-school studies; the son, in business school, will have lunch as usual with his fiancée. After lunch, one finds upstairs that the bedroom has been straightened, and one's freshly hand-laundered, perfectly ironed clothes lay carefully folded or hanging from the wardrobe. The austere white walls and dark wood furniture, the cool parquet floors constantly swept, mopped, or waxed by a softly moving domestic worker, the long, laterally opening, wooden shuttered windows, the shaded tiled terrace, the distinctive, predictable sounds of each street vendor, the back garden with its scent of jasmine, the night breeze gently moving the mosquito netting. Tropical, postcolonial luxury, intimacy, and formality present themselves with mesmerizing calm to the fortunate visitor at an upper-middle-class Brazilian home.

Backtracking, the visitor might note that privately contracted guards watch neighborhood streets or individual houses, whose high walls and barred windows further discourage intrusion. If the home is in an apartment building, tall gates and twenty-four-hour doormen control entrances from guard stations. Inside, two elevators separate residents and their guests from service workers, a (now notorious) system that segregates by color as well as by class or occupation. In this society, such demonstrations of class and status are ubiquitous, reinforced through redundancy, and organized by principles of social separateness and form.

These are recollections from my first stay in Recife. Returning ten years later, I witnessed the following scene. At the Bom Preço super-market checkout line, housewives would be flanked by two to three shopping carts filled to the brim with several foot-long bars of laundry soap, mounds of sugar sacks, cans of cooking oil, sweetened condensed milk and Nestle's powdered milk, extra milk bags to freeze, many kilos of meat, dozens of oranges, varieties of bananas ripe to dark green, and so on. This apparent excess was not merely to sustain large households, but rather to get a jump on the next inflationary hike in prices. I remember thinking one day while standing in the checkout line, "this is not war-time," yet the tactic of stockpiling lent an odd urgency to grocery shop-ping. Several years later, after spiraling inflation and recession had over-whelmed the country for more than a decade, I learned from the news of a more unprecedented response by middle-class Brazilians: all over the country they took to the streets to impeach (ex)President Fernando Collor de Mello for corruption.

These images refer us to historical moments. The first are from the Brazilian economic miracle of 1968–73, a period of remarkable growth of the national product and of Brazil's middle classes. This coincided with the military regime's harshest repression, when outside the pro-tected interiors, one's movement through the hushed streets could be disturbed by the military doing exercises, by the foreboding sight of their bases on the edges of town, by the abrupt car search, or worse. The grocery store and impeachment images belong to the democratic phase, from 1985 forward, when the nation suffered its worst and longest eco-nomic crisis since the 1930s, exerting extraordinary force on people's lives. It is important never to lose sight of the fact that Brazil's crisis disproportionately and severely prejudiced working classes, whose em-ployment itself was most targeted by the recession, whose wages did not receive the kinds of protections against inflationary losses extended to middle and upper classes, and whose living conditions and classist and racial discriminations against them make them victimized by violence of all kinds. Yet during this time the supports of middle-class living—job security, education, home ownership, savings, ease of consumption— were also shaken, for all but the wealthiest. By the 1990s, with "crisis" an apparently ineradicable reality, the means, the meaning, and what I will call for now without elaboration the *project* of this middle class were put into question.

"Go soon, before it [the Brazilian middle class] disappears," "that will be quick work" and even "that will be archaeological research": sardonic comments by my Brazilian graduate-school classmates suggesting that the middle class was nearing extinction set me thinking about the ways to approach my fieldwork of 1993–94, when inflation of 2,700 percent broke all previous records. These scenarios and comments should elicit any number of questions. One might well ask: How many Brazilians in the 1970s lived under such privileged and protected conditions? Did the same people really end up behind grocery carts during the inflation crisis and on the streets protesting? Can the people depicted in each scenario all be said to belong to the "middle class"? These empirically and somewhat skeptically phrased questions touch on what this book is about: how middle-class Brazilians redefined their identities in a context of political and economic instability. It raises questions about a social category that has been central to twentieth-century development, yet seldom studied outside the so-called First World or Global North. In the process, the work uncovers assumptions about the category middle class in theory and popular culture.

Theory offered useful but limited directives for this research. Analytical theorists (e.g., Wright 1989) have identified the complex locations that old and new middle classes occupy in the economic structure. The political economy perspective underscores middle-class heterogeneity and instability; most important, it directs our attention to the fact that class is about social inequality. Theoretical discussions cannot tell us, however, how people experience class or how they "define" it (verbally and actively). My research aim was precisely to understand the native self-understandings and practical realizations of class as these were worked out "on the ground," processually, and from there, to reflect on what that story tells us about middle classes.

This book, then, is an effort to further our understanding of middle classes by locating a particular middle class in place and time and by conceptualizing this social category through the everyday practices and discourses of middle-class people. It identifies consumption and discursive claims of "cultural" and "moral" superiority as foundational to the attainment, maintenance, and performance of middle-class identity and boundaries. Although my work is very much about Brazil and Brazilians, it addresses debates concerning middle classes and everyday life in capitalist modernity elsewhere.

FROM MIDDLE CLASSES TO MIDDLE CLASS AND BACK

The challenges with this research project ranged from the theoretical to the practical. Much of what is said or understood about the concept of middle class refers to Europe and the United States, whose hegemony makes their middle classes the international standard.[1] What happens with these theories when we study a location outside the First World or Global North where, among other differences, the middle class is a minority rather than a sizable demographic group? More generally, what if certain features that underlie and thereby construct this category are altered in some way? Can those under survey still be called middle class? Questions arise over the diversity of the category middle class within and across national contexts.

There are two immediate and apparently reasonable recourses for research on middle classes. One impulse is to rely on subcategories like upper middle, middle middle, and lower middle. Yet if income brackets were all that was needed to clarify the meaning of class, we could contact the internal revenue service and our work would be done. Although such terms can indicate a rich amalgam of subjective understandings, these are rendered opaque by the shorthand phrasing. Is it not the case that to resort to such commonplace terms without analysis begs the question? We know that all classes are heterogeneous. Why the insistence about the diversity of this class in particular?

Besides this latching onto familiar designations of internal differences, a second recourse (which often follows) is to identify one sector, fraction, or subgroup of this larger, amorphous, contentious category as representative or typical. This group, duly described, is then used to provide answers to questions about a generic middle class. I came to realize, however, that the reasoning behind the attempt to find the mainstream group within this heterogeneous class is erroneous and can easily lead to fundamental problems impeding analysis. It is worth pursuing this line of thinking further in order to better expose its problems.

The question of internal variation is pertinently raised in Patillo-McCoy's (1999) *Black Picket Fences,* an ethnography of a black middle-class neighborhood of Chicago bordering the "inner city," where the African American residents are subjected to poor city services, including schools, and to vulnerabilities relating to the proximity of crime and poverty. A heated debate arose in my class after one student wondered whether the subjects of her study could therefore be called middle class, while others attacked the presumption implied by the question. Notwithstanding, one might still hold onto the notion that there are circumstances in which this question is appropriate. One might be persuaded of the need to look for "more mainstream" versions of the class not so much because of the universally accepted fact that middle classes are internally differentiated, but owing to the commonsense notion that some subgroup is the most representative.

The opening paragraphs of this work describe what some would be skeptical of calling middle class—and I include Brazilians among those objecting against applying the term to an upper middle sector with such a lifestyle. As I found, the pull toward a lower sector is strong. It was, in fact, the second scenario, of a middle middle class doing household shopping, that prompted me to conduct the study. Yet although middle-class Brazilians all over the country were in supermarket lines, I decided to work among middle-class people in an area that was undeniably central to the country—São Paulo—rather than in the marginal Northeast. In retrospect, I can say that there is no problem with selecting a group for focus, and indeed it must be done. However, to do so unreflectingly can reify some middle-class people as an unproblematic or more worthy mainstream; it can reinforce rather than analyze a stereotype.

To illuminate our understanding of processes defining middle classes and contestations of the category, my work goes against the understandable tendency to zero in on the heterogeneity of the middle class, which then imperceptibly slides into an almost automatic assumption that there are standards for identifying the (one) "right" middle-class sector. As a later section describes more graphically through social geography, the tellingly arbitrary nature of these assumptions emerges in full force once one makes the move from theory to a qualitative study of middle class. My work confronts unacknowledged assumptions that emerge in contestations over the very designation of the term, over its mere application to a given group or individual. Rather than engage in a defense of this or that sector as middle class, I step aside to point out that the debate confusingly replicates a major preoccupation of the "natives"—that of attempting at all times to distinguish one's own kind from "others." I ask not what are the standards, but what are the processes of power whereby these standards are created and imposed.

Although I make several arguments in this book—notably about the political implications of middle-class consumption—this work is founded on the premise that we need to fundamentally change our approach to middle class as a necessary preliminary for studying it. We need to expose and then jettison the perspective that, without disclosing the terms of its authority, asserts the right to decide, qualify, and legitimate who belongs to the true or standard middle class and disqualify others. If caution is not exercised, we may end up reproducing native constructs as theory. It therefore makes sense to examine the role of native categories of difference and related practices in constituting social identity and reproducing inequality. It is naturally not the case that the native categories themselves provide "the" definition of middle class. But having the native constructs in direct view and bracketed off from the "noise" that theory can make is necessary for us to gain perspective about how native categories operate and, ultimately, how middle class is constituted.

Following anthropological methods, I examine subjective experiences and discourses. I consider middle-class home ownership, consumption, education, and work as means whereby middle-class people, materially and symbolically, attain and perform their class. Through these means, individuals position themselves vis-à-vis others—both of their own class and of other classes—and they understand and locate themselves in local, national, and transnational spheres. In adopting these procedures, I adhere to the conceptualization of middle class as historically constituted (Weinstein 1996) through social, economic, and political processes.

My analysis, though, is somewhat heterodox in comparison with the literature on middle classes and the native emphasis on difference within a broadly defined middle class: I focus as much or more on what is shared by middle-class Brazilians as I do on differences. Again, without ignoring important differences within the middle class underscored by scholars in many disciplines (e.g., J. A. G. Albuquerque 1977 and G. Velho 1981), I

nonetheless suggest that one productive protocol for middle-class research is to consider constructs of middle class*es* in light of a middle class
viewed in the singular. In this way, we may more readily gain an analytical
perspective on native categories of difference rather than reinsert them
in anthropological discourse. Instead of assuming difference, we can
examine problematic connections between groups and social spheres
held to be separate within the more broadly defined middle class. We can
gain critical perspective on the insistence, or better, the investment, by
middle-class people in defining boundaries, finding and creating distinctions (Bourdieu 1984), in constructing their sector as occupying a totally
separate incommensurable universe from an "other" (adjacent sector of
the class or other class). This is one of the ways the class partakes in a
similar social project (see G. Velho 1981, 137; DaMatta 1990; García
Canclini 1995a, 45).[2]

One of the main lines of difference remarked on by all is Brazil's
regional variation. The North Amazonian region, with mineral wealth
and agriculture, and the Central West deep inland, with tropical grass-
lands and agriculture, share frontier-like growth qualities. They still have
sparse populations; most indigenous Brazilians live in these regions. The
colonial Northeast has varying microclimates: in the coastal tropical area
sugar cane, tobacco, and other cash crops predominate, while inland are
semi-arid and drought areas of mixed farming and ranches. It contains
over one-quarter of the nation's population, including a significant proportion of Brazilians of African descent. The Southeast has a range of
qualities: from coastal colonial to inland frontier, from tropical to semi-
tropical climates. It is the nation's industrial center, yet also has strong
agricultural production (coffee, oranges, and more) and the densest population. The pampas of the temperate South region bordering Argentina
have a balance of agriculture, ranching, and manufacturing. In the late
nineteenth and early twentieth century, many European and Japanese
immigrants settled in the South and Southeast.

The regional differences between the colonial Northeast and the
modern Southeast are pronounced. The family and household I became
acquainted with in Recife was of an upper-middle-class urban sector,
whose parents came from the declining agricultural elite of the Northeast. The Paulistanos (residents of the capital city of São Paulo) of my
study were often first- to third-generation immigrants from Europe or

Japan, whose parents had worked in modest occupations in rural São Paulo or the capital city. The generation of my study had enjoyed dramatic upward mobility thanks to their parents' efforts, their racial classification as white (Andrews 1991), and the 1960s economic boom, which produced the largest middle class in Brazil in the Southeast region (Quadros 1991). It is important to recognize these divergent experiences and regional and historical contexts; indeed this work is based on the "situated knowledges" (Haraway 1988)—that is, the contextual understandings—of about fifty middle-class adults aged 35–55, born or raised in the city or state of São Paulo, and living with their families in the capital in the 1990s.

At the same time, it has been well argued that the expansion of Brazil's middle classes during the economic miracle gave rise to collective aspirations and desires, with an idealized standard of how to be middle class (Guimarães 1987; Oliveira 1988), even when most Brazilians have been excluded from it (Faria 1983). Although the image of the lower-middle-class family is amply represented in Brazilian media, it is not the ideal. That status goes to the upper middle class, whose favorable depiction in the media includes those in Northeastern settings. Furthermore, different sectors of this class all over Brazil share a number of privileged conditions, such as being able to live in standardized housing cared for by a domestic worker. However, with due respect for the very different potentials and constraints on members of this heterogeneous class (whose variation will quickly become obvious among my informants), even the prosperous members are not the powerful elite. Furthermore, middle-class Brazilians share in their instability within and across generations. Indeed, even the subdivision of new versus old middle classes splintered in this era when a chemistry major went into clothing sales and an engineer opened a juice bar. Finally, the generalized nature of the crisis of the 1980–90s created conditions whereby a large portion of the class across the nation shared certain significant structural and subjective experiences. Thus partly in reaction to the native insistence on the ways they differ from a generic middle class (which I take to be a symptomatic middle-class preoccupation with symbolic boundaries), and partly in recognition of the important common grounds across these lines of difference, I emphasize similarity and singularity—middle class, not classes.

I chose to open this work with an image of a middle-class home in

Recife first for the simple reason that it was the means I had of connecting with my informants, who had reached adulthood in the prosperous authoritarian time period I had witnessed elsewhere in the nation. I retain this image as one that emphasizes how, compared to the majority of poor Brazilians, the middle class enjoys a lush private space where elevated social status is proclaimed, cared for, and safeguarded. I juxtapose the jarring contrasting images of the commercial site of frantic economizing and the massive middle-class politicization during the period of democracy and economic chaos in the 1980–90s to underscore the change. Regardless of location and detail and, ultimately, regardless of the accuracy of what is recalled of the past, the sense of inversion, as people put it, was shared by middle-class Brazilians across the nation, as their sense of past and hopes were contradicted by the experience of the inflation crisis.

There is yet one final reason why I refrain from directing attention to internal difference alone: I fear the perspective suffers from excessive realism and inattention to the social imaginary. Unlike class in theory, a good part of the middle-class experience seems to be immaterial, a state of mind. It is based on contingencies (in which more than one position is possible); it is experienced as what one would be (in which realism must be relativized or replaced with idealizations); it is formulated oppositionally, on what one would not be; and its constant (re)construction in the media takes on its own "realism." Rather than dwell solely on behavioral grounds, I sought to get a sense of the realm of desire and dream, as Williams (1982) so aptly captured for the emerging middle class of another time and place, and the implications of this ephemeral realm for the individuals and the society. This way, we might better grasp the meaning of *middle class* in a Third World nation bound and determined to participate in the global culture. By highlighting the overall shared patterns, investments, and discourses of middle-class Brazilians and about them in popular culture, I point to the project of this middle class—to participate in modernity. Echoing Velho (1980, 1981) and Campbell (1987), my sense of class motivation moves beyond instrumental status intentions.[3] Rather, I conceptualize it more broadly as a class project, in which the efforts and performances involve material as well as symbolic means and ends. What is more, this project (easy for subjects to recognize, hard to describe) has social and political repercussions.

The perspective of middle class I eventually derived from this study developed first from a decentering move to the so-called Third World or Global South, and second, by a methodology and analysis focused on daily-life efforts to attain this goal despite national constraints. Through the categories, practices, and discourses produced by a particular group of people in a unique context, I identify processes that reveal how this middle class defines itself at a particular moment. However, comparable processes are doubtless operative for "other" middle classes. I refer to issues best shown through the ethnography itself, for example, avowals and disavowals of the material bases of their class; strategies of symbolic boundary making, particularly assertions of distance and superiority through consumption and claims that one's own "culture," "morality," or "race/ethnicity" is distinct from that of others; critical evaluations of the nation, state, and national culture—but here the North-South divide resurfaces, as I allude to ambivalent and negative attitudes. This point brings us back full circle to the question of difference, this time to underscore it. For it is also crucial to see that one's historical and current location makes a lot of difference. Thus I argue, finally, that it is in the tension between the specific and diverging realities and imaginings of middle-class people worked out in a field of local, national, and transnational power, and their sometimes strikingly common preoccupations and tactics that we can get a closer sense of what *middle class* means. Through a dual vision (material/immaterial, commonality/difference, social practice/context), we can better grasp how middle class is constituted as a social group and category, and the difference location makes.

THE MUNDANE POLITICS OF CONSUMPTION AND DISCOURSES ON "CULTURE"

This work conceptualizes the positions of middle-class Brazilians as multiply defined through social, economic, and political processes. My criteria for choosing which areas of daily life to look at most closely derived in part from insights and impasses in the analytical literature on class, which itself had been calling for study of processes and subjectivities (see J. A. G. Albuquerque 1977; Wright 1989; Frow 1993); from the literature on consumption, which constantly associates middle classes and consumption,[4] and from the Brazilian context. Having witnessed

Brazil's growing inflation crisis, I knew that consumption would be a particularly vexing aspect of middle-class life. Nonetheless, I was still unprepared for the great extent and weight of consumption in both private and public realms. Inflation demands an excruciating attention to monetary detail; consumption issues made newspaper headlines throughout the 1980s and 1990s.

Consumption is a major focus for this study. I take the association drawn in the literature between consumption and class one step further, showing that consumption is central to middle-class self-definition, not only in prosperity, as has more usually been shown, but in any and all circumstances, even in recession. While I emphasize the importance of the economic bases of capitalist society, I do not assume that productive activities, usually translated into occupational categories, are the sole foundation of class identity or political practice. Rather, I highlight the ever increasing centrality of consumption.[5] Appadurai finds that the "work" of consumption has become the "central preoccupation of otherwise very different contemporary societies" (1996, 83). I give due attention to the social aspects of consumption, but do not stop at social expressions of identity. Instead I also investigate the ways consumption engages people in ongoing stratification processes. Many previous studies of consumption have been criticized for ignoring its class basis.[6] The fact that consumption is predicated on inequality has not been lost in research into middle classes outside the First World (Appadurai 1990; Abu-Lughod 1990; Lee 1993; Nash 1994; Wilk 1994; García Canclini 1995a; Pinches 1999). Like these decentered studies, I show that the class project to attain social distinction and global modernity through consumption engages middle-class people in the local reproduction of inequalities. In turn, the transnational engagements reinforce rather than reduce hierarchies among nations. Thus I draw out the political dimensions of consumption, both transnationally and nationally.

In wealthy countries with sizable middle-class populations, middle-class people seem to inhabit a kind of buffer zone wherein the political dimensions of daily life can often be occluded. Elsewhere, the politics of daily life and of consumption in particular are quite apparent and difficult to avoid. To consume is itself a political act; as García Canclini puts it, "To consume is to participate in a field of disputes over goods that the society produces and over the ways of using them" (1995a, 18).[7] The question I ask is not so much whether middle classes engage in formal politics, but in what ways their activities and discourses are political. Brazil's democratic era coincided with an inflation crisis of such vast proportions that the politics of consumption and of middle-class life became unusually overt. Indeed, it seems no accident that the biggest middle-class movement in twenty-five years occurred to impeach a president who not only was corrupt, but whose drastic economic policies literally confiscated people's savings accounts, hence directly and severely straining middle-class consumption (see also Meade 1997).[8] The middle-class people described in this work therefore offer particularly wide-ranging, salient, and overtly political expressions of class identity through consumption.

Besides the burgeoning literature on consumption and the ethnography discussed earlier on the black middle class in the United States, other key ethnographies of middle classes offered me suggestions for how to analyze middle classes in daily life. Newman's (1988) work draws out how the middle-class members of various occupational groups affected by downward mobility in the United States interpreted their misfortunes and evaluated their worth in comparison to others of their class self-critically in terms of prevalent ideologies of individualism, mobility, and "success." This work underscored for me the value of examining middle-class Brazilians' interpretations of their circumstances in light of aspirations for themselves and their families, in comparison to others of their class, and in terms of societal ideologies (Ortner 1991; Rapp 1978; Vanneman and Cannon 1987).

The scope of my work is also limited to middle-class people, in this case, people undergoing not individual downward mobility so much as mass downsliding under recessionary conditions. Given the grave inequalities in Brazil's class structure and the generalized nature of the crisis, I was less interested in verifying downward mobility than in asking what material and symbolic measures middle-class people were taking to maintain their standing. The threatening conditions afforded me the opportunity to get at what middle-class Brazilians deemed essential. Practices and discourses undertaken to maintain their own and their family's standing indicated what people regarded as foundational to their class identity. Relevant practices among my informants ranged from dedicating a large portion of family income to children's private schooling and going to Disney World, to elaborate comparison shopping for ordinary goods and transnational contraband shopping for high-status products, to housewives' entering the informal economy, to everyone's criticizing the government. I was especially interested in what interpretive frameworks and underlying ideologies of class would be revealed. Maria Regina and Ricardo's situations are illustrative.

In 1993–94, grade-school teacher Maria Regina, her husband, Ricardo, a technician, and their three girls lived in a two-bedroom apartment in Pinheiros, which they bought soon before the crisis began, with government-subsidized financing. Like hundreds of other high-rise apartments in São Paulo, this one was built in the late 1970s, when the south and west zones underwent the vast expansion that turned the city into the quintessential "concrete jungle" that distinguishes it. The tall, narrow, stark buildings of ten or more stories that uniformly line these streets, each with a guard post at the sidewalk, summon up a strong sense of function rather than style.

What was happening was not an extinction, as colleagues had put it; rather, as I heard repeatedly, the middle class lost its character (*descaracterizou-se*); there was an inversion of class. With spirit, Regina told me: "We got married in 1978, and we have three children, born in 1981, '83, '84. So we really caught the beginning of all this mess of the country. When the children were born, I left the state job. My husband worked all day long. And we sustained our children on this, private school for the three. Today I work from 7:30 in the morning to 7 at night. I give almost fifty class hours per week. I doubled my hours." In 1993 they withdrew the oldest daughter from private school. Ricardo denounced their situation as "completely inverted. Her with two jobs, me with an extra one." From the countryside, Regina likened her workday to rural workers condemned to eat a cold lunch in the fields: "Eu levo marmita. Virei bóia fria" [I carry a lunch box. I became a day laborer].

Another work stimulating my own was Frykman and Lofgren's (1987) ethnohistorical study of the emerging middle classes of nineteenth-century Sweden, which revealed the importance—impossible to overstate—of home life to middle-class constitution. Home-owner demarcations of domestic space and consequent regulations of the circulation of domestic workers, as well as discourses of purity and attendant moralizing condemnation of working-class people, provided striking examples of material and symbolic efforts at boundary making. Accordingly, my work investigates the meaning of home ownership; and it identifies practices and discourses directed toward creating or maintaining social boundaries. I pay particular attention to resentment of poor people and to moralizing discourses aimed at adjacent sectors, for example, claims of different values in education and "culture." Marcos's comments pertain to the latter.

Also living in Pinheiros in one of the more recently built apartments that features a fancy facade but a similarly boxy interior space, Marcos, a young, successful psychologist, spoke of inversion in reference to a new minority that emerged in the crisis: "They took the place of the others with less money, these people who were middle class. . . . Today you see lots of people riding around in imported cars and they don't have the least bit of culture. There is this inversion. It is not only economic, it's cultural." In Portuguese, the term *cultura* connotes schooling and upbringing, the latter associated with "refined" manners and pursuit of high culture. People are seen as having or lacking culture. Note Marcos's disavowal of the material basis for acquiring cultural capital and his sense of what ought to be, conveyed by the term *inversion*.

These ethnographies on material and symbolic dimensions of middle-class work and home life indicate some ways in which social inequality is experienced and reproduced in middle-class private life. Studies of race in Brazil (Hasenbalg 1979; Scheper-Hughes 1992; Fontaine 1985; Andrews 1991; M. Lima 1995; Sheriff 1997; Guimarães 1997; Norvell 1997; Winddance-Twine 1998; Reichmann 1999; Hanchard 1999; Goldstein 1999) directly demonstrate on-the-ground relations forged by upper and upper middle classes interacting with (against) working classes, as do studies of social geography. The global trend to enclosed shopping malls, which developed in the 1980s in Brazil, and the spatial segregation of wealthy Brazilians in gated communities (*condomínios fechados*), or with high-security systems intended to defend homes against burglary, present a disturbing trend in social inequality, as Pintaudi and Frúgoli (1992) and Caldeira (1996 and 2001), respectively, discuss. Caldeira's ethnography of how wealthy Paulistanos have responded to violence by creating high-security systems and segregated living reveals the undemocratic implications of private measures ensuring only the protection of the wealthy. Given the thorough, compelling, and immediate relevance of her work, I chose to attend to ways in which social inequalities were furthered by consumption practices and characterized in discourses of (less wealthy) middle-class Brazilians.

In particular, I focus on practices of local and global consumption that received a great commitment of time and concern. Despite agreement that a study of consumption in everyday life is the "royal road" to understanding middle classes, few analysts, as noted in Morris (1988) and Fine (1995), take the "low road" (but see Lave 1988). Yet the place and import of high-status goods or the frequenting of shopping centers can be only very partially understood if one does not study them in relation to the mundane routines of daily life. While I dedicate a part of the work to the loftier forms of transnational consumption, these need to be viewed against the local world of everyday consumption as experienced by middle-class Brazilians. In so doing, I show how both kinds of engagements further inequalities within and across social classes. Looking at the procurement of goods and experiences in unremarkable sites (supermarkets, banks) and the means employed (comparison shopping, stockpiling), as well as at remarkable sites (Disney) and means (e.g., contraband of microwaves), I also draw attention to the ways that desire and value, and frustration and politics, were developing together, creating a dual vision—of the immediate reality of crisis and the desired reality of the First World.

As the preceding examples show, besides practices in work and consumption, I highlight discourses—arguments pronounced in similar fashion that I kept hearing—about education and culture, about the nouveaux riches and poor Northeasterners of color, about the decline of middle-class liberal professions and the rise of small business, about governmental and societal corruption. These reiterated practices and commentaries were, I surmised, preoccupations motivated by class aims. I maintain that just as certain aspects of consumption were "plotted," so too did informal discourse about one's self, class sector, class, other social groups, and the nation comprise a set of arguments about and constructive of middle class. Thus when I speak of everyday practices constituting middle-class identity, I also mean signifying agents and discursive practices. Unlike writers of works on consumption or class that consider only the ways people actively elaborate identities through practices, thereby unwittingly suggesting that people are only intuitive and/

or that their understandings are irrelevant, I am directly concerned with the stories people tell and hear about themselves (P. Jackson 1993; Campbell 1994). This work illustrates ways in which class is constituted in informal language contexts; it shows that discursive constitution (by middle-class people and about them in the media) is integral to its identity formation.

The media has been an extremely important agent in the process of identity construction, through its *telenovelas* (soap operas) and news reports (Miceli 1972; Lins da Silva 1985; Leal 1986; Kottak 1990; A. Albuquerque 1993; Matos 1994; Fausto Neto 1994; Hamburger 1999). In this social imaginary the Brazilian middle class symbolizes a national ideal in part because of its "modernity." This modernity is most often proved through consumption practices, locally, nationally, and transnationally conferred (Ortiz 1991; García Canclini 1995a, 1995b), or deferred, hence denied. Throughout the work, I emphasize the involvement of the media in constructing images, definitions, and interpretations of middle-class Brazilians. For instance, in recurring newspaper headlines on inflationary hikes phrased like the following—"For the middle class the dream is over" (*Folha de São Paulo* 10/13/87)—the object of dream is always consumption.

Such ethnographies guided my selection of areas of special focus for this study of the politics of middle-class private life; they also provided an important lesson on method and analysis. Significantly, the ethnographies from the United States, Sweden, and Brazil pay dual attention to discourse and practice—each studied on its own terms, but also, and especially, in relation to each other. To examine practice or discourse alone would have severely limited the works; a far more probing understanding was arrived at by analyzing the relation of discourse to practice and vice versa. If we fail to do some of this juggling, we may be in danger of excessive coherence and miss the opportunity so clearly indicated in feminist theory: to examine the complex relationship between experience and discourse, and their political dimensions. Accordingly, I do not relinquish discussion of homes, local and global consumption, work, the media, the national economy, and politics because it is through analysis of practices and discourses in relation to each other and produced within and against a field of power that we can understand the processes defining a given middle class.

LOCATING MIDDLE-CLASS BRAZILIANS IN SÃO PAULO

Before I move into the work itself, there is one final matter to discuss regarding my approach. A project aiming, as mine did, toward an understanding of the native construction of class (in the process of reshaping itself) should hardly make such a definitional judgment a priori. How, then, could I select middle-class Brazilians for the study? Indeed, as is common in fieldwork, my start-up problem turned into data. The following passage is intended not only as a recounting of how I located an actual "informant pool." More importantly, the process made me confront native categories of class and thereby prompted the change in my approach to middle class that grounds the arguments of this book.

When I told academic acquaintances in São Paulo that I was there to study "the Brazilian middle class," but was unfamiliar with this city of 17 million, they immediately tested me with questions of an analytical order: "What do *you* mean by middle class?" and "How do you define the middle class?" or more intriguingly, "*Which* middle class do you intend to study?" It quickly became clear that these advisers had a sense of which sorts of middle-class people belonged in my study. They suggested that I would find the most examples, that is, the most representative middle class, housed in the *bairro* (neighborhood, part of town) of Santana or Moóca. I soon learned that Santana, in the north zone, is famed for its "traditional" middle class, that is, petite bourgeoisie shopkeepers, often immigrants. (See Hansen 1976.) Recently, Moóca, in the east zone, has captured attention for producing a number of nouveau riche families. What strikes nonresidents as curious is that natives of Moóca, upon making it, stay there. "They feel better there," explained a Paulistano who was taking me on a car tour of some São Paulo neighborhoods my second week there. He insisted on driving me (along with his family) to Moóca to see it for myself. I could not then appreciate the nonresidents' astonishment that people who did not need to stay there did, for the area looked to my undiscerning eye like parts of the south zone of São Paulo—new high-rises adjacent to older townhouse-style homes. Only much later when I saw other bairros of the east zone did I realize what this zone, if not Moóca, was known for: slum housing in a vast industrial area. After the tour, I remembered a comment from my 1991 preliminary field trip to São Paulo when a woman asked me what I

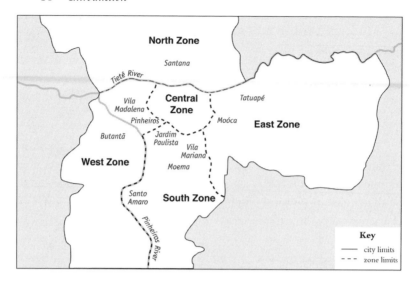

Zones and selected neighborhoods of greater São Paulo. Tourist maps show only the central zone and adjacent middle- and upper-class areas of the south and west zones as "São Paulo."

had come to know of the city. I told her, "Only downtown and the south zone as far as Santo Amaro," adding apologetically that I did not know anything of the north or east zones. This woman, a lifelong resident of Jardim América, raised her eyebrows and said, "Why, there's nothing there." The "Jardins" are those wealthy bairros (called noble in Brazilian Portuguese) in the south zone usually carrying the name Garden X (Jardim Paulista, Jardim América, Jardim Europa). Moóca was intriguing, but I decided that in an exploratory study I did not wish to focus on a curiosity.

The more I was pointed in the direction of the "traditional" middle classes in the east and north zones, the more I wondered about middle classes living in the south and west zones. Although any sector of the middle class would be worth studying, I was then most interested in the "new middle class" (Mills 1969) of salaried workers in liberal and technical professions. This sector is known for a rapid increase and upward mobility in Brazil in the 1960s and 1970s (Bresser Pereira 1962; Pastoré 1979, 1986; Quadros 1991) and is associated with Brazil's modernization and modernity—nowhere more so than in São Paulo, the nation's industrial center. How would members of this group, who had benefited from Brazil's previous economic expansion, respond to this major threat to their class standing? I decided that by working with families whose children attended respected private schools, I would find parents in this "white-collar" category. Their higher income range, as suggested by school tuitions (approaching US$300 per month), would ally the fear I then had of excessive internal diversity.

On learning that I wanted my pool of informants to derive from private schools in the south zone, local specialists were taken aback, then resumed a consistent stance, suggesting a school in the south zone said to be the choice of upwardly mobile immigrants. A few named a school characterized by the traditional conservatism of its upper-middle- to upper-class families. Just as with the indication of certain bairros, here again with private schools, I found insistence that the middle class is heterogeneous, a very different implication. Sectors were not merely varied; some sectors were more qualified, more ideal-typical representatives than others. The latter remained nameless, or were qualified as "alternative" or simply "not typical" middle class. Having come to what I imagined to be Brazil's largest demographic pool for the middle class, I was surprised to hear that its members were confined to a couple of bairros or attended very specific schools and were a very specific subgroup. In fact, some academic contacts even suggested I move out of town altogether, to do the study in Curitiba, Paraná, the city with the highest standard of living in Brazil (and a very white population).

This trail of directives recalls the old TV game show "To Tell the Truth," in which contestants competed to discover the true Mrs. (or Mr.) John Doe from the two impostors. At the end, the game host would demand: "Will the real Mrs. Doe please stand up?" My point is that after the actual and mental drives through parts of São Paulo, I chose a less "real" middle class than the academic standards recommended. At one level, their indication of what evidently was a classic middle class, in traditional petit bourgeois or nouveau riche forms, seemed perfectly reasonable. But I realized that I did not want to conflate the local stereotype with the "representative," so I moved away from the experts' suggestions. In this contrary effort, I learned that the group I was looking for was known by the name of "modern" middle class. Indeed, only when I specified that my interest was to study the modern middle class was I finally directed to the salaried liberal professionals and white-collar business people in the south and west zones who took part in the study.

I assume full responsibility for making a nonrandom and unorthodox sampling. I want to be clear that the subjects in my study were not chosen with expectations of their being "representative," "typical," or "middle middle," much less "mainstream," but rather for purportedly being part of a modern middle class. As it turned out, my arklike group of twenty-four families (chosen from an initial survey of forty-two households) included informants from all over the south and west zones: Vila Madalena and Pinheiros on the west, crossing through the Jardins to Vila Mariana, south to the Ibirapuera area, into Butantã and beyond. Informants' children attended three different schools, and the adults' occupations and material circumstances ranged from low-paid salaried teachers to doctors to small- and medium-sized business owners. One could argue that the families I worked with did exemplify a "typical" aspect of the middle class: its variability and instability. Although I prefer not to rely on designations of lower middle, middle middle, and upper middle, for this tends to reinforce these native categories unreflectingly, I will note that my informants included some families considered middle-class by official Brazilian standards and others who fell in higher income ranges.[9] Combined yearly household incomes for these families of five or six ranged from US$14,000 to US$85,000. Eleven of the families earned US$3,000 or less per month.

This pseudo tour of middle-class São Paulo shows that classism is readily proclaimed in a large, pervasive, versatile, and potent vocabulary even as it is stated inconsequentially. For local intellectuals the tendency was to take the part (the traditional petit bourgeois and the nouveaux riches) for the whole, the one viewed patronizingly, the other scornfully. The terms *traditional* and *modern* dichotomize the middle class into polar opposites; the geographic indicators reveal strong subdivisions of the status hierarchy. My calculated use of the singular provoked strong responses, indicating that I violated categories basic to constructs of self and other: it seemed unthinkable to contemplate the two as belonging in one broader social category. How would the informants I actually found respond to the identification of Brazilian middle class? Where would they place themselves?

This work as a whole is of course dedicated to addressing this question more amply. Yet it is interesting to note here that the people I met gave indications quite immediately. A teacher whose children attended the private school where she taught free of charge and whose husband was a mechanic said: "I don't know what class I am in. I come from a very poor family. I don't see so many changes [since the crisis]. It has always been hard." Lisete's response immediately distinguished her from most in my study, who instead emphasized the negative impact of the crisis and their prior prosperity. Similarly, I found some very wealthy people surveyed (and excluded) were relatively unable to articulate issues about the middle class, speaking rather of the poor (*favelados*). This dislocation left me unsure as to whether they categorized the two together as "popular," or whether they felt uncomfortable (unwilling or unable) to comment on the middle class. One such person did eventually comment from his luxury apartment in Moema that middle-class people were whining (*choramingando*) about some minor inconveniences. In contrast, those people with whom I worked gave incisive characterization of their middle-class identity, always relativized, like Simone's.

Degreed in chemistry, Simone was highly adaptive. First, in São Paulo, she worked at her husband's computer consulting business and lived in Alphaville, a gated community on the west side of São Paulo. Then, when her husband, a government employee, was transferred to Ribeirão Preto (the boomtown of São Paulo's agricultural belt, known as the California of Brazil), she worked as a sales rep selling advertising space. They returned to the city of São Paulo in the 1990s, leaving a trail of white-elephant houses. At the time I knew them, Simone was opening up a clothing boutique, and her family was living in a sparsely furnished rental apartment in Pinheiros, evidently several steps down from their prior lifestyle. But Simone put it differently: she didn't want to be a "slave of a big house." Her quizzical response to the gauche social science question I eventually asked people—"After all, how do you define the middle class?"—offers a perfect recap of the discussion of native constructs of middle class. Simone responded unhesitatingly: "A classe média é um sonho, é ilusão" [The middle class is a dream, it's an illusion].

OVERVIEW

Chapter 1 presents how informants explicitly defined their class: through home and car ownership in particular and through consumer goods and activities overall. The crisis threatened the attainment of these very goods. Informants accordingly qualified their definition in a hierarchy of consumption and investment standards in which the home was sacrosanct, but in which education and their cultural pursuits ranked over more frivolous forms of consumption associated with the nouveaux riches, who were a subject of frequent criticism. A strategy for intergenerational class continuity, education and cultural pursuits were presented as a value that separated my informants from other middle-class sectors. Thus chapter 1 identifies informants' self-definition through material goods, and their (ambivalent) means of reclaiming honor and distinction by upholding education and culture as their unique, higher value.

Chapter 2 concerns the almost invisible processes that reproduce inequalities through everyday acts of consumption. It details the daily complexities of maintaining a middle-class household under wildly fluctuating inflationary conditions, in which devaluations, currency changes, and other effects obliged Brazilians to dedicate enormous amounts of time and concern to money and led to increasing resentment of government failure to achieve stability. Highlighting novel "survival strategies" of various institutions and agents—consumers, merchants, bankers—this chapter shows how class differentiation processes occurred as middle-class people attempted to protect their money and economize. The chapter closes by adding another, and crucial, layer to the inflation crisis: the first government stabilization plan (the Plano Cruzado), which proclaimed a price freeze. This prompted a frenzy of consumption and reactive black-marketeering, and eventually backfired, moving Brazil into ever higher inflation. The government's failure and irregular business dealings bred an atmosphere of mistrust and defensive acts in Brazilian society; these were deplored by informants. This chapter presents further statements and acts showing that consumption is foundational to middle-class Brazilian identity, and that the economic crisis was thus experienced by these middle-class Brazilians not only as a great inconvenience to their practical lives, but more centrally as a threat to the basis and purpose of their social existence.

Chapter 3 concerns redefining practices of middle-class identity in work. It examines the shift from hitherto guaranteed employment in well-paid, secure, prestigious white-collar occupations (as salaries were eroded by devaluation and for some threatened by layoffs) into petit bourgeois and often informal economy production, service, or sales, and it examines diverging attitudes among informants toward this change. Chapter 3 also highlights the media's role in promoting this redefinition of middle-class employment.

In his historical study of Brazil's middle classes from 1920 to 1950, Owensby (1999) argues that they attempted to forge distinctions from and superiority over the working class by classifying their own work as nonmanual and by staking claims to culture and education (in contrast to the illiterate or semiliterate masses). I found the latter efforts very much in vigor in the 1990s, and these were especially directed against the newly rich. However, as the middle class began to lose its grip on liberal professional options (forced to "open one's hand," as the Portuguese expression goes, to these forms of employment and associated status), it seemed that people were tightening their hold on consumption as an ever more important and inflexible foundation to their identity. In this shift, I speculate that women and youth were stretching the outer (lower) boundaries through work in sales.

Thus far, the very active tactics (de Certeau 1984) taken by families to maintain and further their class standing appear coherent, consistent, and suited to times noteworthy for their chaotic and antiutopian qualities. The next two chapters provide a counterpoint to these efforts. Chapters 4 and 5 are paired examinations of the multiple uses and meanings of transnational consumption, in the forms of travel experiences, especially to Disney World, and consumption of imported goods. In chapter 4 I view the trip to Disney World not only as a rite of passage for Latin American teens but also as a kind of "tournament of value" (Appadurai 1986) for adults. In either reading, the trip supports claims to validate and upgrade the family in the local status hierarchy, and hence can also be seen as a family strategy to accumulate cultural capital (Bourdieu 1984). Chapter 5 focuses on imported goods, which represent in a literal and experiential way the acquisition of First World modernity and symbolic positioning in that world. These material and symbolic consumption practices to construct and perform middle-class identity occurred in a context of exacerbated social differentiation. Such transnational activities and goods producing local subjects and localities (Appadurai 1996) should also be seen as acts against the state, held responsible for a crisis prolonging Third World conditions in Brazil as well as for holding onto outmoded protectionist policies for national industries. Indeed, this is a middle class in which the agents were fully aware of the trappings of middle-class life elsewhere—of what "should be" for them, yet had been denied, owing to national impediments. They would not let boundaries stop them; however, imported goods were obtained by contraband. I conclude by qualifying claims that globalization renders the nation-state irrelevant or that indigenization of transnational consumer goods renders the First World influence negligible. Instead, practices are indeed readily indigenized: in particular, the "modern" Disney trip compares and competes with the "traditional" debutante ball. But I argue that far from reducing or removing the social inequalities of class—far from erasing the importance of national boundaries and hierarchies—the transnational shopping goods and experiences reinforce these invidious distinctions, as well as the notion that modernity and its material embodiments are from elsewhere, out of Brazil.

Chapters 6–8 consider the reconstitution of middle-class identity in the public, national arena. The media's central role in representing middle-class identity and in providing social knowledge of the crisis and the government are the focus of chapter 6. I show how the print media insinuated itself into middle-class households by variously alerting readers to safe or dangerous investments and shopping methods, narrating horror stories of middle-class decline, taunting readers with representations of luxury consumption, and presenting governmental policies and scandals with heavy criticism and irony. I argue that since the late 1970s and in increasing intensity in the 1980s, the print media has defined the middle class via consumption by (metonymic) association and has interpellated its middle-class readership continually as consumers. Consequently, it was not difficult to represent middle-class households as the central arena and even the target of the public crisis. This chapter then examines the media's representations of the government stabilization plan (the Plano Collor) notorious for confiscating bank-account holdings and provoking serious recession. Against these conditions, which in this case did directly target the middle class (the working-class poor would not have bank accounts), there was an increasingly militant middle-class stand against the Collor presidency, which culminated in a middle-class youth-led movement to impeach the president for corruption. My study of informant commentary and popular media found a coincidence in perspective in the explicit definition of the middle class through consumption, the interpretation that the middle class was *the* target of the crisis, and the view that the media was a proxy for the middle class in the public sphere.

Chapter 7 discusses the foundation of middle-class identity through discursive practice, in particular, assertions of moral and cultural (class and racial) superiority. I first isolate a discourse of regional identity— Northeasterners versus Southeasterners. I argue that this regional identity is built on scarcely veiled classist and racist lines, operating as much through joking as through explicit resentment of Northeasterners, most of whom are poor people of color. Although this discourse is evidently commonplace in the region, as are recorded instances of discrimination (Guimarães 1997), it was infrequent among my informants. That said, it is arguably as important to note what is not discussed (Lassalle 1997; Sheriff 2000) as what is. This chapter therefore raises the question of white middle-class silence on issues of poverty, violence, racism, and poor Brazilians.[10] Within the confines of my research, the discourse I most often encountered was permeated with moral indignation against rampant government corruption, and with anxiety for their children's fate in what was viewed as an increasingly dog-eat-dog civil society also contaminated by pervasive opportunism and corruption. This second discourse asserts a moral and cultural critique of the government and society; informants claimed that Brazilians were culturally predisposed to inflationary practices and corruption in business.

The almost generalized critique and insistence on their "difference" symbolically positioned these middle-class Brazilians above and apart from those of another region (in some cases) and from their society overall. The antistate, anti-Northeastern, and/or anti-Brazilian discourses, registered after more than a decade of crisis, isolated these middle-class Paulistanos in the nation-state. As it was not possible to tell from commentaries blaming Brazilians for the unending inflation crisis whether the speakers included themselves or not, I infer there was decided ambiguity and ambivalence in middle-class Paulistano discourse regarding their own class, as well as their society and state.

Far from intending a panorama, I wish by the shifting focus of each chapter to understand more adequately the dynamics of class identity. Having these pieces before us allows us to think further, and ultimately, comparatively, about what it means that the most enduring foundation of middle-class Brazilian identity is consumption coupled with a sense of moral and cultural superiority. What are the conditions that render this combination unproblematic for the middle class? How is it that in their story of the nation-state, this middle class represents itself as passive, as if outside society and history? What are the implications of the self-critique revealed in middle-class Brazilian ambivalence regarding employment, consumption, state, and society? This brings us to the final chapter, which shows not how middle-class Brazilians resolved these questions, but instead how they plunged into a new era, and the kind of sense that made.

My field research of seventeen months ended with a quietly dramatic shift from the highest recorded year of inflation and a seemingly unending economic nightmare to the start of low inflation, with a new and promising government stabilization plan (the Plano Real) and new currency, and the election of this plan's designer, Fernando Henrique Cardoso, to the presidency. Chapter 8 concerns this plan, the election, and the aftermath. In late 1994, these changes seemed to decisively set Brazil and middle-class Brazilians on a road to economic salvation and modernity through neoliberalism, preferably and positively called globalization. As the remainder of the decade unfolded, economic fluctuations resurged, once again throwing the middle-class project into question.

1

THE DREAM CLASS IS OVER

Home Ownership, Consumption,

and (Re)definitions of Middle-

Class Identity

The dream ended.
Those who didn't sleep in a sleeping bag
didn't even dream.
The dream ended.
It was heavy, that sleep, for those who didn't dream.
—from the song "O Sonho Acabou" [The dream ended]
by Gilberto Gil, 1972

Milton told me his situation would have been different if he had been born ten years earlier. Milton was an engineer employed for more than twenty years in a bank that served as the Brazilian government's office of housing financing. Given where Milton worked, it was sad but ironic that he and his wife, Aninha, did not own their home. They lived with their two grade-school-aged children in a rented house in Jardim Bonfiglioli, not one of the south-zone Jardins neighborhoods, but a southwestern suburban area (past Butantã) with two-storied houses on quiet streets. To explain his point about timing, Milton told me of his cousin: also an engineer, he had started his career earlier and came to have a firm with forty employees, a big house in São Paulo, a beach house, and a country home. Then, the firm lost during the 1980s crisis, he and one partner opened an antique store in the traditionally exclusive Jardins area, which relied on the labor of the partners' wives. Although this example somewhat contradicts what he was trying to illustrate, Milton nonetheless reiterated that starting ten years earlier, his family could have done well. This set him to recalling the 1970s economic miracle and Brazil's phenomenal growth, and the stagnant 1980s. It was as if he and Brazil could have made it together, but, as in the poem "Miniver Cheevy" by Edwin Arlington Robinson, he had been "born too late."

Perhaps Milton did have a point. Consider João, a graduate in civil engineering, about ten years Milton's senior, who built an ever more successful career in banking, most recently with Citibank. He lived with his wife, Wilma, a homemaker, and two college-bound daughters in a luxury apartment in Vila Nova Conceição, the neighborhood of São Paulo then boasting the highest real-estate values. João repeatedly noted with satisfaction that graduates in the economic miracle period (1968–73) of the dictatorship enjoyed great ease getting jobs. "My whole class graduated employed. One could even choose jobs. The demand for educated professionals was great. . . . It was a golden age, the whole decade of the '70s." He later added, "We passed through a black political period, in an exuberant economy." I excluded this family from my study, but kept in contact with them for they were helpful in providing an outside perspective. João's high income, the family's living conditions, and his and Wilma's unfaltering optimism provided a usefully clear contrast to the middle-class people in my study.

This chapter introduces the question of Brazilian middle-class identity through discourse, first through discussion of informants' homes: those they owned, were paying for, were hoping to buy or to sell.[1] I then turn to informants' explicit self-definition of the middle class and compare it to the media's. The final section considers unsolicited informant criticisms of the homes and consumption of others. This choice of introduction to some families in the study is doubly motivated: indeed, the commentaries and stories about consumption and homes were chosen because this was how these middle-class Brazilians (in a display of commonality) defined middle-classness. Although family history might be the more usual method of introduction, the recollections of my informants, often first- to third-generation immigrants (from Portugal, Italy, Japan, Spain and beyond), were lacking in detail, attesting perhaps to instability.[2] When instead we turned to their homes, to their discourse on consumption and that of others, I received abundant description and stylistic qualities that allowed me to situate these families, if only partially, in the context of the economic crisis.[3]

ARRESTED DEVELOPMENT

Irene and Heitor

Formerly a nurse, Irene was an active secretary for her husband, Heitor, a doctor. They had three young children and were living in an apartment in Vila Madalena bought in 1983 with government housing financing. Irene's buoyant good spirits were matched by her ironic humor, displayed from the very beginning. At our first meeting, Irene played on the etiquette of offering refreshments with a set formality, whether from a white, gilded-rim porcelain demitasse coffee service on a silver tray covered with a lace doily or from a plastic variant. She, too, offered me a beverage, but informed me impishly that it would be served on "Cica crystal," that is, recycled jelly glasses (the standard glassware of the poor). Walking to the kitchen, she tossed back that it would not be served on a tray either. She also reported that when he heard about our interview, her husband, Heitor, was horrified that it was to take place at their home. "Nessa porra toda?!" he exclaimed (the translation, "In all this mess?" doesn't capture the crudeness of the term *porra*). Later on, Irene told me without any drama, just with sheer energy, about their seventy-six-square-meter apartment (a mid-range size compared to those of other families in this study):[4] "We are desperate to leave. As you can see, we don't fit inside it. As you entered, you could see the bookcase with things on top. The bedrooms are full of piles. We don't fit in here. But we can't get out of here either. The investment would be too high. We just have this apartment as capital. With the expenses of schooling—probably with that money we could make monthly payments on a new apartment. But I prefer to stay here and keep the children [at a school] we think is better."

Among the twenty-four families of the study, all but seven already owned a home, and thus had attained the essential status and means of building middle-class culture (see G. Velho 1980; DaMatta 1985; Frykman and Lofgren 1987; Blumin 1989; Wilk 1989; Halle 1993; and Colloredo-Mansfeld 1994). For most, homes had been acquired during the dictatorship (1964–85), a time of rapid economic growth, increase in middle-class employment for both men and women, and broader consumer opportunities. Almost all long-term, unchanging home owners told me, as if paraphrasing each other, that they were lucky to have acquired their homes when they did (often as many as fifteen years before), for they would never have been able to do so since the crisis. The stories of the next two home-owning families show that Brazil's miracle and crisis allowed for—even favored—some unexpected developments.

Maria do Carmo and José Claudio

Maria do Carmo, an immigrant from the Azores, started working at age eighteen. She taught for ten years, then stopped after having her fourth child. (This family had the most children in the study.) José Claudio built up a successful private practice as an obstetrician-gynecologist. They were living in a huge apartment (four bedrooms, five bathrooms) in Paraíso, an upper-middle-class neighborhood of the Jardins distinguished for being very close to the main uptown commercial avenue, the stately Avenida Paulista. To follow José Claudio's story, please note that *correction* refers to monetary correction, or increases in salary, savings, or prices to offset the devaluations. José Claudio told me:

> Nineteen ninety was the only time in my life that I got worried, it was because of the apartment we are buying. There was this distortion. I signed a contract in which my debt could be corrected during the construction of the building via the correction of the savings. When I got the apartment, this correction was no longer valid, because this correction, it was equal to inflation, but there was another inflation index, from civil construction, by the construction company. Obviously they pushed the index way above inflation, and I had to pay the difference. . . . I had expected to pay about 300,000 dollars, but they charged me about 450,000.

I exclaimed, "That can't be true!" Maria do Carmo then replied, "It's really absurd . . . we lived here alone [in the building] for nearly a year [1992]." José Claudio explained, "Many people gave up, lost . . . all but 20 to 30 percent of their investment." In response to my query about the legality of the proceedings, José Claudio told me they had figured that

1. View of the Avenida Paulista. Only a few of the former coffee mansions remain on this street, which is São Paulo's financial center. The South Zone residential area moves south and downhill from the Avenida Paulista. *Photo courtesy of the author.*

2. View from the tenth story of an apartment building in Jardim Paulista, of the South Zone, the zone where nine informant families lived. *Photo courtesy of the author.*

legal recourse would be as much or more of a risk than paying. Resuming the story, he added, "Today my monthly payments are practically half of what I earn, at the time [1990–92], 60 percent, an absurdity. . . . I had to start working more. Luckily I can work more . . . with my private practice."

José Claudio and Maria do Carmo were then 49 and 46, their children teens (one already in college); Irene and her husband, in contrast, had a young family (then aged 8, 6, and 3) and were in their late thirties (then 36 and 38). Heitor was still struggling to establish himself, whereas José Claudio had already done so and could "simply" work more to manage. I saw José Claudio only twice. Arriving in his white clothes direct from work after 8 P.M., he was visibly fatigued. The last time I saw Irene she was exhausted—from being secretary and from chauffering her children to and from schools, extracurricular classes (*cursinhos*), clubs, shopping centers, friends' homes, and more, as mothers often do. Perhaps Milton was right, if even doctors (like Heitor) could be born too late. Contrariwise, as the next example shows, a waiter and seamstress could come to own two homes before the crisis hit them.

Clarinha and José

During our first encounter, Clarinha spontaneously told me her family's house and car history. "We did the following in order to marry. We went out for five years. He bought a car, and I helped. It was an old car, we traded it and bought a new car. We sold the car when we finished the payments and put this money as down payment on a small apartment in Pinheiros [in 1974]. Two bedrooms, kitchen, living room. And we got married. He bought another old car. Our house financing was for two years. We paid for it. After less than a year and a half of marriage, I had my first child. I worked until the last week. He was born, and two weeks later I was already working again."

Currently a housewife (*dona de casa*), Clarinha did not complete secondary school and had worked for eight years as a seamstress. This can be a very meager living, but she had sewn for a boutique on what was for years São Paulo's fashion center, the Rua Augusta. Her husband José's work situation was similar: an immigrant from Portugal at age twelve, he had always worked at a banquet hall in Itaím-Bibí. This family's history illustrated one road to the middle class; they had acquired material means and were intent on providing their children with the requisite cultural capital to consolidate class standing. Their children, Marcos and Márcia, attended one of São Paulo's expensive private high schools, thereby nearly ensuring college entrance.

Clarinha explained that when she worked, she would go to the boutique, pick up the sewing work, and bring it home. "At the time, I had a girl, fourteen or fifteen years old, who stayed with me, so that I could watch the baby. We moved up through our work. We didn't receive help from my parents or from his." After this comment differentiating their family backgrounds from more privileged middle-class families, the conversation switched momentarily to a discussion of Márcia's fifteen birthday party (see chapter 4), held free of charge at the buffet house where José worked. Clarinha then described how she and José repeated their financing strategy, this time selling a car to purchase land in a semiurbanized western suburb where they built the spacious home in which they lived. Sometime in the 1980s, they inherited another plot just two blocks away, and built a house they hoped to sell. Of contemporary design, the home boasted a swimming pool and barbecue area (the rage), and had three bedrooms and two and a half baths. (See fig. 4.) However, José and Clarinha were unable to find a buyer. In Brazil there is almost no financing except for new constructions. Buying a "used" or already built home from a home owner usually requires outright payment in full, an especially difficult prospect during the inflation crisis. Clarinha also felt the house was less salable because it was on an unpaved road.

The upward mobility of this family attests to the fact that not only middle to upper middle classes benefited in the period of São Paulo's boom. Notwithstanding, expressing disbelief that people with lower levels of employment could have the means to send their children to private school, academic contacts insisted that the children must have had scholarships. Although this was not so, tuition was indeed a financial burden that this family was just barely managing. It was clearly a relief as well as a joy that (then) nineteen-year-old Marcos had made it into the Universidade de São Paulo (USP), the public state university, rather than a less renowned and costly private college. Márcia was still in high school, but there would probably be reluctance to spend money on her college education, since she was deemed less academically inclined.

3. View of older and more recent apartment buildings in Pinheiros, of the West Zone, the zone where eleven informant families lived. *Photo courtesy of the author.*

4. View of Clarinha and José's newly built home, in a semi-urbanized neighborhood of the West Zone. *Photo courtesy of the author.*

With no prospect of a sale, the family moved into the newer house in late 1994. Clarinha then spoke to me of her idea of turning the vacated home into a garment-making business if a sale did not go through. She would have more time now that the children were nearly grown. Furthermore, José's buffet employment was suffering from the crisis and from increased competition. Thus the crisis was prompting the need once again for two incomes, and together with the limits on financing, was threatening to turn the second home into either an inalienable possession or a cottage industry.[5]

Although I am not interested per se in ordering families along a socioeconomic continuum, it might be useful to view Clarinha and José as belonging to the newly middle class, Maria do Carmo and José Claudio as moving up and out, and Irene and Heitor as falling somewhere in between. The next example belonged to this last category and was part of the minority in my sample who were not home owners.

Sandra and Carlos

Carlos and Sandra and their two teenagers lived in a comfortable but rented apartment in a small, older complex in the bairro Moema, where newer expensive-looking apartments were being built. Carlos had been in bank administration for seventeen years; a full-time housewife, Sandra was setting up her own jewelry-making business. The styles of this couple were quite distinct. Sandra had a low but sharp voice and a determined manner. An active Spiritist (a practitioner of Kardecism, as were six other informants), Sandra explained that her religious beliefs included a sense of strong personal responsibility, including for the "vibes" one emits. She practiced chromotherapy at the religious center she and her husband frequented. Carlos was soft-spoken and had an air of constant fatigue, evidently related to his heart condition. Although a Spiritist himself, a discouraged manner colored most of what he said. Sandra dwelt not in dreams and laments, but in realism. Like Milton, Carlos emphasized his sense of lost opportunity. The excerpt below reveals his family's difficulties with making a large purchase such as a home during the crisis.

> Carlos: So you start to plan and suddenly you see . . . like us. We plan to buy a house. We have lived here for eighteen years, this is

rented. You try to save money in the bank, but if you do, it's worse. You can't save.

M. O'D.: You have to invest in something.

Sandra: Yes, even if in a lesser good. In Brazil, to save money is not an advantage. We separated off some of the monthly budget, kept saving something. In some of the government's plans, what they call "packages," which were made by ministers . . . new rules were made. These plans fooled with savings a lot. If you reached a certain level, the government would have to give you a lot. They'd say, "Well now, we're giving a lot to these people. Let's make a system to cut this off." Many times the savings, at a given moment, were pushed down [jogado lá para baixo].

M. O'D.: More than once? Because I know in the Plano Collor— [Sandra jumped in as I alluded to the eighteen-month bank-account freeze in 1990 (see chapter 6)]

Sandra: Yes, more than once! The Collor plan was the most. Before this it was done, though in a more subtle manner: "Let's just get part."

Carlos: Delfim Neto, for example.[6] In 1980 somehow the inflation of the year was fixed at 50 percent when in reality it was 100 percent. . . . But I only woke up with Collor. That was a coup. Besides taking everything, he pushed us into hyperinflation.

Although inflation complicated the process, the end of the National Housing Bank (BNH) in 1986, or rather its replacement by a very reduced version, called the Financial System of Housing (SFH), also rendered it more difficult to buy a brand-new home.[7] Six families (one-third of home owners) acquired their homes through the BNH or SFH.

Speaking of these impediments, Sandra and Carlos noted the change from the preceding generation. Sandra commented: "My father was a grade-school teacher, but he had his own house, raised two children, took a vacation every year." Then Carlos recalled of his grandfather: "He was a simple chauffeur, yet had three houses, lived very well, had five children." Sandra joined in, "Even us. We used to buy cars all the time. Now it's a lot harder." Carlos explained, "She says we switched cars, but we didn't have two children then." Carlos lamented not having bought a house when it was more feasible. I watched two of the 1994 World Cup soccer games (in which Brazil won the championship) at the home of Sandra's extended family. Sandra pointed out to me that she and Carlos could not host these potluck-snack events because their apartment would not hold everyone.

Soon after the Plano Real, which as of July 1, 1994, ended three- and four-digit inflation, Carlos and Sandra began seeking in earnest to buy a house. They found the prices high: more than 100,000 reais. (For the exchange rate of the time, add 10 percent to get the U.S. dollar equivalent.) Owing to Carlos's long tenure at his job, he was eligible for a limited period for some bank financing. During a visit I paid at this time, Sandra showed me issues of the magazine *Victoria* (published in Florida), which she subscribed to, featuring romantic turn-of-the-century photography of home interiors. When I asked if she could imagine how she would decorate their house, she said flatly, no, she would have to see the space. The last time I visited Carlos and Sandra, I was told they were holding off a bit on the search for a house. They had been looking during lunch hours and in the early evenings, but Carlos, who wore a pacemaker, had become too fatigued with this tight schedule and added stress.

These stories of both home owners and renters suggest how contingent, transitory, and transient the middle-class state is—and how much it is buoyed by plans and dreams (cf. R. Williams 1982). The crisis interfered with both, perhaps pushing Sandra into a rigidly unimaginative stance. So unlike her was Nicole, an actress and active Spiritist as well, whose family's income was a mere $1,200 per month (the lowest of all families in my sample). Nowhere near able to own a home, Nicole was nonetheless able to "reminisce" freely and fondly, from her small, dank apartment in Santa Cecília, of the American kitchens and white picket fences she had seen so often on TV and in the movies. Finally and most generally, the stories suggest that the crisis sooner or later affected every family—both the prosperous as well as the more marginal middle class—in their own particular moment. Despite vastly different material circumstances, all experienced their homes and home lives held in "arrested development." By its own estimations, the middle class must fulfill home- and consumption-related projects; the crisis complicated or blocked these involvements.

WHAT WE ARE

The middle class of ten years ago, which continues to live off a salary, lost a lot in buying power. Ten years ago, middle class was someone who could buy a car, their own house, maintain their children in private school, frequent, let's say, good restaurants, take a trip once a year. . . . Today, if I had to live from my husband's salary and my city job, my children would not be in [School X] studying, I would not have a car, we would be reduced to one car and I don't know if I would be living on Rua [X].—Lara (architect, married to Rodolfo, an engineer; living with three teenaged sons in a large rental apartment in the desirable Itaím-Bibí neighborhood of the Jardins)

The middle class is able to buy a car and an apartment with a BNH subsidy. —José Luis (engineer, business owner, married to Maricarmen, a Spanish teacher; living with three teenaged daughters in a large apartment near Santo Amaro)

Sorry, we can't be in your study. We don't own a home or a car. We are proletarians.—Miguel (playwright, actor, business consultant, married to Nicole, an actress; living with two teenaged sons in a run-down apartment in Santa Cecília)

Without any prompting, informants volunteered lengthy, descriptive definitions of the middle class, including ownership of a home and car, private schooling of children, and the possibility of spending on leisure activities and travel. When I eventually asked point blank for a definition, the response eventually produced by nearly all informants was that middle class meant owning a house and a car. There were just two exceptions: a sociologist, who gave a Marxian definition, and Simone, cited in the introduction, who said the middle class was a dream. Even the negative formulation by Miguel, cited above, conforms to this fundamental definition.

Informants could have defined middle class by referring to profession, parental education, or neighborhood in São Paulo, but most gave the response as owning one's home and car. This definition may seem too simple or mundane to be taken seriously by social science standards. Yet it offers a concise, unambiguous designation. In contrast to those offered in the class literature, this definition refers to the private sphere and hence is akin to a Weberian understanding of class conditions (see Gerth and Mills 1958). Yet like the analytical view of class, the basic definition makes a clean split between classes; it is not a continuum view of stratification. Note that it places the middle class with the upper class and in oblique contrast to the poor. This definition also indicates (a variously indifferent or fearful) recognition of the hugely differing living conditions by class in Brazil, where the vast majority live in substandard, precarious housing and, not having their own cars, are subjected to a gravely deficient public transit system as well as an alarmingly high risk of pedestrian accidents. While public transportation is a major problem in all Brazilian cities, in São Paulo, where most of the population of 17 million lives in poor outlying suburbs, a conservative estimate for a round-trip commute is a three-hour bus ride. In short, the definition "sides" with the wealthy, yet an important referent is the poor.

Baudrillard (1981, 34) called the tendency to classify middle classes by their possession of objects "naive empiricism." Yet what if the "natives" adopt the criterion to identify themselves and others? Or more correctly, I should note that these middle classes defined themselves in and through the possession first of a home and car and more expansively through consumption, whereas they are interpellated in the media (and by scornful intellectuals) only by the latter: as consuming subjects and then as consuming subjects denied. Like academics, the media offers a "thin description," as it were, and a mocking tone.[8]

From as far back as the 35 percent devaluation of the Brazilian currency in 1979, newspapers have regularly produced state-of-the-middle-class reports. One kind of report is statistical. "Who is paying more? Once again, the middle class" is the title of a *Jornal da Tarde* article (12/30/81) stating that a government measure would adversely target salaried workers and consumers. Another headline announces, "The middle class is poorer and eating less" (*Jornal da Tarde* 1/22/82). Reports tell us generally that the "Buying power of the middle class is falling" (*Jornal do Brasil* 1/9/93) and specifically that "Middle-class income fell 175.41% in 1984" (*Folha de São Paulo* 1/24/85).

Often the body of such articles details how the middle class has changed. Thus, as of the crisis, the middle class has spent more of the household budget on food and less on cleaning and hygiene; has gone without domestic servitude; has had less leisure time out of the house and watched more TV (interesting how this is linked not to the power of TV, but to lack of buying power); has been obliged to take children out of private school; and has become disloyal to brands. One headline reads: "The middle class cuts maid, meat, and even hairdresser" (*Folha de São Paulo* 12/4/83). A "humanizing" variant of these surveys is the life story of hardships faced by middle-class individuals, usually very drippily presented. An impressionist version of these articles declares that the middle class shrunk (*encolheu*) or has been flattened (*achatado*) by the crisis (e.g., "O achatamento da classe média" [The flattening of the middle class], *Folha de São Paulo* 5/12/85).

Leafing through these headlines, one is repeatedly confronted by two words—*paradise* and *dream*. These were diminishing, lost, over. Thus in 1979, just after the devaluation, the headlines read: "The middle class loses paradise" (*Folha de São Paulo* 12/9/79);[9] in 1981, "The middle class is more modest in its dreams" (*Folha de São Paulo* 11/8/81) and, just before Christmas, "Will the glory of the middle class return? Is the rationing of consumption irreversible or will we [*sic*] one day return to the shopping of the past decade?" (*Jornal da Tarde* 12/16/81). The following year, "The dreams and superfluities were abandoned" (*Jornal da Tarde* 7/10/82); then in 1983, "[The] middle class leaves paradise to confront inflation" (*Jornal do Brasil* 8/14/83); after Christmas of 1984, "[A] study finds that the middle class has returned to the paradise of consumption" (*Folha de São Paulo* 1/3/85); but eighteen months after the Plano Cruzado, "For the middle class the dream is over" (*Folha de São Paulo* 10/13/87), and by Christmas of 1991, "The middle class was expelled from paradise" (*Jornal da Tarde* 12/28/91).[10]

What is this dream? Where is this paradise? These are more than barometric readings registering ups and downs of middle-class living standards and money. The formula is invariable. Through constant, metonymic association, the middle class is defined next to dreams and paradise, whose object when linked with middle class is consumption. This clarification is almost always presented in the first sentence of text, as in "Paradise lost. For many the Brazilian middle class didn't even manage to enter into the promised *paradise of the consumer society* . . . and it is being expelled from a paradise from which it only imagined it had entered" (*Folha de São Paulo*, Folhetim, 8/31/80; emphasis added). This media definition of the middle class includes a level of practice (shopping) and an existential one (dreams, paradise).

Without the mocking tone, my informants did share a similar formulation. It is rather striking that their definition is so reductionist. From an affluent perspective, the definition of home and car ownership might prompt a question like "Is that all these middle-class people see as separating them from the popular masses?" While a fear of sliding so far as to have to move to a shantytown is probably unfounded for most, fears of the working classes—even of being momentarily mistaken for someone poor—certainly drives a good deal of middle-class practice at any time. The stark simplicity of the self-definition (have/have not) suggests that the inverse identity is unthinkable. Or better (given the vast gulf between classes and the deplorable conditions of the poor), there is no possibility but to be middle class.[11] And if there is no other possibility, then one must work at assuring that position even in the slightest instances, from dress and decorum to home and car. Anxieties of class were not absent in times of prosperity; instead I found a constant and deliberate attention to form. It is also striking that precisely those things held dear and held to be the proof of middle-classness were threatened in this period, in two senses. First, financing for cars and homes became risky due to inflation, currency changes, and surprise government interventions in the economy. Second, owing to a high risk of theft and burglary, both homes and goods have been increasingly guarded—with extra locks, bars, walls, and twenty-four-hour watchmen for buildings and self-elected car watchmen (see Caldeira 2001). How then, did these middle-class Paulistanos respond to this impasse? Each ensuing chapter pursues this question more. For now, let us look first at their speech.

CULTURA VERSUS CONSUMPTION

A Home and Education versus Consumption

As one looks further into the conversations of informants, their straightforward definition of the middle class grows more complicated through comparisons made with other times and other people. Many of the older generation (perhaps aided by the media) painted a sort of good-old-days picture of the precrisis period, when they never had to count money, pay attention to bills, or restrict their leisure and spending. The crisis affected their potential for having these goods and experiences, and it left the middle class flattened (*achatada*), informants said, using words identical to those of the press. The crisis obliged them to establish priorities in the household budget, spending on what they deemed essential. Predictably for my sample, private school education was deemed a necessity. Informants often explained that this was so given the current absence of a viable alternative in public school education. Many Paulistas (inhabitants of the state of São Paulo) told me how in the past, public schools were good, even better than private, the latter derided with the alliterative expression *papai-pagou-passou,* literally, "papa paid [so (s)he] passed." Now it seems the tables had turned. As more than one informant put it, "It's all I can give my child." The parent generation was putting stakes in what it could still afford—quality education—perhaps with even greater force and intensity than before, considering the cost. At two of the schools, tuition cost nearly US$250 per month in December 1993. Industrial manager Ademar confided that the tuition for their two children consumed one-third of his salary. (However, he later said his monthly salary was US$2,500.) College physical education professor and doctoral candidate Alice said the tuition for her two children took most of her ex-husband's retirement salary (from the military). Many said tuition was their highest expenditure.[12] The schools were chosen by parents with due consideration to giving their children an extra good "start in life" (cf. E. P. Thompson 1976).

Negative contrasts often provide us with a clear means of distinguishing ourselves. Informants would point out that their prioritized choice was completely contrary to those people who "buy an expensive car yet put their children in a public school." I heard almost identical phrasing of this very charged statement over and over, leaving no doubt as to the opinion. New cars but public schools: what a complete inversion of values—putting an ostentatious object of mere status and crass consumption in front of (as more important than) your children's education, culture, and future!

Reinaldo, a professor of psychology, extemporaneously envisioned "a butcher in Moóca (as noted in the introduction, this bairro of the industrial, lower middle class and poor, captured attention for a number of nouveau riche families there) who lives in a badly built house with second-rate furniture, has two new cars at the door, a studio at the beach, and his children study at a state school." This scenario was opposed to "a college-educated professional of the Jardins, Vila Madalena, Cerqueira César, etcetera [upper- and upper-middle-class bairros of the south and west zones] who lives in a smaller apartment, well kept, with better furniture, as is our case, has an old car, but whose children study in a private school of excellent quality." Reinaldo added that college-educated but salaried professionals in the Jardins might not have as high an income as "a butcher-shop owner, a grocer, a bakery owner, who might have five or six times the salary," yet the expenditures and consumption patterns of professionals are much more laudable. Grade-school teacher Maria Regina affirmed that rich people drove up in expensive cars to drop off their kids at the public school where she worked. In fact, teachers repeatedly emphasized the unfavorable contrast between expensive cars and free schools.

Public schooling in São Paulo has been far better than in other regions, but suffered greatly in the past decade. Since the mid-1980s it has been considered *falido* (failed); some said, more dramatically, that it "doesn't exist." Hugely inadequate, undersupplied, and insufficiently staffed, the public school system was called a case for national alarm (cf. *Veja* 2/15/95). Accordingly, informants found it horrifying that those with the means to provide education—which, in this assessment, can occur only in private schools—did not bother, but sent their children to free public schools. Alice put it most forcefully: "It is impossible to put your child in a public school today. It is unthinkable. It is to know with certainty that the child is not going to learn absolutely anything."[13]

Whereas the home and education were constantly upheld in extended conversations, unqualified consumption was not.[14] Although all informants except two said they liked or loved to shop, they repeatedly censured Brazilians for being "consumerist." One young woman said, "Brazilians are very consumerist, aren't they? They like to have nice clothes, dress well. The house is falling down, right, but they need clothes." Using hyperbolic comparisons of consumption practices to expose an inversion of values (and lack of sense) was an extremely popular rhetorical tactic. Bia, a young psychologist who previously worked in the personnel department of a firm but was assisting her husband, Marcos, in his highly successful practice as a psychotherapist, said: "Sometimes I find the Brazilian people really superfluous. . . . [They say:] 'It's expensive, but who cares, I want these pants anyway. I want to travel. I'll go without eating for three months, but I'm going to travel.' I don't know if it's a small group that is noticeable, but I hear this kind of conversation a lot. 'I prefer not to have a maid—whatever—to not eat well, to not eat filet mignon every day, but I'm going to travel. I'm going to buy clothes I

like,' understand? And then [the person] doesn't have his own home."
The typist who transcribed this material for me (and struggled greatly to
support her family, as her husband's health problems prevented him from
working) objected that she had never met a soul who had gone without
food in order to travel. Bia, however, was unique among informants for
choosing travel as an example of a misguided expense. For most, travel
was an elevated use of money. For instance, one woman said: "We went
to Europe instead of buying a car. There are people who insist on having
status, a new sofa. We prefer to travel."

It is interesting that while making these diatribes against consumerism, no one pointed out that during high inflation one could not simply
store money. One could invest in some banking scheme set up during the
inflation years to protect money against inflation, or even earn through it;
one could "invest" in durable goods, which in Brazil do not devalue as in
the United States; or one could spend diversely, as chapter 2 discusses.
These matters were perfectly clear to people; however, the rhetorical
aims here being quite other, such justifications were not offered. That is
to say, the arguments evidently were made to critically appraise—and
identify—other Brazilians essentially through their (vulgar, materialist) consumption practices in contradistinction to one's own honorable
investments in housing, education, and enlightened consumption: in
culture.

In a formerly slavocratic society, where educational levels (McDonough 1981; Plank 1996) are lower than one might expect from a country
with such a large economy (aside from the worst years of the crisis, Brazil
has ranked among the top ten world economies), having or not having
cultura (i.e., education and fine upbringing) functions as a stark division in
the social hierarchy. When the description is applied to the poor majority, it connotes ignorance, lack of education and manners (in the eye of
the beholder). In reference to the nouveaux riches, lack of interest in
education is added to the familiar view of unrefined spending and style.

One further point seals "culture" as the homogenizing value for this
group of informants. Along with criticism of the merely material was an
appreciation for another kind of good. When I asked what, if anything,
the person missed not having, the response was theater/cinema and
travel—the reduction or privation of travel especially hurt. What can be
seen simply as leisure was often presented in its enlightening aspect, its

absence experienced as cultural deprivation.[15] Thus Lara regretted not having time to read, to study English, to take gymnastics. Alice, who also regretted not being able to study English, contrasted her consumption habits to others: "I spend money on newspapers, magazines; they aren't going to do that. I adore art. Classics, sculptures, I love it. If I had the money, I would be surrounded with things like that. They wouldn't spend money on such things." She added, "I would never go to a *churrascaria* [barbecue] restaurant because I detest it.[16] I prefer to stay at home. They go. For these people this is sufficient, but not for me. So there are these tastes, these values that are different." Unlike most informants, Alice did name the material support for culture. She noted of clothing: "I want a given piece of clothing because it gives me quality, it falls better, it's a different elegance." Recalling a dress she had wanted while window shopping, she added, with wry amusement, "My eyes don't fall on the dress selling for 4,900 [cruzeiros reais], they always fall on the one for 16,000!"[17]

Cultura versus Cars

A man with a car don't need no justification.
—Hazel Motes, in *Wise Blood,* by Flannery O'Connor

Although cars were part of a positively asserted, unqualified baseline self-definition of these middle-class informants, in most other contexts cars generated vehement criticism. People often noted the national obsession with cars, explicitly calling them high-status symbols. Whereas homes of the wealthy in Brazil are often hidden from view, with protective walls and gardens, cars offer ready opportunities for nonverbal, unambiguous public display of wealth. Cars too have a bottom-line variant (have/have not) and then many gradations. At the top are foreign cars, which can easily run the equivalent of US$30,000, owing to import taxes (75 percent at the time of this study). More generally, high status accrues to any new car (often called *carro zero,* car with zero kilometers) or "car of the year." Not having a fairly new car (not to mention not having one at all, which for middle-class Paulistanos is unthinkable) can be a source of embarrassment. The attention to car upkeep in Brazil is impressive; it gives one the feeling that most cars are new. (The same goes for household appliances.) For about one-third of the families in the research, however, the strategy used with regard to cars was simple: keep the same old car. Noting the Brazilian fixation on cars, Alice, adopting the standard formula, said: "Here in Brazil there are people who live in a rental apartment, or in a house falling to pieces, horrible, in a bad state, in order to have the car of the year. For the Brazilian, a car is very important. It is the highest status symbol." She was living in a rental apartment herself and had a ten-year-old car, which she said embarrassed her teenaged sons. With gleeful malice, another divorced woman said that her ex-husband, who had for years rationalized getting the car of the year, now had to get "the car of the year before."

Ademar managed a firm that manufactured cutting tools for export to the United States and Canada. Since 1989, the firm had reduced its employees from 180 to 49. Grim Ademar and cheerful Mara and their two teens lived in a huge concrete complex on the Avenida Francisco Morato (almost a freeway in speed of traffic and volume). Their apartment seemed institutionally drab and meager in furnishings. Note how Ademar worried about working-class car owners in his definition of the middle class: "Ten years ago, what characterized someone from the middle class? You had a car, you belonged to a [social/sport] club, you had your children in private school, you lived in your own apartment or house, you traveled. Today you don't travel anymore. Car? Everyone has them, better or worse. Your own home? Yes. The poorer class also got these things [foram conquistas que a classe mais pobre conseguiu]. *Today, the middle class is not very characterizable* [não está bem caracterizada]" (emphasis added). Ademar, whose own financial situation was among the more modest of my informants, disparaged the industrial workers at the firm he managed. They constantly complained and had a pessimistic outlook, he said, and yet nineteen (of forty-nine) owned cars: "Only cars falling apart. They use them to come to work. Keeping up a car is expensive. But they are improving their lives. But if you ask them how they are doing, you get that gloomy response [é aquela tristeza]." Ademar exaggerated. Although formal-sector working-class people may have cars (perhaps obtained from the efforts of several household wage earners), this is certainly not the case for the working poor overall, for whom car ownership is not within reach. Sixty percent made minimum wage in the early 1990s, the equivalent of a mere $70 per month. A new "economy" car ran about $8,500.

Readers might imagine that the references to people lacking decent housing and education but spending on cars and clothes could apply to either the working class (unable to make the big purchases) or the newly rich. However, Ademar notwithstanding, given the implausibility of poor people buying cars at all, much less new cars, I always took such statements as referring to the latter.

Evidently, the seeming progress of working-class people diminished Ademar. He was, however, fairly unique among my informants in his expression of resentment at the (imagined) upward mobility of the working class. His wife, Mara, in contrast, an apartment-complex super occasionally employed as an attorney, also felt the gap between themselves and the poor was narrowing, yet her statements lacked sign of resentment. "I think that today, the middle class hardly exists anymore. It is getting closer and closer to the poorer class [classe mais pobre]. There isn't such a big difference anymore between the poor class and the middle. There is a big rift in relation to the richer." Note also the words of Ursula (married to Reinaldo), degreed in biology, but working at a bank. After first comparing her family to the poor, she immediately qualified her statement: "We thought we were middle class, but I feel kind of poor! I don't feel miserably poor—it would be a sin to say we were poor, since there are so many people with great problems, you know?"

In sum, most often the nouveaux riches were the favorite target for ridicule, and not only by those with lesser incomes. It was Marcos whom I quoted in the introduction, referring to the upwardly mobile: "They took the place of the others with less money, these people who were middle class. . . . Today you see lots of people riding around in imported cars and they don't have the least bit of culture. There is this inversion. It is not only economic, it's cultural." The car, material proof and symbolic icon of wealth, was also ubiquitous in the commentary of intellectuals. The media shared this preoccupation with the nouveaux riches and especially with foreign cars: both were so constantly remarked on in the press, one would have the impression that they were numerically important rather than simply there at all—outrageously so, given the deplorable economic conditions.

In short, for this middle class, there is an "other" middle class stereo-typically imagined. Though reduced in material resources, this middle class distinguished itself by maintaining a cultural standard for its family project (Romanelli 1986) and social project (G. Velho 1981). Informants scorned another middle class for its lack of project and poor values—or rather, for its frivolous consumption and poor taste. The combination of one's own downward mobility (or stationary position) versus the ascent of others was evidently irritating. The context had made the possible expressions of consumption (and by close extension, identity) uncom-fortably close to people whose tastes "should" be worlds apart. Again, this was a frequent stance excepting those in my study who might be labeled nouveaux riches and who tended not to draw invidious com-parisons. There were several (of varying financial situations) who indi-cated their dissatisfaction without targeting another social group, refer-ring instead somewhat vaguely to systemic societal problems or the crisis overall. The better-off informants frequently capped any discussion about reduced budgets or rising others by noting their "privileges": namely home ownership and the ability to educate their children in private school.

By now it should be obvious that all this makes for a fairly "classic" representation of a middle class. The group as a whole showed they were grasping ever more firmly onto education and cultural enlightenment both as the means of consolidating middle-classdom and as the badge of their social standing. But their discourse had some twists and turns, so let us backtrack to review these formulations. The informant definition of home and car ownership was advanced in absolute terms without any denial or qualification of their materiality. In positive formulations relat-ing to their own cases, informants also presented consumer goods and activities in an unqualified manner. However, as we saw, the very same markers underwent a reevaluation when applied to "others." Others were criticized for not having a home, not because they could not afford it but because, by this representation, they were seemingly able to buy or improve a home, yet did not place this as the top priority, as the most worthy good.[18] Similarly, others were criticized for owning a new car, and for placing that and other frivolous consumption over education or home ownership. Revising the earlier absolute definition of home and car ownership to incorporate these statements, we find that these middle-class speakers constructed a morally superior position on the (quasi-sacred) supports of home ownership, educational investments, and cultured consumption (plus ownership of an old car), in contradistinction to those who had a new car and engaged in vulgar, superfluous, materialistic consumption, but did not have a "decent" home, education, or culture. In the balancing and rebalancing of the scales of distinction, the speakers knew what constituted cultured, tasteful, moral consumption.[19]

The very eschewing of the material, the protesting of the cultured over and against the material, point us to the familiar Weberian argument of social honor over economic class. They also point us to Bourdieu's concept of misrecognition (Bourdieu and Passeron 1977). I cannot avoid highlighting these obvious rhetorical strategies, for they were so generalized, both in content and in style. Indeed, it is perhaps more noteworthy that the argument relies on hyperbole, in particular on a fantastical construction (rather than on empirically compelling evidence): "The house is falling down, right, but they need clothes." Why this exaggeration? The great attention to intraclass distinctions attests to the centrality of symbolic boundary making in this context of downsliding, which, as stories of nouveau riche families indicate, also had surprising aspects, allowing a few to gain wealth under these conditions. The way these matters are taken so personally bears witness to Miller's observation that "consumption has become the main arena in which and through which people have to struggle towards control over the definition of themselves and their values" (1995a, 277; and see Bourdieu 1984). Here that struggle has concerned the immediate social sphere. As we shall see in the following chapters, "this struggle," as Miller goes on to say, "is often posed against larger institutions such as capitalism and the state."

This discussion of the home calls to mind the classic study *A Casa e a Rua* (The home and the street, 1985) by Robert DaMatta. The anthropologist argues that the Brazilian worldview is strongly marked by the oppositional categories of the title. Thus the home would be the calm and safe haven of people whose social stations are known, respected, naturalized. The architecture and social use of the space reinforce the separation from the street and the stranger. The street is the agitated place where unknowns in a heterogeneous space mix in ways that are materially and socially dangerous. DaMatta observes that

> What is curious, fascinating, miraculous—and perhaps this is really the Brazilian miracle—is that we don't perceive these radical changes in our behavior as having any politico-moral or ideological implications. That is, we live in a divided universe and we don't realize it. So, when we speak of *change, transformation, modification, reform* or *revolution,* we are referring almost exclusively to the sphere of problems that emerge in the public world: the universe of politics and the street. The home and the supernatural are very rarely incorporated/envisioned [englobados] in our transformative proposals about the world; they are the place where time doesn't pass and history rarely knocks at the door. (1985, 114; emphasis his)

Thus Brazilians would be dichotomists for whom the interaction between the spheres, or the contaminating of the sacrosanct private sphere, could not occur.

DaMatta's frame of reference for his essays tends toward crystallized representations in Brazilian society; his examinations are of the "traditional society" as depicted by Gilberto Freyre and Jorge Amado. DaMatta examines a social world that is already there, and the ensuing concepts and relations. The social actors are already "bourgeois," their homes were long since built, the insecurities and dangers were kept outside on the street.

This chapter took a look at middle-class families whose home lives were not already there. Their homes were built, bought, rented, and in the case of one family in the study, lost from the time of the Brazilian miracle to the crisis. Their private sphere was invaded by the crisis, just as it had been fostered by the miracle. Yet it is curious, and bears witness to DaMatta's original insight, that middle-class people attempted to maintain these dichotomies—or boundaries, even when they visibly, overtly collapsed—and these same people knew this, as their ambivalent, occasionally fantastic discourse implies.

2

SHOPPING NIGHTMARES,

BANKING GAMES,

GOVERNMENT PACKAGES

Local Shopping during Inflation

In 1984, inflation was officially at 100 percent, and more realistically at 200 percent. In less than eighteen months a grade-school teacher's salary of somewhat more than five minimum wages, or US$550, would decline precipitously.[1] The teacher could draw a graph depicting how his or her salary was steadily, indeed increasingly, approaching zero. Yet that near-zero would be registered in millions of cruzeiros. How to manage living expenses under these conditions of rising prices and devaluations?[2]

Donas de casa (homemakers) knew that one should start the week's shopping by going to a government-subsidized outlet (e.g., COBAL Brazilian Food Company) to buy sugar, margarine, rice, manioc flour, and other dry goods. One should then go to another subsidized market called Sacolão (Big Bag) to buy (somewhat overly mature) fruits and vegetables at one price per kilo. If one wanted something special (e.g., fresh eggs, chicken breast, regional fruit), one should proceed to the traditional farmers' market, which has both open-air and building sections. In this weekly routine of price-controlled shopping lasting a good part of the morning, the very last stop would be at the Pão de Açúcar (Sugarloaf) supermarket to get what was not found at the other markets. There one would encounter the unforgettable sight recounted in the introduction of housewives with several grocery carts piled high at the checkout counters.

This chapter is dedicated to studying routine middle-class consumption under Brazil's inflation. In much of the literature on consumption in middle classes, the context is an expanding market for upwardly mobile sectors, whether for mass consumption in Western Europe and the United States, or for a privileged minority elsewhere. In those circumstances of increased discretionary income and/or cheaper goods, the act of shopping, for all its social significance, seems an optional pleasure.[3] Conditions in Brazil from 1980 to 1994 were almost diametrically opposed to this scenario. The crisis began with a "high" inflation nearly 100 percent in 1981; by 1993, the last year before inflation was halted, it exceeded 2,700 percent (see graph on page 63). The currency suffered continual devaluations, periodic decreed maxi devaluations and extinctions. The national currency changed six times in eight years.[4]

Several questions arise regarding Brazilian daily life in this extended disruption of habitus (Bourdieu 1977). What were the meanings of consumption for middle-class Brazilians, and how did this experience affect them? But first, more directly: what went on in the inflationary marketplace where, as one Brazilian concluded, "saving or not saving is the same thing" (Standard, Ogilvy, and Mather 26 February 1987)?[5] This statement might sound implausible. But as we will see, it was not that saving versus spending did not matter (nor did the speaker say that). Rather, where the currency was increasingly devalued and savings often useless, Brazilians formulated a number of unique strategies and tactics (de Certeau 1984) to counteract damages to income.

This chapter concerns a specific moment in the consumption process—shopping while the inflationary context demanded a focus on procedures of exchange. The first two sections detail the complexities of maintaining a middle-class household under inflationary conditions, highlighting local practices that were either novel or specific to the middle class. From the money perspective, I describe responses to inflation in commerce and banking. The third section then incorporates a layer crucial to understanding the inflation crisis, the government's involvement. Between 1986 and 1993, there were nine intervention plans aiming to lower inflation and stabilize the economy. Yet until the Plano Real of 1994, all of these "economic shocks" failed. I focus here on the first such plan and the changes it provoked. (See chapters 6 and 8 for two other plans of great significance.) In the final section, I discuss how these household tactics were experienced by my informants. Their statements reveal that consumption is foundational to their identity; and thus that the economic crisis constituted far more than an inconvenience to their daily lives, but more centrally was a threat to the basis and purpose of their social existence.

My descriptions are necessarily detailed for several reasons. Although I focus on procedures leading up to shopping transactions rather than on the eventual use and meanings associated with consumer goods, I am not concerned with how these methods inform marketing analysis. Instead, I wish to demonstrate as graphically as possible what is meant by the intensification of daily life in a particular environment and then consider the social effects. Provided with microlevel descriptions, we can turn to how these survival tactics—these attempts to exert control over a precarious daily life—influenced middle-class Brazilians' outlook on the nation and society, class identity, and political culture. Thus, for this chapter, I have recourse to de Certeau's (1984) distinction between "tactics"—means employed by ordinary folk, here heads of households and individual merchants—and the far more potent "strategies" undertaken by those in power, here major banks and the government. Overall I follow second-wave feminism by examining the mutual constitution of the personal and the political and the relationship between experience and discourse. This chapter emphasizes an area neglected in much consumption theory relating to middle classes, that is, the low road of the most mundane routines of daily life.[6] I stay here with the unadorned local world of everyday consumption as experienced by middle-class Brazilians, and I incorporate the voiced perspectives of the people concerned, a necessary inclusion toward understanding consumption and wider economic process.

THE SHOPPING SYSTEM: CONDUCTING "MARKET RESEARCH", STOCKPILING GOODS, MINIATURIZING REAL ESTATE

The shopping procedures described earlier were based on a general recognition of what goods to buy most cheaply and where. Those with larger households developed more elaborate processes, involving "market research" (*pesquisa de mercado*), which is literally the expression used in

Portuguese to refer to comparison shopping prior to buying, and stock-piling (*estocagem*) or monthly buys (*compras do mês*). A popular expression was coined to mock stockpile shopping: the ant effect (*efeito formiga*).

Small-businessman Adalberto gave the most detailed explanation of shopping. His bulk shopping was done every forty-five days, and meat was stocked in the freezer every two weeks, leaving weekly shopping for fruits, vegetables, dairy, and bread. For perishables, Adalberto did not simply go to a nearby Sacolão outlet; he went straight to the source—Centrais de Abastecimento Sociedade Anônima (CEASA), the food distribution center, in São Paulo's west zone. Adalberto compared their prices to the neighborhood open markets, which have become very expensive. "I do CEASA on Saturday. There's an open market right nearby [the apartment] on Saturday, too. If I put 50,000 cruzeiros [reais] in my pocket and go to the open market, I don't get the shopping done with 50,000. If I put 30,000 in my pocket and go to CEASA, I do the shopping for two weeks."

Besides the Sacolão outlets and municipal supply centers, two other kinds of stores call our attention: the Lojas Americanas and its rival Lojas Brasileiras (both national chains) and the "hyper" supermarket chains (national or regional). Lojas Americanas and Lojas Brasileiras (American and Brazilian Stores) are modeled on the U.S. drugstore—minus the pharmacy—drawing shoppers not only for incidentals, but for household supplies on a regular basis. Also inspired by and modeled after those in the United States, hypermarkets grew in the 1980s as the internal crisis deepened. São Paulo boasts many hypermarkets, for instance, the Extra (formerly Jumbo). The ground floor is monstrously huge, but until the full opening of the national market to foreign perishables in 1994, it had a dearth of brands and mediocre produce. Brazilian supermarkets have long carried household goods like bath towels, pots and pans, flip-flops, and so on. Hypermarkets expand these aisles to an entire second floor. Stock personnel had to work quickly to keep up with Saturday shoppers grabbing sale items; for instance, a large metal crate holding one hundred beer bottles was depleted in a minute. Despite as many as forty checkout counters, at prime time the wait at supermarkets could be lengthy.

Market research goes beyond choosing the store by its general price reputation. Rather, it consists of making item comparisons in three or more stores prior to making the big periodic household purchases. Research was not just a smart idea; without it, one could commit serious blunders. The average-sized supermarket in my neighborhood, for instance, counterbalanced its special offers with highly overpriced goods. Full-time housewife and mother of four Maria do Carmo called this a lure (*chamariz*), noting that the supermarkets bank on shoppers picking up other items for convenience. In so doing, any savings might be worse than cancelled. In what became a sort of classic media depiction, middle-class Brazilian housewives (*brava gente!*) were shown with notebooks and calculators in hand in the aisles of drugstores and supermarkets, jotting down the various prices of a set list of goods a day or so prior to buying. In this they were assisted by these same large businesses, which had local TV advertising of weekly specials complete with prices, and by the newspapers, which periodically published lists comparing prices on the most commonly bought goods in as many as ten outlets.

Indeed, in terms of sales, it was the large businesses that drew the stockpilers. Such businesses profited primarily but not only through economies of scale. Business owner Antônio explained that since many supermarkets operated on thirty days' credit, they could profit even without any markup on the wholesaler's price, since the balance owed would have devalued. Not incidentally, some of the wealthiest people in Brazil are supermarket owners, for instance, the Diniz family, of the Pão de Açúcar chain, which ranks as Brazil's twentieth largest company (*Veja São Paulo* 11 / 17 / 93, 18).

There were times when a delay between doing research and buying was not possible, when the indispensable pocket calculators were outpaced by the price-marking machines.[7] Informants recalled store employees continually changing prices with their sticker machines, and lucky customers grabbing items yet to be marked up (perhaps on the backs of shelves). They also angrily recalled having seen products whose three to six stickers plainly registered inflation on household goods. By the 1990s, however, apart from large chains where the laser-equipped UPC readers were introduced, in many stores a code number or letter rather than the price was on the item. At the register, the clerk would consult conversion tables applicable for that period (a maximum of two weeks) to quote the price. Some price leaps that had been unpredictable in the early 1980s were still very large but more tamed by the 1990s. Thus in 1993 the price of gas tended to rise about twice a month. On the fated day (and not before) came the announcement, "Gas prices are going up 30 percent as of midnight tonight." Car owners would scramble to the stations, waiting at times for more than an hour to fill their tanks in the time remaining. Bus riders had to endure large hikes as of the last Sunday of the month.

Lest one imagine that comparison shopping was overzealous, note that both in 1993 during high inflation and instability and after inflation ended as of July 1994 forward, the price variance of a given item sold at various locations could run as much as 170 percent. By contrast, the variance in a stable capitalist economy runs 20 percent or less for consumer goods (*Veja* 1/22/92, 78 and *Estado de São Paulo,* 9/11/95, 1). The price disparities provoked commentary. One day Flávio (a medical doctor) announced to his wife, Sumiko (a social worker), that he had just compared prices for tires at three locations, two of which were major department stores, Mappin and Mesbla. The prices were CR$60,000, CR$75,000, and CR$150,000 (in U.S. currency, the range was roughly from $40 to $100). This variance demonstrates the logic of prices being raised "according to the store's wishes," a friend explained wryly— in other words, any which way. Teresa (private-school director) reported the price of one product being CR$3,000 in a supermarket and CR$6,000 in a pharmacy. She said, "You turn the corner and the price is higher, you turn another and it's cheaper, so you see, you spend a lot of time with this." Regarding price variance over time, *Veja* (1/22/92, 62) reported a man's having bought a carburetor piece in 1988 for CR$900. Fourteen months later he purportedly paid CR$72,000 for it— a 7,900 percent price increase versus an inflation rate of 800 percent during that period.

Disparity in prices and price increases beyond the inflation rate may reflect the fact that the official inflation rates were a composite, an average of increases of a variety of goods. Individual items could be well above or even below the published rates. The enormity of price differences, however, points to merchants' self-protective pricing against future inflation. According to economist Fábio Sá Earp, in *Na Corda Bamba: Doze Estudos sobre a Cultura da Inflação* [On the tightrope: Twelve studies on the culture of inflation], an important interdisciplinary collection of essays by Brazilian scholars concerning the inflation period, "Agents . . . progressively became aware that the official inflation was not accompanying the evolution of the real price of goods—and they moved, therefore, to develop a defensive behavior, always trying to readjust above the prices. With this, the very system of prices transformed into a fiction, rendering inviable the use of any standard of value. The result . . . hyperinflation, [which] is characterized by the absence of parameters of reference, hence *the end of positive economic calculations and the concentration of survival strategies by agents in paranoid defense of buying power*" (1993, 106; emphasis added). Earp's wartime metaphor suggests a qualitative difference took place in predispositions concerning consumption, and draws our attention to attitudes developing in response to the inflation crisis. I will return to that discussion in the last section of the chapter.

The discussion thus far has focused on grocery shopping. The very banality demonstrates how pervasive, indeed invasive, the crisis was; it also illustrates the overriding means of combating inflation. Although the strategies of the different agents (consumers, merchants, bankers) were diverse, they can be grouped under one guiding principle. With money value disintegrating as the clock ticked, the principle governing these many protective acts was the same: avoid cash, or better, convert away from the currency in circulation to a more reliable, steady repository of value. The rule is easiest to see when applied to shopping: one should convert into goods. If not often appropriately termed an investment, these might be called acts of salvaging against future inflation. With high, unrelenting inflation, this principle had generalized validity.

Where possible, household discretionary income was used to buy durable goods, in what I call *miniaturization* in real-estate investment. In Brazil, although the car of the year is best, cars do not depreciate as in the United States. Given inflationary distortions, the resale value (in real terms) might be equal to or better than the original price. Telephone lines, which are bought and sold in Brazil, also became a lesser but still significant "investment."[8] As Sandra put it, one needed to invest, if only in a "lesser good." Since one could not necessarily or only invest in expensive resalable commodities, the best bet at a lower level was to buy anything nonperishable. Thus, without expectation of future exchange, one would also resort to converting currency into laundry detergent or Guaraná soda to preserve value.

Research and buying for household goods at diverse locations was a tactic of those middle-class families on a tight budget—an observation confirmed by the fact that those who adopted the shopping system had to spend time to save money. However, it is obviously the case that miniaturizing as a means of economizing requires a sizable discretionary income, as does stockpiling (see Bowlby 1988). Even if one had the money to buy groceries and the car to transport them, in tropical areas one needs to have containers to store and protect perishables against insects. Poor people lack these means of economizing, and many middle-class people came to lack them as of 1990, when the Collor presidency ushered in Brazil's worst recession since the 1930s world depression.

THE MONEY SYSTEM

Buying over Time and Taking Turns Buying

In Brazil's inflation, protections of money also conformed to the principle described above; that is to say, one should avoid converting to cash unless and until absolutely necessary. Conventional wisdom would suggest that the most obvious strategy under inflationary and recessionary conditions is not to buy. Merchants adopted a credit practice entailing the postdated check, in a modified and truncated form of the installment plan to encourage shoppers to buy.

One of the curiosities regarding money that caught my attention on arrival to do fieldwork was gas stations advertising for drivers to fill their tanks now and pay eight days later. How were errant customers tracked down? By this (in fact illegal) use of postdated checks, I learned, consumers (partially) avoided the devaluation of cash, and merchants encouraged people to buy. So, for instance, a car driver would fill her tank with gas on June 10 and pay for it with a check dated June 17. The congenial gas-station owner would hold this check until that date and then deposit it. In a monthly inflation of 20 percent, the buyer would have paid roughly 5 percent less for the gas than the price offered.

Forms of this system became commonplace in many retail sales, both in large department stores and in small shops. Thus someone buying an outfit, a pair of shoes, or a shirt would pay half the amount with a check dated the day of purchase. The buyer would also write out a postdated check for the balance. Very often, the check-writing customer realized a significant discount—at least this was the logic of this promotional scheme. We might suspect, though, that the retail price had already factored in such devaluations. At any rate, prices placed next to goods in a store window would often have an amount written in big letters, for instance, 199. In the small print, one would read 2 x. Graphically, that would look like this:

$$2 \times 199.$$

The smaller "2 x" might well be in dark ink, with the price listed (just half) in bold red. (See fig. 5.) In my opinion, this advertising style worked mainly as an initial attention catcher. An informant assured me that it had a persuasive psychological impact: "It gave the *illusion* of low prices."

This illusion was momentarily tricky, whereas conventional install-ment buying, or layaway plans (*prestação* or *crediário*), was very risky.[9] With the latter, customers effectively spent a lot more than the asking price of the item. As bank administrator Carlos explained: "For example, a tape deck for the car. It costs 200 dollars [*sic*] if you buy it outright; if not, you pay in three installments of 90 dollars."[10] Formal installment plans would also include interest applied as well as the store's reckoning of future inflation (defensive pricing). In Brazil, the forecast of inflation, as of the weather in the United States, was best made after the fact. Bank interest rates in Brazil are higher per month than U.S. rates per year. (In May 1995 Brazil's interest rate on bank loans was said to be fourth highest in the world. At 64 percent, it was close to Mexico's, yet both stood behind the former Soviet Union's 242 percent [*Estado de São Paulo* 5/9/95, 1].)[11] Enticing for speculators, these rates were awful for the ordinary customer.

Merchants were not the only ones who developed creative tactics against the economic conditions. In response to the lack of reliable fi-nancing offered by merchants, a popular practice proliferated in the pop-ulation. The solution to the problem of wanting to buy something for which one could not amass the total price at one time was the *consórcio*, or consortium system. Developed in working-class sectors, where it had been used for large purchases, for example, cooking gas tanks (which ran about $35), the consortium had already been extended to middle-class households by the 1970s (Hutchinson, Cunningham, and Moore 1976), where it was used initially for a few specific purchases, principally cars. As small-business owner Renato explained, a consortium was a way around

5. Window display of a fourteen-inch TV with remote control. Only the 204,450.00 cruzeiros reais (printed in bright red) can be seen from a distance, making the offer appear to be a great deal. The 2x is printed in small dark ink. *Photo courtesy of the author.*

the installment/layaway plans controlled by businesses. "It's a group of fifty people, all make payments. Let's say you are buying a car in fifty months. You divide the value of the car into fifty payments, and each participant pays an installment the equivalent of one-fiftieth of the car. When the price of the car goes up, the payments do accordingly. So you always pay the current price. And when your name is drawn, you get your car and continue paying. This is a system that the middle class has used a lot in order to buy cars." When I inquired as to why the system developed, he explained: "It's because the interest that you pay today in financing is more than the inflation correction on the monthly payments for the car. If you go through financing, the company will require 60 percent interest or 50, when the monthly inflation might be 30 percent, 20 percent. . . . You can't buy a car on installments, you don't know where the payments will end up." This system expanded in the middle class during the crisis in response to greater and more diverse needs. Maria Regina (a public grade-school teacher) and Ricardo (a technician) reported using the consortium method to redo their kitchen and buy chocolates in bulk.

Having seen a number of middle-class and merchant tactics, let us turn now to the strategies employed by banks and the government.

Banking against Devaluation

Unlike Israel and Argentina, where dollarization became widespread (de facto and de jure, respectively), Brazil's high inflation was singular for not provoking a reversion to a foreign currency; dollarization never became generalized.[12] Instead Brazilians managed to avoid the national currency through their own banks. Banking services that protected clients' money against inflationary losses (and, through money market/ speculative possibilities, allowed a minority to increase their returns) also followed the principle of avoiding cash.

In 1991, a form of short-term savings called Fundão (Big Fund/ Fount) was created.[13] For just sixteen days the money had to be untouched, to avoid taxation. The Fundão was corrected closely to accompany inflation—that is, until the moment when a disbursement was needed, in which case a transfer was made automatically into the nonprotected portion of the account. In U.S. banking terms, one might liken this to an interest-bearing checking account, joined to a noninterest portion of the account. The comparison is somewhat distorted, however, as it was not a question of "interest" but rather, monetary corrections set to accompany inflation. These corrections never met inflation, but rather remained at some percentage lower than the actual inflation. Learning about the Fundão resolved another source of my curiosity when I first arrived in the field: people patiently writing checks for the equivalent of just two or three dollars. As long as it was not cashed, this money was mostly protected against inflation. As Rio de Janeiro inhabitants especially will add, the ubiquitous use and acceptance of checks allowed Brazilians to carry very little cash on their persons, which somewhat alleviated fears of being pickpocketed or assaulted. Bank "protections" were not available to poor Brazilians, who were unable to meet the minimum balance requirements of approximately one minimum wage or other bank requirements.

The money calculations did not stop there. It is important to underscore that made-out checks were no longer protected against devaluation. Thus the recipient of a check should ideally have run immediately to the bank to deposit it. Indeed, merchants in this period would make two trips daily to the bank to deposit checks. Contrariwise, one would hope that checks paid out would be cashed with the longest delay possible. For the same reason, a rule universally adopted was to pay bills on the last possible date, to take advantage of the fact that the sum owed suffered devaluation. (Thus a bill sent October 1 for $80 would be paid at the devalued amount of $64 when paid on the due date of October 15 in a monthly inflation of 40 percent.) A drawback of the Fundão was that a minimum amount had to be registered in the checking portion of the account; at my bank it was close to $25—for convenience, we will call this sum CR$25,000. Thus if a check came to CR$12,000, and the running account had been drained except for CR$2,000 by a previous transaction, not CR$10,000 but CR$25,000 would "spill" from the Fundão into the running account, leaving CR$15,000 unprotected henceforth.

It might seem petty to focus on these minor losses of monetary correction, but they quickly added up. This brings us to consider the money system from the perspective of banks. Since the government had committed to guaranteeing these protectionist rates to depositors, the limitation on some portion of the monies deposited (i.e., the checkable accounts) constituted a service charge and gain for the banks. Banks also benefited from small–scale transactions of another kind. In Brazil, one pays gas, electric, phone, and condominium bills at the bank, not directly to the company. Holding onto these monies for two days or less, as was usual, afforded banks great profits. They could use them in their own transactions, and due to the daily inflation, effectively pay the nationally owned utilities companies that much less. Indeed, the government was the major source of profit for banks, providing one-third of their profits in 1991 through the "overnight," that is, extremely high interest paid by the debtor government for extremely short-term bank loans (*Veja* 8/11/93, 50). Economist Garcia reports that "41 percent of the financial revenues of the largest six Brazilian banks in 1993 came from those 'inflationary' gains" and it has been calculated that "2 percent of the Brazilian GDP has been yearly transferred on average to the banking system in that form" (1995, 17).

While it would be relevant to go into much greater detail about the intricate and diverse means of protecting money and, for those with enough to invest, the speculating methods that developed, further dis-

Inflation Rates in São Paulo

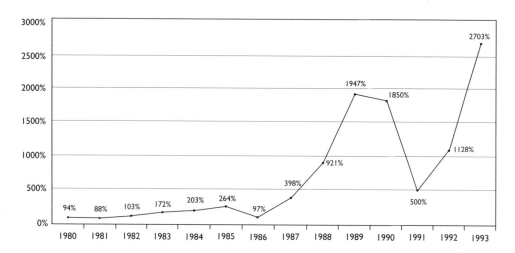

Source: DIEESE (Departamento Intersindical de Estatística e Estudos Sócio-Econômicos), December 1993.

cussion of money is perhaps not necessary to underscore the following. The financial services described thus far were highly profitable for those few speculators, national and international, who were able to meet the higher minimum investment requirements, take higher risks, and get the greatest returns, and for banks' own operations.[14] Although banks are not expected to be charity institutions, it should be noted that banks in Brazil came to specialize in certain income-capturing operations, eliminating unprofitable lending functions such as for housing, sanitation, agricultural credit—that is, financing for social and productive causes (DIEESE September 1990).[15] Furthermore, although the government initiated inflation, the banks did profit from it. As *Veja* reports: "In 1992, with inflation over 1,000 percent, the banking system profited 56 percent more than in 1991, when inflation was 475 percent. Conclusion: banks make more with high inflation" (8/11/93, 57).[16] Banks accumulated huge profits through the microprocesses of holding momentarily onto monies passing through their system. The former president of the Central Bank, Ibrahim Eris, said it distinctively: "It's almost impossible for a bank to suffer loss under inflation of Brazil's kind. If some Franciscan monks left the monastery and were called to open a bank, in a few days they would realize a profit" (quoted in *Veja* 8/11/93, 58).

It would be misleading if the preceding descriptions gave the impression that the systems for handling shopping and money during the crisis were functional, rational routines. Things were both far more complicated than these descriptions convey and far less "rational." The strong devaluation of money meant it came close to losing its functionality not only as a store, but also as a standard and measure of value—or rather, as price. As one informant put it, "Let's say you go once and spend ten dollars on groceries. Another time you have no idea what you will be able to buy with that amount." Those coming from a country with a stable currency and negligible inflation would carry with them a conception of the true cash value—that is, the base price—of a given item and noted endlessly that Brazil had become much more expensive.[17] When shopping for some cheap item, one would be quoted what seemed a jarringly high price. For instance, a plastic ground adaptor was not 69¢ but $7, and pronounced to be a good deal by the salesclerk—a judgment relating to the immediate context, not a long-established price in a non-inflationary economy. Part of the problem was that it was extremely hard to compare prices with things bought previously. If one had good recall or even a sales receipt, the basis for calculation was still obscured due to inflation, currency changes, or a combination of these. Thus homemaker Clarinha, mother of an eighteen-year-old and a nineteen-year-old, recalled that the college entrance exam in July 1993 cost CR$38,000, whereas it had been CR$4,000 the previous January. Were these the "same" prices, correcting for inflation, or had there been an additional increase? In relation to many minor but ubiquitous aspects of home and street life, it was possible to lose a sense of whether something was cheap, reasonably priced, or quite expensive. It no longer was a question of the cash value of the item; rather, one had to ask, "What is the price *today?*" (*Como é o preço hoje?*). Younger informants had experienced only high inflation. Thirty-year-old saleswoman Helena told me of a friend living in Switzerland who had made the following astonishing report: a can of mushrooms had cost 75¢ ten years ago and still did today. Her husband, Adalberto, added, for emphasis, "Not ten days ago, ten years." To call shopping procedures a system also overlooks the irrelevance for some. Yet again, an informant put it best. When I asked Roberta, a single head of household, about the timing of her shopping, imagining people could most opportunistically shop just before the end-of-the-month price hikes, she said dryly: "It's very simple. I shop when the monthly salary comes in." The term *system* is misleading for yet another reason: it implies stability of practice. If a practice became entrenched to the extent of being accomplished without premeditation or reflection, it was later disrupted. The attempts of householders and small-businessmen to impose control, their daily tactics in the fight against inflation, were often thwarted or had to be abandoned or revised. It was not just that new tactics were devised and incorporated into daily life; rather, things started out one way, and then, with each government "stabilization" plan, these tactics had to change, and things had to be done another way. Disruptive changes owing to nine government intervention plans occurred over and over in a period of less than ten years, becoming a central factor in the crisis.

GOVERNMENT INTERVENTION

The Plano Cruzado

Brazil's economic instability came to be characterized by spasmodic, surprise government plans, which provoked dramatic changes for daily life. Although until 1994 every plan failed, even backfired, each was intended to positively intervene against the chaotic economic environment. The first government plan to combat inflation was the famous Plano Cruzado. This plan was an ingenious and perhaps necessarily unorthodox way of countering Brazil's form of inflation. Before we turn to this first stabilization plan and the public responses to it, a few words on inflation vocabulary and the effects of inflation are in order.

In Brazil's economic crisis, we are not talking about simple demand inflation. Rather, in general, inflation involved a devaluation of the currency, hence a rise in prices. Brazil's situation was not called hyperinflation, however, since its inflation, although often high and wild, did not involve resorting to foreign currency, and it had certain controls. Put simply, one of the most important aspects of Brazil's inflation was the fact that the economy had regulatory mechanisms to accompany and buffer inflationary increases. Anti-inflationary policies were put in place by the military dictatorship against the high inflation of the early 1960s and against the 1973 oil crisis, and emergency measures were added in the

1980s. Major buffers against inflation were wage and price adjustments for inflation applied with reference to inflation indexes (monetary correction/indexation). Once acclaimed for being a form of social welfare, many economists now argue that these governmental protective measures (and demonetization in the financial sector) fostered inflation in Brazil and were responsible for turning it from an acute into a chronic form (Cardoso 1992; Bruno 1988; Sachs and Zini 1995; Garcia 1995). In other words, the adjustments for inflation themselves came to create a sort of tide of price increases in some areas responded to by increases in others. Although this form of inflation has received the dull name of inertial inflation, or stagflation, the social costs have been dramatic.

It is important to note that inflation affected the entire Brazilian population and that this impact was highly differential. The disparity in means to protect oneself had to do with salary corrections. Salary adjustments always lagged behind inflation, so over time losses would accumulate—invariably the losses were greatest for those with the least. Until as late as 1993 those earning between one and six minimum wages (figures varied, but anywhere from US$50 to $500 per month)—at least 70 percent of the population (Instituto Brasileiro de Geografia e Estatística [IBGE] 1994)—received quarterly corrections only, whereas those with higher income received monthly adjustments. Obviously such delays set this already poor working population onto a path of irrecoverable loss, debt, and hardship (see Nash 1994). Although some maintained that poorer Brazilians were not as touched by the crisis since, as the argument goes, they spent their money immediately, this is inaccurate. The more-than-decade-long inflation crisis exacerbated already grave social inequalities. A World Bank study of 1996 ranked Brazil first in the world in income concentration; it had been second. This process of income transfer and concentration occurred in part through the insidious shopping and banking activities described here.[18]

By the 1990s, the distortions and inequalities of the anti-inflationary measures were exposed in the media. As *Veja* (6/9/93) caustically described indexation for lay readers, "This is the mechanism of automatically correcting the prices and contracts with reference to inflation indexes.[19] It protects those with money to receive and prejudices those with bills to pay, principally salaried people, whose earnings aren't indexed." That is, the bills one received would have been adjusted for inflation; one's salary adjustment might not come until months later. Inflation one month might be 25 percent, but one's bank would adjust the Fundão at 22 percent. There was always a lag time between corrections, and adjustments usually did not favor the ordinary citizen. The complexity was such that different sectors of the economy had different indexes (totaling eleven) and time frames for adjustment. Indeed, in this flight-and-chase syndrome, time became the key element.

Provided with such information, outsiders can easily wonder: Why not stop all this nonsense? Why not have everyone just stop raising their prices? Indeed, in lay terms, President José Sarney's plan tried to do just that—by imposing measures requiring all to stop raising prices. On February 28, 1986, prices were frozen and a new national currency, the cruzado, was inaugurated.[20] The price freeze (and fixing of the exchange rate) was an unorthodox measure aiming to reduce or eliminate inflation (DIEESE March 1986). Orthodox measures reduce fiscal expenditures, decrease money supply, and apply wage and price restraints (Cardoso 1992). This heterodox plan instantly earned the minister of finance who designed it, Dilson Funaro, *Veja* magazine's admiration for "manag[ing] something no one thought possible in Brazil: he's a populist finance minister" (*Veja* 3/19/86).[21]

Public Responses to the Plano Cruzado: Sarney's Inspectors

The first important response to the Plano Cruzado price freeze was a frenzy of consumer sprees. This was not surprising, since the freeze was coupled with wage increases for low-income earners. As of April 1986 some economists were worried that excessive consumption in itself would provoke inflation (demand inflation). The excesses ranged from meat consumption, which doubled in the middle class (DIEESE July 1986), to amassing of consumer durables. Limits were then imposed on buying in quantities.

More intriguing than this proof for the theory of repressed consumption was consumer "activism." Sarney made all citizens his inspection agents. Popularly called *fiscais de Sarney,* all citizens were authorized to denounce any store selling a good at a higher price than that assigned to it by the plan. Complaints by Sarney inspectors (more often women) succeeded repeatedly in shutting down noncompliant businesses. The plan provoked great enthusiasm, not only for the expanded buying power, but also for this unique consumer empowerment. In response to the militant consumers, businesses developed "shortages."

Truly a surprise measure, the Plano Cruzado came at a moment when some merchants had not yet corrected their prices upward for inflation, so those items frozen at low, devalued prices especially hurt some store owners and producers of certain items. Some real scarcity did result from excessive buying. Yet both real and artificial scarcity at times led to black-marketeering, referred to as usury fees (*ágio*). Meat, chicken, and dairy products, which were central to the consumer jubilee, became scarce. These products are staples for middle-class consumers, but out of reach for those whose poverty restricts them to rice and beans. This brings us to the differential impact of the plan.

Mechanical engineer Euclides and his part-time employed wife, Gilda, reminisced during one of my visits to their three-bedroom apartment in Pinheiros. Though my description of their home suggests spacious comfort, with three teenaged daughters in eighty square meters, their space was at a premium. The recollections of Euclides and Gilda underscored that the plan was for the people. Euclides immediately called it "populist, it was intended to please the people, it raised everyone's salary. If I had to buy something over time, the inflation projection lowered that debt. If on the first of April, I had to pay one hundred, I would pay eighty-five; there was a 15 percent discount. A month later it was 15 percent lower still. So the deal doubled. Whoever had money, had more [quem tinha dinheiro, o dinheiro sobrava]." When Gilda recalled the fiscais de Sarney, the following discussion ensued:

> Euclides: What happens when there's a shortage of a product? The price goes up, isn't that so? There was a supermarket in Curitiba that raised its prices one night, and suddenly a guy appears saying, "I'm a fiscal de Sarney, I'm here in his name, and I close this supermarket."
> M. O'D.: What guy? Anyone?
> Euclides: Yeah, any citizen. He closed the store, and the people, everyone got together, you know? The press covered it, Sarney covered it. All the merchants, they went under [ficava com a maré baixa], everyone was an inspector [fiscal], everyone who went to buy, went with a list [of published prices]. . . . There were shortages, because the demand was big. You can imagine with this mass of population that

hadn't been in the consumers' market, they suddenly have a bunch of money, and go after this consumption.

M. O'D.: So it was a party!

Gilda: It was horrible.

Euclides: There was meat shortage. The butcher shops that followed the rules could hardly sell. I remember that a kilo of *alcatra* [prime cut of beef] cost thirty-one cruzeiros—that was the supplier's price.

M. O'D.: There was no profit.

Euclides: There was no way to sell. On the other hand, there were people who black-marketed, who bought from a supplier that didn't pay taxes, did the transaction in the middle of the night, and the guy sold. If an "inspector" arrived, he'd buy the inspector. I remember that in the Plano Cruzado, my recollection was of lines at the butcher store, the whole day long.

Other informants also especially recalled the long lines at butcher shops, and the scramble to get milk before it ran out for the day. Gilda remembered that there were restrictions prohibiting people from buying in bulk, yet the shortages persisted. Said Gilda: "It was almost Christmas and there was no sweetened condensed milk, which we use a lot, and there wasn't any!"

The era of the Plano Cruzado is most often remembered by the middle class for benefiting "the people," owing to the price freeze. Although it eliminated the need for middle-class individuals to make price comparisons and initially allowed for sprees, the plan soon became more of a hassle than a help, as it entailed waiting in lines, food shortages, and the dilemma of black-marketeering. Furthermore, it was only a partial stop to inflation since the price freezes affected a finite array of goods—the basic basket of food and household items. The plan, then, did have a fleeting populist side to it, and curbed those with higher consumption potential.

Why did the Plano Cruzado fail? In simple terms, the solution of shouting "everyone stop!" requires a de facto agreement of the agents concerned. As Sachs and Zini explain, "These plans (wage and price control plans) collapsed for several reasons. . . . On the political side, they engendered significant pressures from affected business interests that undermined public support and credibility in the controls. Economically, controls led to shortages, black markets and growing economic distortions with each month in which controls were in force" (1995, 8).[22] The

Plano Cruzado and later plans with price freezes were intentionally abrupt, so as to prevent last-minute markups. However, these surprise plans went seriously awry. By mid-1987, the Plano Cruzado had backfired: prices had skyrocketed, moving Brazil into inflation greater than 50 percent per month. In later years, mere rumor of a plan—or rather, of the price-freeze element of a plan—came to prompt defensive price markups, as economist Earp cited earlier noted.

WHAT INFLATION DOES

As inflation came to saturate daily life, informant frustration with the everyday hassles of shopping and banking grew. Stockpile shopping tried Maria do Carmo's time and patience: "I think, for example, you stock things, like food, it's absurd, when there's a sale, you have to run. My maid sometimes arrives saying, 'Look, aren't you going to go to Tulha [supermarket]? Today there's *tornado,* there's a sale!' And so you go and everyone has already taken everything. . . . *This [stockpiling] is terrible too, it's no good for anyone, because everyone will start doing it.* . . . It's terrible, this business, you fill your cart full and at times you don't want to. You have to. The difference of one market to another is huge" (emphasis added). She intimated that stockpiling was a way of furthering inflation rather than simply guarding against its effects.

Adalberto's comments on comparison and bulk shopping in May 1994 reveal both frustration and antigovernment sentiment:

> I'd like to see the Minister of the Economy go personally to the supermarket to shop, just to see. I shop every forty-five days, there are things that go up, it is not like they say, 40 percent, 50 percent, it's a soap that was 126 cruzeiros [reais], you go to the supermarket forty-five days later, I did this, I know, I paid 120 for Lux soap. Forty-five days later it was 560. This isn't only a 100 percent increase. . . . I paid 760 for a can of soy oil, Lisa [a common brand], and forty-five days later, I paid 1,370. That is nearly a 100 percent increase.[23]

Adalberto may have ignored or misunderstood that the inflation rate is a composite (hence a given price could be above the rate, or he may not have factored in devaluation); or this might be an example of defensive overpricing by merchants. In any case, his good recall of actual prices fueled his suspicion that the government was not acknowledging the real inflation. At one point, Adalberto moved from an unenthusiastic comment about the budgeting control one derived from comparison shopping into a defiant rejection of the government's capability of ending the crisis: "Control between quotation marks, because one supermarket asks one price, another asks an entirely different one, so you are obliged to go all over, worse than a peon [que nem um peão aí] to get the cheapest things. Now, from this perspective, what is the vision that I have for the future? Very bad, I don't believe in absolutely anything more that this government might do." Like Adalberto, many informants cited examples of "absurd" prices or trends, then launched into critiques of the government. The monetary crisis deflated pride and trust in the nation-state (see Simmel 1978, 161).

Douglas and Isherwood (1979) have argued that the function of goods is to make sense of the social world and its categories. Brazilians felt that their country's monetary situation was "illusory" or "unreal"—which I read as "should not be real"—and found that it entailed futile efforts (see also Dominguez 1990). Thus Maria Cecília (owner and director of an English-language school) said: "Savings is a very illusory business. . . . All this craziness of going out, investing, savings, CDB [bank-deposit certificate], is a mechanism for you not to lose what you already have. This is nothing that is going to help you live better four or five or ten years from now. This money that you're simply fighting not to lose, not to devaluate, it's nothing that is going to increase." The nonproductive, speculative financial market is known disparagingly in Portuguese as the *ciranda financeira*. *Ciranda* is a ring-around-the-rosy type of game; the phrase thus condemns the vicious circle of financial markets. For ordinary banking services, Brazilians had to wait in lines in monumental buildings, or crowd into modest ones, in a process endlessly repeated, reaching heights of lost time around the first of the month and when the utilities bills were due. One major headache produced through inflation was the payment of monthly installments. A novelty in Brazilians banks was a counter set up by the waiting line for customers to consult a clerk who would make the calculations from relevant tables in order to update their regular bills and translate them into the currency of the moment. Euclides commented dryly that the lost time in bank lines was itself inflationary.

Put together, these statements add up to more than an ad hoc collection of perspectives. Reviewing them, we can see that *no* effort to guard households against inflationary losses went unremarked by informants. They offered disparagingly critical commentary denying the validity of each and every tactic: doing research and comparison shopping offered no real control; avoiding money through banking was an illusory hoax and countered productive activity; the time spent on all of this was wasteful and decadent. And converting into goods was consumerist.

A legacy perhaps dating from the Plano Cruzado forward is the so-called fever to consume (*febre de consumo*), a malady said to afflict many middle-class Brazilians. Indeed, unpredictability most likely prompted what one might call immediatism in buying. Although unplanned, this tactic refers not to impulse buying exactly, but rather to opportunistic shopping owing to a serendipitous combination of having the money at the time a good offer is found. Sounds simple, but it was rare and unforeseeable.[24] Here is the testimony, perhaps rather extreme, of a woman who participated in a focus group one year after the Plano Cruzado:

> I changed my thinking about life lately. Until, let's say, about two years ago, I prepared myself for the future, I was a very secure person. I achieved a lot with this, but I then came to the conclusion that it wasn't worth it, for the times we were going through. . . . So, today I live for the day. So, let's say, if I think I have to have a car, I don't want to hear about tomorrow, and what I'm going to have to eat. Today I'm going to have a car. If I hit on the idea of taking a trip, I'm going to catch a plane and travel, you see? I don't want to hear about getting into debt, what is happening is I'm living for the day. (Standard, Ogilvy, & Mather, 2/26/87)

This practice of immediatism likens middle-class people to those for whom having money is always unpredictable and savings and planning inapplicable. A pithier rationale for spending offered by another female focus-group participant in 1987 was partially cited at the beginning of this chapter. Her full statement was "No one is concerned to save money because we know that *saving or not saving is the same thing*" (emphasis added).

Unlike these defiant focus-group participants, my informants were at pains to criticize such tactics. Disregarding the principle of countering inflation, namely to avoid money and to convert into goods, my informants often disparaged Brazilians for their fever to consume. The recourse to conversion into goods and other spending can simply be read—as economists do—as a symptom of the gravity of inflation. While my informants clearly understood the rationale for this practice and occasionally defended the recourse, they also degraded *other* Brazilians for their consumerist practices in implicit contradistinction to their own more honorable restraint.

Besides pointing to the self-indulgent or superficial aspects of spending, my informants also found consumerism inflationary, and hence damaging to the national economy and society. They underscored that even those tactics employed in a positive effort to salvage against inflation caught one in a vicious cycle, ultimately defeating the purpose of combating inflation. (See chapters 6 and 7 for further discussion of what became known in the media and scholarly circles as the culture of inflation.) Alternatively, the government plans themselves defeated middle-class adaptive tactics. The Plano Cruzado soon made stockpiling impossible. The Plano Collor, as we will see in chapter 6, defeated tactics of consumers and businesses alike by withdrawing most of the national currency from circulation. Many informants noted in frustration how one would go to bed with the situation one way, only to wake up the next day to an entirely new one.

From what perspective can we analyze the middle-class commentaries? The negative appraisals might call up explanations of a social or psychological nature. Some commentaries obliquely expressed injury to social status. What irked among other things was being reduced to economizing (i.e., the underside of what Bourdieu [1984] called making a "choice of the necessary"). Aninha (a homemaker) once lamented, "At times I feel like a witch for controlling so much" [Às vezes me sinto bruxa de tanto controlar]. Even if economizing was erroneously presented as new, my informants believed that the crisis had prompted this, and they tried to impress on me that such economizing had not been necessary to them in the past. Although recollections of easy times in the past may have been distorted, food and other household goods, which used to be cheap for middle-class people, did become weighty expenses. To be obliged to count pennies, even for food, was a mark of declassification for the middling sectors. Statements against the government surely provided a dignified means of venting indignation at having to scramble and spend inordinate time and thought in money dealings and shopping.

Boutique-owner Simone's comment shows that the changes were threatening to her sense of social boundaries and values: "I think one has lost a sense of values, no one knows the just price of anything, you don't know. For example, I'm talking about a problem with maids, maids became expensive—are they really expensive? I start to wonder, if she thinks that [is nice], I'm going to think it's junk [uma porcaria], but I can't pay much more either [than she]. So, there are no values, there aren't any more. This inflation, I think it does us in [acaba com a gente mesmo]." Helena was disenchanted with the void left by economizing: "So, you see, you're obliged to wear the same pair of shoes for a year, for six months, depending on how you wear them, or two years at the most. In the past, you'd open the closet, in the middle class, and you had . . . I once had four pairs of shoes, a bunch. So, this discouraged [desanimou], you see? *There is nothing left for the middle class to do, what for?* It's just go to work, come back home tired, then get into a series of things—for those who don't have a maid for instance, there's a lot to do" (emphasis added).

These middle-class Brazilians drew overt connections between being middle class and being able to consume. The same was true in negative formulations. Ricardo's outburst contains an extraordinary repetition of nine negatives in a few quickly stated sentences:

> At times we lose our sense of it [perde a noção], not of status, but of class itself. What am I? When you don't manage to invest in something at the end of the month, when you break even and the overdraft is in the red, then you can't consider yourself, you don't know, you can't maintain the middle-class standard. You can't go to the theater, you can't go to the cinema. You can't say that you are middle class. Leisure doesn't exist. Not that we don't have activities . . . we go to the park [Ibirapuera]. But to buy five ice creams you have to think twice. If it is the end of the month, forget it. [Not to] have an ice cream on the corner. *Caramba!*

One last commentary was even more striking in the connection drawn between being middle class and being able to consume—and that not being able to consume negated some significant part of life. Like Ricardo, Alice was one of the worst-off financially in the group of informants. She was not bitter about her work, which was satisfying, nor her apartment, which was rented, cheaply furnished, and located on the "wrong" side of the street (i.e., on the other side of the very rough, rundown, and noisy Avenida Santo Amaro, which separates the lush and ritzy Vila Nova Conceição from the dreary Vila Olympia). A college instructor and graduate student, Alice was indignant about the low pay for her field but directed her anger generally at Brazil for not providing a decent living. Alice's ex-husband, a retired military officer, paid for their two sons' education, health care, club membership, and allowances, but she shouldered the daily expenses on the equivalent of US$1,400 per month income from two teaching positions. Alice's glowing happiness was a startling contrast to her dramatically critical words and economic challenges. Completing her Ph.D. dissertation, giving full-time care to two teens, and working at two institutions, Alice said she had worked hard to attain her education and employment, yet felt she was so poorly remunerated as to be unable to enjoy a decent standard of living. Her very first remarks to me, when I asked what changed for the middle class over the crisis, were as follows:

> I think the worst change is despair. I am basing this affirmation on myself. The economic changes are reflected in changes in buying, in consumer goods. And this inevitably is going to reflect on hope. The future doesn't have an outlook/any prospects [perspectiva] today. This has been the great dilemma of the middle class today—the lack of outlook/prospects [não-perspectiva] for the future. It's the disbelief in the nation, a disbelief in the people, and in themselves. Because you want to do something for yourself, for what you believe, for your country, for your children, but you aren't sure these things can happen.

Again, the comments presented here were recorded after more than ten years of inflation, nine failed government plans to counter it, five devalued currencies, and the highest inflation yet; they clearly register informants' frustration and resentment at this impasse. Their remarks show that the association between middle classes and consumption is subjectively, even existentially, experienced by them as foundational— whether affirmed or contradicted. These middle-class Brazilians linked consumption and money matters to their sense of social status, national integrity, even to what makes sense and gives life value.[25] Without ignoring the unself-conscious sense of entitlement expressed in several of the

3

THE DISCRETE SALES OF

THE MIDDLE CLASS

Gender and Generation

in a Globalizing Economy

The first potential informant interviewed in 1993 pressed on me three issues of the magazine *Microempresas* [Microbusinesses], saying, "This is what you need to know about what's happening to the middle class." I soon learned the significance of her assertion. The Brazilian middle class has been the beneficiary of prestigious formal employment in government and the private sector, of privileged consumption, and the standard of stability and progress. Brazil's chronic high inflation and recession eroded the salaries and security of middle-class employment. The key to better withstanding the crisis was hard but simple: generate more income, by working more hours in the same area, if possible, or by adding new sources of income. While fully half of my informants kept the same employment—itself an accomplishment given the recessionary conditions—the others either increased hours at their jobs or created new employment. One-quarter (13) started moonlighting, part- or full-time businesses at some point after the crisis began in 1980.[1] Prejudicial salaries made self-employment a more attractive risk, and for some, the sole alternative. Eight of the forty-seven informants had lost a job in recent years.

While laid off for several months in 1992, technician Ricardo began filming parties. When his job was reinstated, it was as a consultant, and he suffered a 30–40 percent salary cut. Although he later became a salaried employee at Gessy Lever, Ricardo continued his filming sideline and investment in it. He said, citing an aphorism, "A scalded cat is afraid of cold water." That is, after a layoff, formal-sector work became untrustworthy, and the crisis rendered moonlighting both more necessary and attractive. Ricardo's form of self-employment is called a *bico de emprego,* literally a beak of work, or *biscate* (odd job). The expressions connote marginality in work and scale. *Microempresa* connotes higher stature as an enterprise, yet the miniaturizing term is somewhat ironic.

The shift of the new middle class into moonlighting, small business, and sales is the focus of this chapter. The once privileged, now declining class of liberal professionals and managers was treading water, and a new commercial class (i.e., petite bourgeoisie and service and sales personnel) was moving forward with the current in the flexible, globalized economy emerging in Brazil. While the global trend and national crisis provided sufficient inducement for this shift, such a change did not occur in a discursive vacuum, nor evenly across the board. Both men and women entered into small businesses, but my hunch is that women and youth were widening the categories to include hitherto "lower-class" sales positions, acting as the vanguard of the emerging informal, flexible sales economy. However, this turn to formerly lesser occupations was being elevated, not merely because it entailed work against hardship. The news and entertainment media positively promoted the movement toward flexibility with the same gender and generational coordinates. Furthermore, such avenues of work in commerce were uplifted through their association with new consumption goods and practices. Indeed, in fetishistic fashion the goods (and associated sites) might be said to confer status on the (sales)people. Finally, this move toward flexibility in middle-class work raises the following question: To counterbalance that shift, what would then become inviolable in middle-class identity?

LEARNING TO MAKE OUT

At our first meeting Aninha (married to Milton) told me that as of the Collor presidency (1990–92) she was no longer able to find work in her field of industrial design except for sporadic freelancing. She had once tried to work in a boutique as "a salesperson, in a beautiful shop in the Jardins, a chic one, but it is not my profession, and I couldn't . . ." Her voice trailed off. Then she resumed, "It's great to work with the public, though. I like it." She later contradicted this last remark, confiding that the job she had taken and quit was at a lingerie store on the once elegant but now rundown Rua Augusta. Her look of disgust when recalling having to wait on (middle- and upper-middle-class) customers clearly conveyed a sense of personal affront or indignity. Besides, the pay was low, so that she began to ask her husband for gas money. Aninha explained: "But then the whole thing became sort of disconnected [*meio desconexa*]; it became senseless, so I think that I spend less by staying at home, taking the children to school, and doing work at home than I would working outside the home." Like other homemakers, Aninha emphasized her strategic role as an economizer—an act that required a good deal of time and expert accounting due to the chaotic inflation. Once, after picking me up along with her kids after school, Aninha delivered some new clothes to someone's home. This unexplained stop led me to suspect her of selling clothes as a sideline, but given Aninha's evident discomfort over work outside her field, I did not probe this further.

With his brother in Germany and father in Brazil as partners, Euclides, a second-generation Japanese Brazilian, opened a gas station. An engineer, he lost his first and high-paying job with the state oil monopoly, Petrobrás, owing to involvement in a student organization during college. Euclides announced that his salary has been $60,000 in the late 1960s, but it was now one-quarter of that, and that his patrimony had not changed one bit in fifteen years. Whether or not this information was accurate, the overall message of downward mobility was clear from this head of household and father of three. Euclides's full-time employment remained in engineering. He himself never mentioned the gas station. His wife, Gilda, barely spoke the first time we met, beyond saying she was a housewife. The next time talking with me alone in their apartment in Pinheiros, she told me how for years she had been, as she jokingly put it, a "madame" not working at all; then "one fine day" she decided she wanted to work. She and her father-in-law began to manage the station. She worked there every morning. Unlike the invisible lace-working housewives in Narsapur, India (Mies 1982), Gilda, working in the open congested air of São Paulo, somehow managed to do gas-station work discretely and—outside Euclides's presence—discuss it with an air of happy nonchalance.

Lara told me all about her work right away, when we first met at her office, even before I could ask any questions. An architect, Lara was working half-time (at modest pay) for the city government, and with two women partners, running an architectural firm. They had an office in the upper-middle-class Jardins area, in the bairro of Itaím-Bibí, at a short walking distance from her home. When she was first married, Lara worked for a construction company. But after having two children two years in a row, she felt the babysitter was not able to handle it, and she quit for one year. However, as she put it, "in those days, I was really a kid, I think I didn't have much patience. That wasn't a very agreeable activity for me—to stay at home taking care of them, but on the other hand, it was a responsibility, they were my children. I took a civil service exam because at the time the city was offering a job at six and a half hours per day. This matched what I needed."

Lara was reminded, then, of problems at home, and recounted the following horrifying incident. She returned home one day to find firemen at the apartment building, people outside, but her maid and three children indoors, unaware. Said Lara, "I almost killed the super. He had an obligation to knock on people's doors and warn them. Second, I fired the maid. Third, the problem [of childcare] remained." Her mother stayed with the children for a time, but she herself was busy. "I don't even like to remember those days," said Lara of the preschool years.

Her business started in 1981, when poor people of the region where she worked on city projects came to ask for help planning homes. When she and her sister-in-law began, Lara's children were small, all sleeping in one room, leaving her bedroom for an office. Exuding radiant high spirits, Lara recalled their early days. "We worked on projects from 7:30 P.M. until midnight, or 12:30, every day, including Saturdays and Sundays. We worked in my bedroom, in my apartment. It was an 'extra' that we had. Extra money that helped us a lot. To pay medical bills, *it was I who paid*" (emphasis added). The business took off in 1987 with a large project for an industrial company lasting two years. At this point the women rented an office, but were afraid they would not be able to keep up on rent. Lara's father then sold a house in Tatuapé (a bairro in the far eastern part of São Paulo, where Lara grew up) and this money and hers enabled them to buy a small row house on a cul-de-sac (*vila*) with a low selling price, which they then converted to an office.

Why the differing responses to their work? Aninha's shame, Euclides's silence, Gilda's private, but ready admission, Lara's pride? It is possible that Euclides omitted information about his business because it was inconsistent with other commentaries on downward mobility, possibly offset by the gas-station income (sans employee overhead). Yet it also seems likely that this business—even if fully legal and his—went unmentioned because from Euclides's point of view, selling gas did not confer dignity on him or his family. (Might it not make him, as a former executive at the national petrol company, seem ridiculous?) We might recall in this light Ricardo's statement in exasperation at his and his wife's work situation: "It's completely inverted. Her with two jobs, me with an extra one." For these men, most likely male honor as well as class-related social status was at stake.

Aninha's work experience at the lingerie store made her serve people she did not consider her social superiors. It appears that certain traditional venues placed some too unmistakably into subservient working-class positions. If so, then Gilda's carefree manner over gas-station work would require explanation. Most likely the facts of family ownership, transgression of her hitherto traditional housewifely role, and entrance into a distinctly male milieu gave Gilda a defiant spirit not unlike Lara's.[2] Lara's shift did not entail downsliding into a field "beneath" her college degree; on the contrary, her move into business ownership was a big step upward in every way. Furthermore, given the apparent prosperity of her home and family background, and her husband's good salary, Lara's move to part-time self-employment appeared less motivated by economic need than occurred with my other informants. However, Lara herself emphasized that her family would not have the home, car, and schooling they did if they had to rely solely on her city job and her husband's salary. She firmly declared, "I only manage to maintain myself in the middle class with two jobs."

The shift to business ownership may seem to automatically confer honor. My impression, however, from the affectionate but amused references to the stereotypical immigrant shopkeeper (e.g., the depiction of the Lebanese bar owner in *Gabriela, Cinnamon and Clove* by Jorge Amado) en route to upward mobility is that small-business owners are viewed favorably, but as lower in status—owing to some nonexplicit combination of ethnicity, generational depth in Brazil, and economic and cultural criteria. Yet once mobility is attained, those in question—normally, the sons and daughters of these small-businessmen—are eligible to join the ranks of liberal professionals. Thus whereas Lara's move was up—she remained liberal professional after assuming business ownership—other businesses (such as Euclides's) could entail demotion—or would have, until the conditions justified the lowering of this standard. However, in this recessionary state, entrepreneurship was undergoing a widening acceptance and valorization.

Indeed, an entrepreneurial—or rather, selling—spirit seemed to be turning up almost everywhere, and among women with the fewest restrictions. Formerly a secretary at the state university, Helena came to manage a microbusiness that sells bathroom accessories. She explained that she had had no experience with sales, in fact had been very embarrassed (*super acanhada, envergonhada*), but received encouragement and was doing quite well. Two housewives were planning businesses. Sandra was actively working out a means to make and sell her own jewelry. Clarinha, formerly a fashion seamstress, was thinking of designing and making clothes out of the second home her family was no longer living in and was having difficulty selling. And Sumiko, a social worker in her early fifties and eligible to retire after the required thirty years of service, confided her dream of becoming an international (United States–Brazil) contraband merchant of consumer durables (see chapter 5).

Most certainly, for middle-class professionals sales represented the potentially bigger declassification—and hence the avenue for women. At the same time, for many women, paid work per se was a welcome change. The women with outside employment were almost unanimously enthusiastic about their work. Without any prompting on my part, women brought up their work, in some cases—like Lara's—giving entire histories at our first encounters. Only a few men told me about their work without my asking—precisely those who had their own businesses. Most men (and all had full-time work) were by and large unenthusiastic about their jobs. My impression from such responses was that the crisis deflated salaried men's contributions, even though men were most often the bigger breadwinners, and validated women's contributions, no matter what they did. Aninha and a woman whose marital separation obliged her to work in a boutique near her home (where her eight-year-old son had to stay with her after school) were the exceptions in my study.

REDEFINING/REDEEMING COMMERCE

Now that paradise was lost, what was there to do? *Se virar*—Get by/make out, as an informant put it. That is to say, adapt to the crisis in the 1980s, and then to the recessionary, downsized, and globalized economy of the 1990s. In this shifting economic environment, commentaries and stories circulated of middle-class workers who were defying their declassification in the decadent economy by taking initiatives outside the formal sector of salaried employment (see Hart 1992).

After describing her work, Lara emphasized the illegality implicit in these business ventures:

> Most people became aware that it wasn't worth trying to make demands [reivindicar]. The solution had to come from the bottom up. How would you get this solution? Everyone became aware that the income from salary was no longer enough to live on. Everyone went into a third line of work, what I call "bico." Because generally you don't pay taxes and it's sort of clandestine. Just like I did projects in my house, clandestine, not paying taxes, nothing. There were people who started making cakes, selling hotdogs, clothes.

I asked, "People you know?" Lara responded, "Yes, people I know. For example, my sisters-in-law, they learned how to make candy. When it was Easter time, the poor things spent nights up, making Easter eggs. And their husbands sold them in their companies, as an alternative to the market, which was much more expensive." Lara explained that the money earned "wasn't even to maintain their former living standard, but to fill needs." She cited dental care as an example. She also noted how people made trips to Paraguay; contraband merchants traveled there by bus and then resold merchandise in Brazil. "Careful with that tape recorder!" she warned me jokingly, and added, "Because, you see, at the same time that the Brazilian population got poorer, the population continued to have Christmas obligations, and so it sought alternative solutions other than the [formal] market." Lara then justified the irregularities:

I don't pass judgment [não recrimino] when I see people working illegally, without paying taxes, first because it's a case of need. Second, we
lived through something that came from the top down. Because the
Brazilian has good character [tem boa índole]. If you had a dignified,
decent government, everyone would collaborate. I have no doubt of
this. But the way things are, nobody feels like obeying the law. There
isn't much law in this country. . . . It's a misgovernment [desgoverno].

Although no informant ever mentioned it, one could include as an
example of middle-class illegal business the extremely common practice
of doctors who charged two rates: one with a receipt, the second a
discount (up to 20 percent off) without a receipt, by which the doctor
avoided taxes. Previous expansion of middle-class employment relied
on government jobs or state-assisted development; the work here described—bicos de emprego and microempresas—were created in spite of
the government. Lara's defiant or self-righteous attitude regarding businesses outside legal norms of incorporation or involved in tax evasion
registers antagonism against the government, held responsible for the
chaotic economic environment.

Lara was fairly unique in defending illegality; most informants were
at pains to show their unflinchingly high ethics. In all cases, however,
understanding of downward mobility and how to counteract it differentiates these members of the Brazilian middle class from the groups Newman (1988) studied who underwent downward mobility in the United
States. As Newman shows, such misfortune befalls individuals or certain
occupational groups, which hides the extent of their occurrence. This
obscurity, coupled with the ideologies of the self-made man and the
work ethic, supports an interpretation of downward mobility as individually caused. Brazil's crisis affected the majority of the population, ob-
viating individualized self-blame. (See chapter 7 for further discussion.)

Whereas Lara emphasized and defended the informal-economy aspect of her own business, and that of far less glamorous cottage industries
and contraband sales, Adalberto bemoaned the plight of middle-class
professionals. Adalberto (married to Helena) started his own business in
1989, and like Lara and the few other business owners, told me all about
it right away without my elicitation. Adalberto did mechanical design
related to computers; for instance, he designed the model of the series of
plastic cards for telephones and photocopies. Although the first two years

were rough, by 1994 his business held promise, which his previous salaried employment as a mechanic did not. Their family lived in an apartment in Pinheiros that they inherited. A young couple with two grade-schoolers, Adalberto and Helena emphasized that they would never have been able to buy an apartment and that their children had tuition scholarships, owing to their friendship with the school's owner. Enthusiasm for his own business did not prevent Adalberto from directly condemning the degrading of these professions. He asked with characteristic rhetorical flourish:

> Middle-class people, people who had a more European education, let's say, what conclusion can we draw, over what this generation, children, grandchildren are going to do from now on, if I know engineers who are car mechanics, if I know doctors who are elevator operators? Do you know what an elevator operator is?! They make the elevator go up and down, doctors, a guy who studied five years in college. . . . Waiters, civil engineers who are waiters, a friend of mine, personal friend, a civil engineer, sells fritters now at the market. . . . Where are we going to end up?

This led immediately, without break, into a description of the poor who raid for goods (*arrastão de trem* was the expression Adalberto used), just like on the beach or on the bus. "Do you know what this is called? It isn't banditry, it's hunger!" And yet, Adalberto added, he warily put his daughter on the bus to go to school, thinking of these dangers. (Pickpocketing on buses in São Paulo was frequent; residents of Rio de Janeiro would say it was continual.)

Adalberto's reference to doctors notwithstanding, in the popular imagination, the most dramatic move out of one of the traditionally "noble" professions was from engineering to quasi-marginal sales or services. It was from José Luis, an engineer and board member directing a successful engineering firm, that I first learned of the engineer who had turned to juice. "A while back there was an expression, a very common one, because there was a real fact—*o engenheiro que virou suco,* literally, 'the engineer who turned to juice.' It was an engineer who was finding everything very difficult, he built a small luncheonette, where his strong point was selling orange juice." The expression alludes to a movie title, *The Man Who Turned Into Juice,* a story of a poor Northeastern migrant who works himself to the bone in São Paulo industry. The later mock horror story satirizes middle-class downsliding by comparing the professional workers to those of the humblest means. Yet I must underscore that the sales were not just from a mobile juice cart, such as are found in declining downtown São Paulo, but rather from a permanent store on the most important uptown street in the city, the Avenida Paulista. Hence the business must have provided an excellent revenue. This fact-based tale received national press coverage (probably in *Veja* or a Sunday newspaper feature); however, I found just one reference to it in an article titled, predictably, "The dream of engineering is over," in which a line of text reads, "Here's another one who 'turned to juice' " (*Jornal do Brasil* 11/12/87).

Another small-business owner (of an English-language teaching school) commented on the growing number of liberal professionals in small business. As Maria Cecília put it, "São Paulo at the beginning of this year had two hundred thousand unemployed executives, that's a lot of people! The opportunities to open something outside the area are running out [se esgotando]; for example, what there are of engineers, architects, administrators who opened a luncheonette, coffee house, pizzaria—tons of them! São Paulo is already saturated with this." Her husband, an engineer, lost his job after eighteen years but was lucky: he was reemployed elsewhere in six weeks' time at a higher salary. Not without amusement, Maria Cecília told of her neighbor, an engineer who "opened a bakery, pretty, like a bread boutique." The most famous baker in Brazil is Vera Loyola of Rio de Janeiro; her "bread boutique" (in the fancy Rio de Janeiro suburb of São Conrado) placed her as a leading figure among the nouveaux riches, now ironically called the new emerging society (*nova sociedade emergente,* as coined by society columnist Hildegard Angel, for *O Globo* newspaper).

Aside from these rather satirical modes of discussing middle-class employment, the media also took on an important "straight" role of offering strategic vocational counseling. It did this in two successive ways. Initially it presented human-interest stories of the downward paths being taken by unfortunate white-collar professionals.[3] During the 1980s, there were frequent reports of college graduates who, unable to find a position in their field, resorted to odd jobs (*biscates*) of all kinds, including shockingly degraded jobs such as being autonomous garbage collectors/recyclers and car watchmen.[4] For instance, the *Jornal do Brasil* announced forbodingly, "The profession of garbageman brings teachers, mathematicians, and philosophers to the streets" (11/10/85). A *Veja* feature story told of teachers selling anything: instant coffee, macaroni, sanitary napkins (12/9/92).

The Brazilian media ostensibly charted these human-interest stories, saying merely "Middle-class people are doing X." But could this not also imply "Middle-class people should do X" (where X refers to "just about anything to make a living")? In Barthes's (1967) analysis of *Elle* magazine, he shows that the texts accompanying fashions tend to state "X is the fashion," or "people are wearing Y." By saying X and Y are being worn, the "fashion makers" pretend to be charting a trend whereas what they are in fact doing is attempting to set one.

By the early 1990s, as neoliberalism appeared more definitively on the horizon, variously sad or mocking tales of the "outcaste" state of the middle-class professional were replaced by forthright advice in the form of cheerful how-to instructions. Newspapers brainstormed ideas for microempresas; for instance, how to make and sell American-style cookies in one's very own cottage industry. To those laid off or fired, the news media advised against holding out for the dream job (as if that were possible), recommending a jack-of-all-trades approach. Similarly it said, don't hold out for the level of your previous salary: take less! Such reports can only remind us of Aninha's unattainable dream job; Ricardo's imposed salary cut; Lara's sisters-in-law making Easter eggs. The variation in news style, from melodramatic over downsliding to ironic over the nouveaux riches to cheerleading for those in cottage-industry ventures, also recalls the array of informant responses: Adalberto's outraged outburst—"Do you know what an elevator operator is?!"—Maria Cecília's sardonic comment about liberal professionals becoming bread-boutique owners, the spunk and determination of housewives to start their own businesses or sales.

In sum, although informant assessments differed, the press—itself offering a "plurality" in the style of presentation of human-interest stories, from drippy to cheery to sarcastic—quite invariably produced one plot: downgrading of the liberal professional to a job in commerce, which could prove, if not glorious, lucrative. Thus I argue that the media was an integral and important catalyst in the trend toward petty commerce, making it inevitable and desirable. But the media did not act alone.

A new valorization of consumption facilitated a loosening of what had seemed to be inflexible middle- to lower-class occupational boundaries in Brazil. Sales work became capable of reclassification upward. The very quality of the merchandise could confer status: cell phones were a prime example of high-tech value, but even bathroom accessories could be transformed into a sophisticated aesthetics. The sites of consumption could also elevate the occupation. Sumiko's daring idea for sales would involve international travel, and the goods would have a First World provenance. In keeping with Marx's presentation of commodity fetishism, the commodity itself and the sites of consumption were acting as agents conferring honor back on the merchants and salespeople.

YOUTH, PARENTS, ADVERTISING, AND SALES

Each of my visits to Mariza and Renato's fell on a Friday evening. Each time I was served a variety of hors d'oeuvres and imported liquor. According to Renato, some things cannot be substituted. Mariza was a school teacher and director. With his brother, Renato co-owned and ran a welding business his father started. On my first visit to their luxury apartment in the upper-middle-class neighborhood of Moema, where they moved expressly so that their daughters would associate with that (upper) social circle, I met their younger daughter, Luciana, who showed me pictures of her forty-day stay on Fernando de Noronha, an island off Paraíba famous for its diversity of flora and fauna, and for the expense.

The most extraordinary news was that Luciana had earned the money for the trip by selling sandwiches at the Shopping (Center) Ibirapuera—not at a café or fast-food shop, but on her own, store to store, much like hippie beach vendors. She was so successful that she expanded, incorporating cakes into her basket, *which the maid prepared* (and for which she received some compensation). Luciana was eventually caught by shopping-center security, but by that time she had made many friends. Luciana had sold mostly to sales personnel, so that she then worked for two months as an extra during the Christmas rush. Renato said he would have been too embarrassed to do such a thing, but he saw with satisfaction that his daughters knew how to fight (*sabem lutar*).

The family's elder daughter, Silvana, was in her first year in advertising at the respected private college MacKenzie, known for business administration. Renato did not like Silvana's choice of major but said he would not impose his wishes on his children. Silvana had three jobs at the time, two related to advertising, one teaching English. Renato pointed out that his daughters did not have that middle-class malady of being spoiled children, who then turn into adults waiting for the government to act without doing anything. His daughters could look out for themselves, they could get by, they knew how to make out (*sabem virar*).

Renato began work at an early age at his father's store. In college, despite an interest in medicine, he completed a degree in economics, as this would be most applicable to his future as a business owner. Twice he told me the exact same story, once in 1994, and then on a return visit after my fieldwork, in 1996. Renato asked a doctor friend of his whether he woke up with a positive outlook on the day's work; the friend said yes. Renato himself said he did not get out of bed looking forward to the day's work. Mariza, who worked part-time as a teacher, part-time as a school director, always looked fatigued. She told me that she had come from a poor family, and that she had always been tight with money.

The next time I was at the family's home, Silvana arrived at about 11 P.M., announcing that she was going to Guarujá for the weekend. A beach town frequented by upper-middle-class Paulistanos who have apartments there, Guarujá is about an hour's drive from the capital. She and two girlfriends would stay in their apartment, nineteen-year-old Silvana explained, and their three boyfriends would stay in another person's apartment (how convenient!). She asked for an advance of "twenty dollars," stating the dollar value explicitly, then left to make a call from her bedroom.

Her parents, impassive until then, indicated that they were upset and explained why. Renato told me that he had already gone through this so much that finally he threw up his hands, telling his daughter to just go ahead and do as she wished without asking. Still, they were very displeased with her lack of consideration. It was that she had just announced this plan, with no warning, very late. Furthermore, the short trip entailed a drive through a range of hills, which could be dangerous at night. Mariza went into Silvana's room; I heard loud voices.

An issue in all this was the boyfriend, Renato meanwhile explained. They did not like him, he was not welcome in the house. One thing they did not like was that he was very possessive/jealous (*ciumento*). Renato told me that he had asked Silvana, "What will happen when you finish and I want to send you to the United States for three years?" He noted that he had no connections, but knew that postgraduate training abroad was a way for people to get good jobs. A bit later he said he was concerned, he did not want his daughters to be housewives, then he came to the point: he was concerned about pregnancy. In fact, he had told Silvana that if this occurred, "Many things you would like to have happen in your life will no longer be possible." (Although abortion is illegal in Brazil, this was a striking way of stating the outcome of pregnancy.) The episode concluded after Renato gave his daughter the twenty dollars. He then reported to me that he had told her she had been inconsiderate, and that she was lucky he had gone to the bank. (I privately debated whether this was said for effect, since it seemed Brazilians had to go to the bank almost daily, or whether it simply referred to the rule of carrying very little cash on one's person.)

Renato expressed two views about his daughters' work: he was concerned that his daughters become liberal professionals, which he himself had not been able to do. Although the field of advertising was distasteful to him, he wanted to ensure that Silvana would have a successful career, which might require foreign training, given the high competition and small number of jobs. The few sought-after high-paying positions in advertising most certainly required connections. Besides this concern about the feasibility for her in her chosen field, Renato's worries for Silvana clearly involved elements of his own frustrated career outside the liberal professions. Yet Renato also demonstrated pleasure and pride that his daughters were not afraid of work. In both cases he valued the wherewithal to make out—perhaps less out of a sheer admiration than assessment of the economic environment.

We have seen middle-class adults reluctantly or gladly undertaking forms of work previously classified as beneath them, as well as ways that various agents and discourses render it acceptable. As Renato showed so clearly, many informants appeared to accept the prospect of their having to adapt their work and perspectives; however, they still set their stakes for their children's futures in college education. The degree of anxiety, however, appeared to vary according to the parents' longevity and security within the noble middle class of liberal professionals. Besides Renato, other nouveau riche families in the study lacking either education or connections also displayed strong concerns that the children enter into "new middle-class" professions traditional to the upper middle class—or rather, those fields that still were viable. The children themselves were fully cognizant of their prospects. Thus Marcos (son of housewife Clarinha and maître d' José, who came as a youth from Portugal) told me his field of production engineering at USP promised "100 percent employment." Former salesman Nando and school director Teresa (daughter of a Portuguese shopkeeper) had their three daughters training rigorously for college (also toward engineering fields in the case of the high school–aged daughters). These same families also invested in manifesting their heightened status symbolically, through debutante balls, as well as the "obligatory" Disney trip (see chapter 4).

Nevertheless, like Renato, several other informants worried that the decline in education and noble professions and the increasing commercialism would be damaging to the nation's future course. Maricarmen (an immigrant as a child from Spain) was shocked that college hopefuls were going into advertising: "It's a dream for you in this country to want to be in advertising. . . . Either you expect to import everything, or they're going to advertise for what?!" Other engineers told me critically there was a time when the financial market offered higher returns than any productive activity. Sandra spoke approvingly of the United States, where, she said, people admired honest working people—as opposed to Brazil, where laborers were not respected. These middle-range, liberal professional parents stressed honorable, productive work and money earned without corruption (see chapter 7). These informants upheld their own work endeavors (lucrative or not) against unproductive speculative and corrupt activity damaging to the national economy.[5]

In contrast, the better-off liberal professionals and larger-business owners in this study did not display worries about whether their vocational choices were pragmatically sound. Sumiko (married to a medical doctor) was proud of her eldest son's choice of philosophy as his college major. Citibank executive João and homemaker Wilma were calm and assured that their daughter in advertising would go to the United States and later succeed—quite possibly they had connections. Lara did worry—that her son should not choose architecture, because he preferred art. These parents wanted their children to find fulfillment; the others certainly had such dreams for their kids too, but (conflicted or not) were steering their offspring onto a pragmatic route—of having to make it—anyhow.

For their part, the youth themselves seemed bent on commercial and service vocations: advertising, hotel management, tourism, and psychology were all on the rise. In fact, relatively speaking, the most competitive field for entrance into USP in 1994 was advertising. (In Brazil, students apply to the academic departments for acceptance into college.) Thus 3,340 students applied to enter the advertising school of USP. Since only 40 could enter, the ratio, 1:84, was the toughest of all. Similarly, the newly popular field of tourism had room for just 1 of every 50 applicants. In contrast, the School of Medicine, which remains the top choice in numbers of applicants (14,000), accepted 1 in 29 (USP 1994 figures).

Television showed support for the trends into small business, service, and sales here identified. A 1993 prime-time soap opera (*novela*), "Fera Ferida" (Wounded and Wild), airing after the 8 P.M. news and geared to adults of all ages, had the mayor's daughter, no less, actively running a cottage textile industry—in very humane conditions and with a tasteful product, to be sure. In the next 8 P.M. novela, a remake of an earlier one on Spiritism, "A Viagem" (The Trip), the older and younger major male characters were in the classic fields of law and architecture; the corresponding main female protagonist, however, was the owner of a video-rental store (offering glamour through its modernity). In the 7 P.M. time slot geared to youth, the main plot of another 1993 novela ("Olho no Olho" [Eye to Eye]) showed psychic powers to be the special talent of youth. Although perhaps an ironic commentary on what might be needed to make it in Brazilian society of the 1990s, dance-hall ownership was clearly presented as an attractive occupation for young men and women, as was waitering, long the exclusive province of working-class men. Likewise, popular nonfiction sources (like *Vejinha São Paulo*) regularly produced blatant "lives of the rich," quasi-advertisement reports of young eligible men who had made their fortunes in business.

Brazil's path to globalization developed from a particularly acute and nearly chronic economic crisis. Through it, the protected middle class lost its hold onto sure paths of upward mobility, was deprived of security and drained of financial resources, bringing it into a perfect position to accommodate flexibility. While the categories petite bourgeoisie and new middle class remain important native classifications and, with qualifications, can indicate economic position or potential, they do not separate out families or even individuals, who may well move across these categories within their lifetimes, as is amply clear even from my sample. Although views conflict, one could find, especially with respect to women and youth, a lowering of liberal professional standards and a broadening of the occupational categories included as middle class. The "vanguard" appeared to be saying, as did Mariza of counter sales, "Middle-class children do it now, look at our daughter." From this perspective, the defining criterion could become extremely flexible, following the decree of the speaker: "If we do it, then it's a middle-class job." These ventures—legal and not—might in the early years of the crisis have been the discrete sales of a dishonored bourgeoisie, prompting shame or ambivalence in the people involved. But they quickly became visible, and thanks to the media's encouragements, the fetishlike conferral of honor on salespeople by consumption sites and goods, and the boldness of women and youth, informal businesses and sales were gaining a chic appeal. As employment became flexible, consumption—or better, certain kinds of consumption—became ever more inflexible to middle class identity.

4

THE INTERNATIONAL

IN DAILY LIFE

Of Debutantes and Disney

Accounts of living through high inflation and recession normally feature austerity. Indeed, middle-class Paulistanos have economized and worked more since the economic crisis of the 1980s and 1990s. Still, one might also ask: in a context of high economic instability, to what leisure pursuits, if any, were middle-class Brazilians committing themselves? In what arenas and through what means were symbolic claims to middle-class identity being formulated (Bourdieu 1984; Appadurai 1986; Lamont and Fournier 1992)?

Threats to class position have led to a reinforcement of "classic" middle- and upper-middle-class ways and means (Leeds 1964; Bourdieu and Passeron 1977), as we have learned, primarily through expensive private primary and secondary education to ensure children's entrance into the better colleges and universities. In the more competitive and restricted economy of the 1990s, the great concern for education was significant, timely, and obvious. What I found surprising was the strong involvement in symbolic pursuits abroad. Continually encountering instances of transnationally obtained goods and experiences, I inferred that nonlocal, nonnational elements are vital to contemporary Brazilian middle-class identity, figuring importantly in the local status hierarchy. In this chapter and the next I investigate current forms of transnational consumption through fieldwork episodes and from the perspective of the actors involved. I attempt to find not one but several motivations revolving around this consumption. One episode in particular struck me, owing to the apparent frivolousness of the foreign experience.

EPISODE 1: DISNEY VERSUS FOREIGN EXCHANGE

One night after watching TV at Gilda and Euclides's, she and Martha, soon to be a high-school senior and the oldest daughter in a family of three girls, drove me home. In the car Gilda told me that they wanted Martha to be in an exchange program with an American family and wondered if I could help set this up. Several weeks later, having found a willing family in my hometown of Minneapolis, I called Gilda with information about our friends and their daughter about Martha's age. She countered with the following: "Euclides insists on going to Disney [World]" [Euclides faz questão de ir a Disney]; "he is going no matter what" [vai de qualquer maneira]; "he refuses to give up the idea of going to Disney" [ele não vai deixar de ir a Disney]. In other words, Euclides was determined that the family should go to Disney, even if that meant, as Gilda explained, that Martha would have to postpone the exchange for another year. Gilda did not at any moment say that the kids had been pestering Euclides to make this trip. Rather, she stressed that Euclides had established that if just one trip were possible now, that trip would be to Disney.

Later, I became intrigued with the fact that although an educational experience abroad was desired for the eldest daughter, the father gave priority to Disney World, a place more "invested" with parental hopes than one might expect. How to understand this? It was not attributable to the parents' frivolousness or carefree financial circumstances. We saw in chapter 3 that salary decreases eventually prompted Euclides to find an additional source of income, one that in turn required Gilda's unpaid employment in the family business. Why was Euclides prepared to violate the unassailable middle-class principle of education first and foremost?

In a recent essay, Colin Campbell (1994) examines some of the motives behind consumption, especially the conspicuous variety. He criticizes Veblen's theory of status emulation for imputing motives without regard for subjectivity, and psychoanalytic and Marxian theories for assuming that people do things without knowing the "real" reasons. Campbell conceives of motives as beyond instrumental, means-ends purposes (which he calls intentions); for him, they involve moral and ethical concerns brought to bear both in motivating the act and in providing a meaningful explanation for the actors. Although Campbell's focus is the individual subject, he presents motives and justifications as developing through the cultural context.

Unfortunately, during fieldwork I was inhibited from questioning Euclides. Besides being intimidated by his severity and less than forth-coming manner, I was reluctant to set him up with a question like "Why do you want to go to Disney?" It can be hard to get at motives when self-evident reasons provide barrier explanations, or when one is otherwise hindered from probing. I therefore needed to have recourse to sources other than Euclides for interpretation of the "Disney motive." Martha's testimony after the trip confirmed that one imperative was social. She said: "Now that practically everyone has gone, we couldn't really con-tinue without making the trip." Martha quickly added a sentimental motive, pointing out that the trip "united" the whole family. Other perspectives on this phenomenon will emerge as we compare it to the debutante ball, or coming-out party, now celebrated as the fifteen-year-old party (*festa de quinze anos*) in Brazil (*quinceañera* among Latinos and Latin Americans).

DISNEY VERSUS DEBUTANTE BALLS: PERSPECTIVES ON ADULTS

Teresa and Nando's second daughter, Juliana, celebrated her fifteen-year-old party in September 1994. Teresa had worked for more than twenty years at the Colégio Objetivo, teaching and writing curriculum for this chain of schools. At the time I met with her, she directed a branch in a town about an hour outside São Paulo, with the assistance of Nando, a longtime salesman who lost his job in the early 1990s. They lived in a modest middle-class bairro far south in town (Planalto Paulista). The upward mobility enjoyed by this family was shown in their housing: they extended their row house by buying the one next door and integrating the two.

Highly ritualized, the phases of the debutante ball unfold like a stylized pageant. The event culminates in the midnight descent from a stage of the fifteen girlfriends (*damas*) and then the fifteen-year-old, who has changed costume from one prom-styled dress in the color she chose for herself and friends, into another gown, white of course. The girl-now-turned-young-lady (*mocinha*) dances three waltzes—first with her father and godfather (or other relative) and then with a young man—as if for the first time.

The banquet hall this family rented (at Mac Buffet on Rua Augusta) charged the equivalent of US$7,000 for the hall rental and (the more economical) buffet-style food service. To this must be added the costs of invitations, music, flowers, photos, filming, presents to the damas, and unlimited wine and whiskey—all of which increase the sum significantly. Teresa said the event cost the price of a new car. Perhaps the closest U.S. equivalents besides the debutante ball itself are the bas mitzvah and the Italian-American wedding reception. The current smaller family size (usually three children), in those families with more discretionary income, allows for a rather high concentration of expensive attention on the children. Elaborate birthday parties are held for one-year-old babies in Brazil, attended by a broad circle of family, friends, and associates. Though a few informants mentioned having attended debutante balls, just two of the twenty-four families in my study, both of whom had experienced remarkable upward mobility, had held them. (Chapter 1 discussed the upward trajectory of Clarinha and José, whose daughter, Márcia, had been a debutante.) These same two families plus seven more of the twenty-four had gone to Miami-Orlando in the past few years. Among the many ways one might internally divide the middle class, the accomplishment of Disney might have been as reliable an indicator as any in the 1980s and 1990s.

Without assuming that the intention went beyond a desire to shower love on the children, one can imagine additional motives and benefits for the parents who take their families to Disney. The pressure and possibility to see Disney has perhaps been strongest in the upper middle class, which "rubs shoulders" with a wealthier sector (sometimes called *classe A,* a kind of tongue-in-cheek adoption of the term used in market research for the highest social class). Euclides's teenaged daughters attended a school in which classes A and B "mixed." Thus Euclides *was* investing in Martha's education—in Brazil. Quite possibly he as well as his children experienced peer pressure. By making the Disney trip, the family followed a strong, recent precedent.[1] In 1985, 86,576 Brazilians entered Florida; in 1990, following the opening of MGM studios, the figure rose to 207,156; and in 1994, the year of Gilda and Euclides's trip, 334,793 passed through (Florida State Division of Tourism, U.S. Immigration).

Even discounting the very wealthy and business travelers (including informal-sector buyers), these figures are impressive. Of these, probably most first-time visitors went to Disney. By 1997, 400,000 Brazilians were going to Disney annually.[2]

Comparing the Disney trip with the debutante ball brings the specificity of Disney for Brazilians into sharper focus. The debutante ball is coated with family love, sentiment (especially in the father-daughter waltz), and unity (as a total experience, and specifically, as the family together greets all incoming guests). Thanks to Martha's clear statement, we see that Disney can also be idealized as a moment for family unity (for comparison, see Willis 1995). Like the trips to Europe in previous eras by elites with daughters who had just finished school or with sons about to enter a profession, Disney marks a turning point. It has become a highly desired rite among upper-middle-class Brazilian (and generally Latin American) teens, a quasi requisite for social validation. Like the debutante ball, the trip to Disney could be viewed as a teenage rite of passage (van Gennep 1960). As such, the trip should accomplish a change in status. Ideally, it should signify the incorporation of the teen and family into the higher stratum—or more realistically, into a new or particular branch of it—or at least express how the family wishes to represent itself or with which reference group it identifies. Although both the debutante ball and the Disney trip may be called rites of passage, some qualifications are in order. First, teenage rites of passage are understood to occur universally; the ball and the trip, for reasons financial and other, do not. Second, the Disney trip is for boys and girls, unlike the debutante ball in honor of girls alone. (I will return to gender in the last section of this chapter.) Finally, the Disney trip is also central to the parents' class identity. Like the debutante ball, this packaged "magical" experience, arranged by parents for their children, attests to concern for the children's social positioning and the parents' own.

At the risk of juggling too many anthropological concepts, I consider each event hybrid, involving a rite of passage for the teens and more. Appadurai recently suggested that the "rite of passage is concerned with the production of local subjects" (1996, 179). He asks us to see how such rites locate us spatially as well as socially and goes on to consider the "global production of locality" (188ff.). This description also leads us to ask what it means that the Disney rite of passage is accomplished on foreign soil. Several have proposed seeing the Disney experience as a secular pilgrimage (Moore 1980; Worsley 1981; Fjellman 1992), an apt characterization that registers its significance and the fact that it is not universally attainable. I draw on Appadurai's "tournaments of value" as a further means of clarifying and distinguishing the motives behind the two coexisting and competing events—Disney and the debutante ball. Inspired by the example of the *kula* system, Appadurai describes the tournament of value as

> complex periodic events that are removed in some culturally well-defined way from the routines of economic life. Participation in them is likely to be both a privilege of those in power and an instrument of status contests between them. The currency of such tournaments is also likely to be set apart through well understood cultural diacritics. Finally, what is at issue in such tournaments is not just status, rank, fame, or reputation of actors, but the disposition of the central tokens of value in the society in question. Finally, though such tournaments of value occur in special times and places, their forms and outcomes are always consequential for the more mundane realities of power and value in ordinary life. (1986, 21)

With these concepts in mind, let us further refine our understanding of the two rites, with attention to the adult perspective. One basic difference between Disney and the ball is that the latter is a pageant for immediate display, involving guests who are actors and witnesses of this highly ostentatious and highly controlled event. The rounds of debutante balls can be readily seen as examples of status contests. The family trip to Disney, recalled in stories, photos, camcord films, and theme-park T-shirts, makes for a fragmentary circulation of status claims.

The spectacular nature and the attendant conspicuous consumption in the debutante ball, or rather, those produced by *nouveau riche* parents, further differentiates it from Disney. With $15,000 burned in one night's festivities, the family proves they have no need to store every value in tangibles. Faced with the prospect of one or more expensive debutante balls and the decline of the fad among youth during the 1970s, upper-middle-class parents started to substitute a trip to Disney—which included sons as well as daughters. Herein lies one practical reason for Euclides's decision: all three children—by chance, all daughters—and

Gilda went to Disney in one trip. In contrast, on the night of second daughter Juliana's debutante ball, Nando was already talking about how he needed to save for his third daughter's party.

It might strike one that the debutante ball is the higher-status event because, in Veblenesque reasoning, it is more wasteful, but that inference is questionable on several grounds, only one of which is monetary. Although some families find both rites desirable, others would repudiate the old-fashioned debutante ball in favor of Disney. The debutante's ball is quickly dismissed as square (*careta*), corny, or kitsch (*brega*) and scorned by some Brazilians of the milieu, if not the financial level. An academic friend called it *brega-chique,* as did the press.[3] For their part, the ball critics wish to take or do take the Disney trip, readily affirming or confessing their enjoyment. Why do some embrace, some eschew debutante balls? Why the ready acceptance of Disney? Taking into account the history of the ball may provide clues.

I was unable to ascertain when the festa de quinze anos was first practiced. Those Brazilianist sources I consulted, such as Pinho (1970), Pierson (1972), Azevedo (1986), Needell (1987), and Lopes (1989), mention balls in general for members of high society in different eras, from the late nineteenth century forward, but not coming-out parties. A feature story on the debutante fad in the Sunday magazine of the *Jornal do Brasil* (11/4/90) claims that the first Brazilian debutante ball was held in 1944, and notes that it was rare for a girl to give one by herself. These Rio balls were held only in the Copacabana Palace, according to one of the "original" debutantes. In the 1960s and early 1970s in Brazil, social clubs would put on a yearly party for fifteen-year-old members at which the birthday girls all wore white. Wealthier families would hold a party in the home or even rent the social club for an evening in honor of just one debutante. The banquet-hall rentals evidently are a variant of the latter.

The popularity of the debutante ball in the upper middle class rose after the nation witnessed the maximum debut—when President Juscelino Kubitschek's two daughters were invited to share in a debut at the palace of Versailles in June 1959. The current craze is associated with a TV depiction of that era. According to the press, the TV miniseries *Anos Dourados* (Golden years), a nostalgic depiction of the 1950s that aired in 1986, triggered the revival. If in the past only "traditional families" (i.e., the minority of elite families, such as sugar-plantation owners) could partake in them, later that identification may have been the inspiration for its widened popularity among youth.[4] Although the debutante ball may initially have signified emulation of Europe (see, e.g., Miles 1992), it is most likely experienced at the present as a tradition in emulation of the Brazilian upper class. Calling fashionable practices emulative of the upper class (following Simmel and Veblen) has been greatly criticized (see, e.g., Hebdige 1979; McCracken 1990; Campbell 1994); however, since the people involved convey that intent, it would be unwise to overlook that explanation. One middle-class family who put on a ball said, with no evident irony, "Our family has a traditional [elite] mentality" [Somos uma família de mentalidade tradicional] (*O Globo* 7/16/89).

Disney appears to offer a clear set of competing contrasts. Travel abroad per se accrues cultural capital. Acquiring this form of capital became an especially noteworthy accomplishment during the economic crisis. And Disney is associated with modernity and a transnational social circuit. Thus the Disney trip positions Brazilian travelers symbolically among the citizens of the First World. According to the local classification system, therefore, the debutante ball is traditional, and the Disney trip modern. Those who scorn the debutante ball probably find the emulative quality of the traditional ball somewhat ridiculous. What this perspective conveniently ignores, however, is that the Disney trip also refers to the local status hierarchy, and gaining validation for class standing via foreign experience has had a long tradition among local elite (see Needell 1987), one now spreading out into the population. Though still confined to the more prosperous middle class, Disney has become increasingly accessible.[5] Package deals now allow payment over several months, as do international credit cards made available to Brazilians since 1990, features that also bring out that Disney is an investment. A major tour agency, Soletur, advertised two different options for a Florida trip of "14 days, 11 nights [*sic*] at 4 x US$621 without interest, or downpayment of US$373 + 15 x US$198." The former total price would be US$2,484, the latter, US$3,343. The package included "Miami, Fort Lauderdale, Orlando, Disney, Epcot Center, Universal Studios, Sea World, Busch Gardens, and a layover in Key West" (*Jornal do Brasil* 11/20/96). *Veja* (4/11/90 and 10/3/90) declared the Orlando–Disney World trip cheap after the Plano Collor took effect (March 15, 1990), for thereafter dollar prices fell.

Let us dwell further on the terms *traditional* and *modern* in light of Appadurai's definition of tournaments of value, which states that the "cultural diacritics" of such events are well understood. Although the status connotations of the debutante ball are clear, issues arise when nonelites claim that identity in performance. Further complications arise since the term *traditional* can refer to elites, as is most usual, but also to the petite bourgeoisie. Thus the press points out that debutante balls occur in traditional and modern middle-class neighborhoods—the former in the sense of petit bourgeois, mainly lower-middle-class neighborhoods well separated geographically (by zone) from the "modern" ones, these stereotypically middle- to upper-middle-class areas of white-collared employees and liberal professionals. Rio newspapers note that balls were being held in the Baixada Fluminense, among "high-middle-class" (alta classe média) families (*Jornal do Brasil* 9/28/87), as well as in Ipanema—that is to say, in an area known mostly as a working-class suburb as well as in an upper-middle-class one. Likewise, the *Estado de São Paulo* (9/29/89) located debuts variously in the (traditional) rural areas and in the (modern) central south zone of the capital. A later report in Rio informed readers that debuts were being held not only in social clubs, but in samba courts (e.g., at the Escola de Samba Beija Flor, *Jornal do Brasil* 11/4/90). That being the case, one wonders whether those who scoff at the festa de quinze anos are more bothered by its adoption among the nouveaux riches or by the poor. The popular spread also indicates why the debutante ball cannot necessarily be seen as higher status for monetary reasons: one can stretch the debutante ball greatly, but although travel abroad has become more feasible for Brazilians, there is still a bottom-line cost. Interestingly, whereas the traditionality of debutante-giving families is disputed, the assumption of modernity through Disney is not subject to doubt or debate.

Those of a "modern mentality" who insist on demarcating differences by rejecting the more ostentatious, elite-styled pageant underscore the unease produced in this era of heightened social differentiation provoked by inflationary conditions. Hence the constant struggles, on material and symbolic planes, by those less favored financially to separate out the rising-class members, or better, to delegitimate the candidacy of nouveau riche people for higher social status. Through enactment of competitive rites and evaluative idioms—through these rites of passage/

tournaments of value—middle-class families, some more stationary, others wealthier, take differing routes and make conflicting claims to social distinction (Bourdieu 1984).

Explanations of status competition and search for cultural capital give the activities purpose, but the concept of symbolic / cultural capital does not greatly surpass what Campbell (1994) considers to be instrumental intentions. Nor does it adequately address the intensity of the adult desire to go to Disney. Moore suggests that the popularity of theme parks is a response to "endemic crisis in our lives caused by geographic and social mobility" (1980, 216). For Zukin, themes ranging from old-fashioned small-town America to futuristic Epcot Center exude control and security. This touristic experience chosen by largely white visitors, reports Zukin, offers both escape from "individual social realities" (1990, 44) and, interestingly, "ultimate predictability" (45), thanks to the "friendly face of power" (1991, 228).

In a wide-ranging exploration of Walt Disney World, Fjellman calls Disney an "antidote to the normal, everyday experiences of many of its middle-class guests. They need only to submit to Disney's total control of the operation and to the commodification of their own experience" (1992, 403). In this "symbolic essence of childhood" (10) produced by Disney, in this "utopian" world, all is safe and clean (12), and all is superlative. Fjellman points out that Disney provides not only these experiences, but also the responses to them, in its literature telling guests that "Everyone loves Y," that there is "More vacation fun than ever before" (15), and so on. Disney epitomizes postmodern capitalism, and is a late development of commodity fetishism, in which consumption has "metastasized" (4), rendering Americans the subjects and objects of consumption. The irony, then, is that the supposed antidote to the postmodern anomie is a heavy dose of the problem—consumption, in aid of Disney's reason for being.

The authors of *Inside the Mouse* (Klugman et al. 1995) study a range of features engaging Disney goers, such as Disney's designation of technology as the historical agent and people as consumers in a controlled environment. As Kuenz puts it, Disney offers a "system of social relations based on consumption" (1995, 57) and "purposeful consumption" (187). Referring to Disney, Featherstone observes that "such postmodern spaces could be regarded as commemorative rituals which reinforce, or help regain, a lost sense of place" (1993, 180). Of course, this would be an "ersatz nostalgia—nostalgia without memory" (Appadurai 1996, 82). Observations keying into appeals for American visitors, such as the nationalist representations helping them feel good about themselves and their history (Klugman et al. 1995, 60) and the construction of nostalgia through consumer goods and sites, again raise the question of the experience and messages for foreign visitors.

These analyses of Disney in itself move us toward consideration of motivations not covered by status emulation and competition over symbolic capital, namely, the possible "side effects" and "fringe benefits" of these travels. Not only does the Disney ideology match Martha's characterization of family unity; the Disney experience and wider U.S. stability held special meaning for Brazilians, who have lived in a chaotic political and economic environment plagued by wildly fluctuating inflation and failed government stabilization plans. One might wonder whether Brazilian travelers thought of ex-President Collor while at Disney. An article in *Veja* (9/9/92) during the Collor impeachment movement described the two-million-dollar garden that the Collors had landscaped at their home (the Casa da Dinda). Featuring five artificial waterfalls and a lake, fifteen tons of stone, tropical trees from outside the region—including a pau-Brazil tree (which needed to be brought from Africa since it is extinct in its native land)—a quartz grotto, and special nightly illumination creating a fairylike wilderness, this garden was expressly likened to Disney's Typhoon Lagoon. News like this must have fueled Brazilians' indignation against the monstrous extravagance of the president who had confiscated all but the equivalent of US$1,200 from their bank accounts and plunged the country into the worst depression of the century (see chapter 6). *Veja* condemned Collor but exempted Disney from criticism: it was built not for a single owner's babylonian-styled pleasure, but rather for the profit of a company and thousands of tourists.

Let us consider the touristic experience further. Mass, semipublic recreation is itself a novelty, since middle-class families in Brazil, always a minority, have hitherto avoided mixing with other social sectors.[6] Brazilians whom I met demonstrated anxiety about whether they had adhered to imagined norms while traveling in the United States, and seemed anxious to avoid other Brazilians who, they claimed, were unconcerned about such norms. I debated whether these were exaggerated or unfounded worries, until I read in *Inside the Mouse* that Brazilians had become notorious among Disney workers. "They turn up everywhere in worker narratives, always playing the part of the out-of-line guests who use language or ethnic difference to excuse unacceptable behavior" (Klugman et al. 1995, 150). The author of this chapter, Jane Kuenz, aptly notes that whether or not the workers are capable of distinguishing Brazilians accurately, they universally designate the "difficult Disney guest" (151) as Brazilian. I have no doubt that my informants would be horrified to learn this. And indeed perhaps they did.

A front-page article in the travel section of Rio de Janeiro's daily newspaper, *Jornal do Brasil,* titled "Disney—Well-behaved" (11/20/96), reports that Disney produced a video shown in hotel rooms frequented by Brazilians, the goal of which was to teach Brazilians good theme-park/tourism manners. Disney also held related seminars in seven cities in Brazil for more than two thousand tour guides, established a limit of twenty-five people per group in visits to Disney World, created a checkin especially for groups of Brazilians, and was, at the time of the report, planning to have special visiting hours for Brazilian groups, who, it found, like to stay late at the theme parks. When the enterprise sent telegrams to the major Brazilian media announcing that Brazilian tourists were "bad-mannered, noisy, and undisciplined," its PR effort to couch the training in manners as treatment of Brazilians as VIPs was exposed. This Rio news report claims that Brazilian summer visitors represent 70 percent of Disney's market in groups. Regardless of the accuracy of this figure, the Brazilians who visit the theme park in tour groups were the issue for Disney. The Brazilian media rose to the defense of its compatriots. Yet the accounts on either side recall yet another anthropological concept associated with rites of passage and pilgrimages: liminality. Indeed, this feature story brings up a fascinating thought—Brazilians' appropriation or inversion of Disney. Even if the adults were only letting go in a controlled environment, their impact on the Mouse has been impressive.

Envision, again, how different the adult experience at Disney is from the debutante ball. In the latter, the family is continually performing for guests in a scripted, choreographed rite. The Disney trip, conducted by the family off by itself, isolated in time and space from the local and national milieu, lacks engagement in the obligatory social exchanges as well as the anxieties and entanglements entailed in hosting a large party.[7]

Several families in the study described their U.S. trips to me, certainly prompted in large part by my presence as an American, though never by my question. Clarinha showed me a video of their family at Universal Studios. Another woman twice recalled with great amusement misadventures in Florida. At each recounting her children were very circumspect; perhaps the enthusiastic parent seemed a bit ridiculous to them. Gilda wrote me the following letter telling of her family's experience of Disney: "We returned from the U.S. January 30 [1995]. I loved Miami, we had a three-day cruise on the ship *Seaward* to Cancun. It was wonderful. In Orlando we loved the parks, especially Busch Gardens. If you haven't been, it's really worth going, very entertaining, and fun to scare yourself on the roller coaster. We bought a lot of things because there it's very cheap, and we really took good advantage of it. They were unforgettable days, I loved the trip."

Besides the liminal experiences afforded by pilgrimage to the magical site, there is a very material fringe benefit of going to Disney—or rather, to the United States. By not declaring goods bought in the United States exceeding $500—that is, by circumventing the stiff protectionist customs tariff policy in vigor until today—Gilda and her family joined other Brazilian travelers and informal-sector merchants in a national pastime: U.S. discount shopping. Experiential consumption is part of a global trend (see Featherstone 1990; Urry 1988, 1990; Lee 1993; Rouse 1995), but this pursuit has not, as we will see, displaced the importance of consumption of durable goods. The unfailing interest these Brazilians show in having consumer durables likens them to middle classes cross-culturally. However, there are some significant differences relating to their national location. That is the topic of the next chapter. For now, I wish to raise another contrast between the Disney trip, which concentrates goods within one's own family, and the ball, which circulates goods among participating families who offer and receive birthday gifts.[8]

EPISODE 2: THE TEA PARTY

Daughter of a Portuguese immigrant, Teresa delighted in offering elaborate meals. A week or so after Juliana's fifteen-year-old party, Teresa held a tea party. The table was set with huge amounts of hors d'oeuvres, a homemade chicken pie, imported cheeses, eight different imported teas

(Celestial Seasonings), and later a choice of desserts. Food was served on silver trays; our dishes were blue printed china. A charming hostess at this European-styled meal, Teresa encouraged the three guests—two of her dearest friends, Marlene and Cristiana, and me—to indulge in all.

It was only after we adjourned to the living room that I discovered the purpose of the visit: to inspect the gifts Juliana had received for her birthday, with the benefit of Marlene's expert eye. She, I learned, owned a jewelry store. One piece shown early on caught the greatest attention. Marlene said she was unable to read the numbers on a heart chain necklace with her contact lenses on, so she began to take them out. "Imagine!" Teresa kept exclaiming (in surprise and protest at the inconvenience and fuss). Teresa said that she was to see the gift giver that evening and would tell her that she planned to replace the necklace because it was almost identical to another piece received. Juliana (who had arrived late into the tea) asked her not to, saying she would not be able to face the friend. In response, the other two women reminded Juliana of her mother's tact. Yet evidently Teresa's plan was to let the gift giver know that the gift was unacceptable. Finally, someone was able to decipher the numbers on the chain, which was pronounced gold; the dangling heart, however, was not.

The women conferred on the principles of gift giving: it should be according to means. Cristiana recalled that a plastic item given to her was precious because it was from her maid. While this was excellent, it was inadmissable for someone who could afford more to be cheap. Teresa noted that she herself had given a fine gift to the heart-necklace giver (or rather, to her daughter), who evidently could have returned in kind. Marlene pointed out that people had come to expect lovely gifts from (wealthy) Teresa.[9] After this debate, the other jewelry boxes (about forty) were opened for inspection. In each case, the criteria for appreciation seemed to be gold versus costume, with Marlene verifying the gold factor, and then brand. Concerned that some gifts had lost their brand labels, Teresa chastised Juliana for throwing them out. The latter claimed that some had come without. Coffee was served in the living room, and the inspection turned to purses; we viewed just a few of the 180 that Juliana had received. For her part mostly silent, Juliana was delighted with a velour top she had received from a *chiquérrima* (ultrachic) boutique at the Iguatemi Shopping Center.

Elaborate reflection on this party seems unnecessary; suffice it to say first that making intraclass distinctions through consumer goods can be an absorbing task for the adults. Second, the event registers again the aptness of seeing the debutante ball as a tournament of value: there is a circulation of "positional" or "marker" goods (Featherstone 1991, 18) in these rounds of balls, allowing for measured comparisons.

DISNEY VERSUS DEBUTANTE BALLS:
PERSPECTIVES ON TEENS

I have concentrated on Disney and debutante balls from the perspective of parents, owing to the curiousness of their strong desire to participate in them. However, it is time to reflect on the interest these rites hold for the youth who, after all, provide their reason for being. The media ponders the resurgent popularity of debutante balls, finding nostalgia understandably stemming from parents, themselves children in the 1950s when the event first spread in the middle classes. But why, the press wonders, do young people now want debutante balls? After finding it peculiar that youth of the 1990s should have such an old-fashioned, corny, nostalgic desire, the media portrays youth as seeking more romantic, showy, or even Cinderella means of presenting themselves to each other (cf. *Veja* 11/9/94; *Jornal do Brasil* 11/4/90; *O Globo* 10/29/86) and indicates that there is a heightened conservatism in this generation. One young debutante's view somewhat shatters the notion of romanticism: in her words, "Only those who can't, don't [debut]" (*Jornal do Brasil* 11/4/90). Martha's comment regarding her family's need to go to Disney, cited earlier, indicates the accomplishment of Disney to be a sine qua non for social respect in her milieu. Again, what is interesting here is that from the perspective of youth—as with adults—the social imperative is so compelling and clear as to preclude any need for verbal explanation. It is noteworthy that the desire for the ball and/or for Disney unites two generations at this contradictory historical conjuncture. In a reassertion of family, these middle classes publicly celebrate their relative wealth and social mobility; economic and social capital are perfectly coordinated.[10]

Because Disney is gender-neutral in the sense that both boys and girls are treated to it, it would seem that the Disney substitute has made a definitive break with tradition. In contrast, the debutante ball appears replete with patriarchal over- and undertones. Even as we reject Lévi-Strauss's gender objectifications in his alliance theory (1969), we must still acknowledge that historically the marriages of white elite Brazilian women have been key for family strategies either to expand or to consolidate wealth. Until this century a young elite woman's marriageability was enhanced by her social graces rather than her education. If elite women in the early part of the century did study language, literature, music, and perhaps painting, topped by a trip to Europe, back in Brazil they would find their final vocations: to be perfect wives and mothers, revealing the education to have been a finishing school whose main purpose was to make an upper-class match.[11] According to Needell, "Arranged and early marriages, a private but superficial education, a jealously guarded childhood and adolescence, and a strict regimen of prejudice surrounding virginity, Society, and marriage, all directed toward preserving family status and lineage" (1987, 136–137).

But things have changed. Currently, the young middle- and upper-class debutantes—just like the Disney goers—attend college; any marriage would occur years after the fifteen-year-old party, and potentially stem from a different circle than that of the ball goers. Young women's education and aims have changed as well. In 1965, the female-to-male proportion in higher education in São Paulo was just 28.5 percent (Saffioti 1978, 177). Although Rosemberg, Pinto, and Negrão (1982) also emphasize gender inequalities in Brazilian education, their figures show that of the group who attended college in the 1960s, that is, the upper middle class and elite—there was a fairly substantial showing of women in law (21 percent), architecture (27 percent), and medicine (16 percent) (55). More recent studies show, in contrast, considerable rigidity by gender in majors, but "an unusually high degree of gender equity in enrollments" (Plank 1996, 177). Thus let it suffice to report here that the marital purpose is now detached from the ball; those families who have them do not necessarily have traditional or narrow goals of marriage for their daughters. Parents in my study were overwhelmingly concerned that their daughters attend college and find a viable profession. Teresa had her daughters on a very tight, disciplined homework schedule in order to ensure that they would pass the difficult college entrance exams. Juliana herself was on a rigorous route to engineering.

Furthermore, it seems that the girls themselves have brought the coming-out party up to date. The first time I went to the home of the other family who had had a debutante ball, Clarinha and her seventeen-year-old daughter, Márcia, pulled out a photo album of Márcia's *festa de quinze anos*. Paging through the elaborate photos in astonishment, I observed, "By comparison, a wedding is no bigger an affair." This remark came back to me when reading news stories about debutante balls. Said one carefree fifteen-year-old girl, "I can marry several times, but a debut, there's only one" (*Jornal do Brasil,* Sunday magazine, 11/4/90). As a sidebar to this hilarious comment, allow me to point out that when divorce was first legalized in 1977 in Brazil, only one remarriage was allowed. A constitutional change later removed restrictions on the numbers of divorces and remarriages. Just as in the previous discussion, here too with respect to gender, the term *traditional* can be seen as the flip side of the coin, rather than the irreconcilable opposite of *modern*.

Having considered meanings and benefits of the Disney trip and the debutante ball for parents and their teens, let us return in closing to Appadurai's suggestions that divorced from everyday matters, such tournaments are centrally concerned with power and value (Appadurai 1986, 21). The mundane outcomes of these symbolic/material struggles for the next generation are as yet unknown, but considering that Teresa and Nando ran a private school and that their party guests included colleagues, their daughters' classmates, and parents, there is no question that putting on the ball conferred prestige and a boost for their business, which relied heavily on informal reputation. The Disney trip is understood to improve social contacts as well. Thus, in line with Brazilian precedents and theorists, one might well argue that the accomplishment of either symbolic rite (which, as adults and teens testify, is nearly obligatory for social advancement) is put to social and economic advantage. Though there need not be a final decision over which will prevail—the ostensibly traditional or the presumably modern rite—one thinks of Edith Wharton's satire of the nouveaux riches, *The Custom of the Country* (1913), which acknowledges how their often greater wealth among established elites affords them staying power within exclusive circles. As still fourteen-year-old Juliana told me some weeks before her ball, without the panache of the debutante cited above, but evidently with her parents' assurances to back her: "I can travel any time, but I will only turn fifteen once." Indeed, this family had already gone to Disney.

5

INTERNATIONAL BARGAIN

SHOPPING AND THE MAKING

OF MODERNITY

I met a girl . . .
who was going with a boy who was
so very intelligent,
so very different
Wearing an unbuttoned shirt and
a certain kind of American pants
[he'd] bought through contraband.
—from the song "Tradição" [Tradition]
by Gilberto Gil, 1993

In 1991, checking in at JFK airport to board a flight to Rio de Janeiro, the middle-aged Brazilian man in line in front of me tried unsuccessfully to get the airline agent to dispense with the excess baggage charge—or perhaps it was excess weight, for the item in question was a microwave oven. Later, in São Paulo, I recounted the incident to a Brazilian friend. I noted that the man had tried everyone's patience with his erroneous assumption that he could talk his way out of the charges. Paulinho did not react until I derided the Brazilian travelers who return from the United States with mountains of merchandise. Then it was my friend's turn to become impatient. I later realized the North American arrogance of my position: after all, we are faced with the option of buying a readily available, reasonably priced microwave oven—or not—but in any case, we do not have to carry our houses on our backs intercontinentally.

The microwave incident was critical for me, as the confrontation made me start to think nonironically about the relationship of middle- and upper-middle-class Brazilians to global things and experiences.[1] In a country where housing financing was nearly lacking, and where savings accounts only partially diminished losses, a strategy of spending discretionary income developed. This fever to consume (as Brazilians put it less rationalistically and more judgmentally) extended to international travel and goods. Despite inflation, recession, and salary devaluations on one hand and Brazil's restrictions against, and heavy taxation on, imported goods on the other, Brazilians have been pulled into the expanding transnational consumer market during the crisis.

What is at stake in the consumption of transnationally obtained goods by middle- and upper-middle-class Brazilians? I argue that the answer is both social distinction (Bourdieu 1984) and the attainment of modernity (Romanelli 1986; Philibert 1989; Friedman 1989; Wilk 1994). These global consumption practices are central to the realization of middle-class identity, both as symbolic means of presenting and proving status outwardly, and as the material means of securing and leading a modern life at home (Frykman and Lofgren 1987). By highlighting the recent trend, I do not claim that the middle-class focus on foreign-obtained consumer durables first developed during the economic crisis. Needell's (1987) work shows elite consumption of European goods in turn-of-the-century Rio de Janeiro. An especially memorable passage reporting Carioca use of woolen suits from England strikingly shows the relevance of status imitation through fashion in a way that was entirely at odds with common sense. Studying middle-class Brazilians between 1920 and 1950, Owensby (1999; see especially chap. 5) has argued similarly that class-related concerns regarding differentiation impelled the absorbing pursuit of consumer goods and furthered it; items representing modernity (notably in the 1930s, the radio) held these Brazilians in "rapturous thrall" (116). Thus at least as of the first republic (1889 forward), foreign goods (first European, then U.S. American) have been significant to bourgeois-styled and later middle-class Brazilian social reproduction. My task is to consider the current relevance for middle-class Brazilians.

I have chosen to focus on the means of acquisition of these goods (rather than their eventual meanings and uses), or what Kopytoff (1986) might call the "prehistory" of things, in order to center on shopping and the realm of desire.[2] As we will see, the translation of these desires into efforts at attaining them turned middle-class Brazilians to informal-illegal means, hence, into legal conflict with the state. There are many ongoing debates concerning consumption and transnationalism. One position rejects the interpretation of consumption as merely status-seeking (see, e.g., Miller 1987; McCracken 1990; Rutz and Orlove 1989; Friedman 1989, 1991; Campbell 1994; Lofgren 1994; Wilk 1994). Another finds that as consumption expands, status concerns become blurred or passé, in favor of varied expressions of personal identity and/or lifestyle (see, e.g., Featherstone 1991 and Shields 1992). This position recalls the idea that "democratization" occurred with the advent of mass consumption (for discussion and critique, see Ewen and Ewen 1982). From the perspective of consumption in the period under question, I argue once again that status concerns remain crucial for middle-class Brazilians, perhaps even heightened by the new consumption opportunities, but that is not all: their consumption goals are driven by the desire for modernity.

Rouse (1995) has recently analyzed the directions taken by the dominant transnational bourgeoisie toward inculcating the sense that one's "worth" is related to engagement in particular forms of consumption, including new global experiences. As Rouse puts it, there has been "an extension and intensification of a general ethos of consumerism, an attempt to persuade more people in more profound ways that their worth as persons is intimately linked to their capacity to acquire and consume particular kinds of goods" (365). Lakha (1999) points out the relevance of global consumption for contemporary Indian identity. Certainly Brazilians are responding to the expanded consumers' market and related media, which engage social imaginings worldwide (Appadurai and Breckenridge 1995) about what must ground the middle class and what special experiences it should have. The material presented from my fieldwork does not suggest middle-class "resistance" to the global process—in fact, it is clear that the actors in question not only have been incorporated but have jumped head first into the "global flows."

Let me here add a number of qualifications. First, the terms, urgings, and intensity of the desires for Disney, for Florida, for foreign goods, as well as the meanings and uses they acquire are in good part homemade.

Both local and global conditions came to make the United States a giant bargain basement for Brazilians shopping for consumer durables. Second, although I agree with Rouse's statement that the new consumption practices bring people in deed, if not in intent, to "counter . . . established ideologies of citizenship" (1995, 358), he finds the nation-state quickly becoming passé, given the current conditions of globalized capitalism, whereas I do not, or rather cannot. In the period under question the Brazilian state remained well in view as a player—or better, as an adversary in conflicts over the acquisition of these goods.

Paired with the preceding chapter, this chapter also considers side effects related to obtaining foreign-made goods and foreign travel. Middle-class Brazilians became ever more interested in acquiring the goods and experiences of the transnational, but the state's "outmoded" position (both through the economic crisis and continued tax impediments to obtaining imports) continued to hinder them. The power of the state was therefore contested by consumers ready to buy. I suggest that notwithstanding the creativity of the social meanings and uses associated with these highly desired goods and travel, involvement with these goods keeps the state relevant, but as a devalued, negatively compared entity in this recent era of globalization. I have chosen episodes from fieldwork and other fragments to provide concrete dramatizations of these wider conflicts and issues. The chapter closes with discussion of the implications of the ethnographic material from this and the preceding chapter for theories of consumption and globalization.

EPISODE 1: CHRISTMAS SHOPPING

I was invited to spend Christmas 1993 with a family at their country home (*sítio*) outside Embu, a town adjacent to São Paulo. Sumiko, the daughter of Japanese immigrants, a social worker, and mother of three, and married to a medical doctor (Flávio), picked me up around noon of Christmas Eve day. We stopped by her parents' house to pick up a pork tenderloin (*leitão*) and visit for a bit. While there, I noticed an article in one of the daily newspapers (*Estado de São Paulo*), about a credit-card company that had just held a number of raffles. The winners were to go immediately to New York City, that is, the next day, to spend US$4,000 in one day's shopping. The news pointed out that this meant the winners had to spend $240 per hour (over a sixteen-hour day) to avoid suffering any loss. This dramatic calculation struck us as particularly funny. On the TV report, one winner, a delighted teacher, was shown at the Shopping Center Norte, which is the most "popular" (i.e., of the people) center in São Paulo's north zone. (All contests and contestants were in shopping centers.) On the way to Embu, I discussed the raffle with Sumiko. She said doing the trip for herself would be fun, but she would have her children in mind.

After dinner on Christmas Eve, Sumiko casually passed her sixteen-year-old daughter, Fabiana, a gift: the perfume Volupté. Later Sumiko told me that it had cost US$70, and that she had ordered it from a *muambeira*. A muambeiro/a is the person who carries the *muamba*. These are the quainter, lighter terms for contrabandist and contraband and are used preferentially for such cases. (Meaning *booty, muamba* is a Brazilianism, probably of African origin.) Sumiko explained to her daughter that she had asked the muambeira to open it because she had heard of a case of someone buying perfume only to find a candle inside the box. Sumiko had also ordered CDs from the muambeira from a Christmas list prepared by her two sons. After the gift openings, Fabiana and her grandmother rewrapped the presents. I witnessed something similar at the home of another family (of Italian background): after each use of the European glass coffee pot (the push-down kind), Sandra carefully put it back into its original case.

INFORMAL IMPORTS

Let us consider first the presentation of international shopping practices in advertising. Clearly the intent of the Christmas promotional trip to New York City was to boost both credit-card and shopping-center usage.[3] The $240-per-hour calculation seemed designed to encourage readers to concretely imagine what their shopping strategies and buys would be in a more risk-free state than Brazil. As we have seen, in Brazil during the last decade buying anything became complicated. This was particularly true of consumer durables. In the United States people have the option of buying large appliances through layaway plans or credit-card loans. These same purchasing methods were the riskiest during the 1980s and 1990s in Brazil. Layaway plans entailed paying according to merchants' forecasting of future inflation. In an economy of high and wildly fluctuating inflation, the smart shopper would have to have more than a calculating mind; (s)he would have to be clairvoyant. Given the risks of buying through layaway, exorbitant interest rates (38 percent per month in 1991 and 20 percent in 1995), the increasingly high cost of living, and the potential for assault on Brazil's streets (cf. Caldeira 1993),[4] the United States came to offer easy sale prices, as well as a playground for leisure.

The ad scheme served best, I would say, to incite desires for shopping sprees in the United States, not specifically to use credit cards, its express purpose. The promotional hype was otherwise in tune to the Brazilian context, however. To buy frenetically, as the winner would have to do, was compatible with the strategy known as immediatism in buying that expanded during the crisis (see chapter 2). Furthermore, TV presentation of the winner simultaneously acknowledged and abolished class barriers: what could be more (lower) middle class than a school teacher, for whom the possibility of a trip to New York City was remote?

For those not able to travel, imports could be obtained, albeit informally (illegally), either from *muambeiros* or, for a limited set of goods, from employees affiliated with the airport duty-free market. (This was the way Maria Regina and Ricardo bought a microwave.) Sumiko's Christmas shopping method through professional contrabandists was just one among instances I continually encountered during fieldwork. I already had some knowledge of arrangements middle-class Brazilians had developed to acquire goods abroad from prior visits to Brazil, when I received requests to bring in a Nikon camera and lenses; high-top Converse All Star sneakers; a hand vacuum cleaner; two large bottles of Swiss Formula hand lotion; a water purifier (to guard against the cholera epidemic of 1991); and a laptop computer. The loophole for foreigners was that they were supposed to be bringing in goods for their own personal use, not for resale. Brazilians devised an array of means to ensure their own smooth walk past customs.

Clearing customs in Brazil is a gamble, during which one of two scenarios may occur. Getting the green light means a traveler gets to enter the nothing-to-declare line and sail through. In a red-light situation, the traveler may opt to work with the official inspecting all baggage in order to get off free or with a payoff, rather than paying a tax that would effectively wipe out the savings originally accrued. (Agents even have a catalog from a Miami publication with prices on relevant merchandise to consult for accuracy in verifying declared retail values.) I strongly suspect that the stoplight system is not random as purported, but rather that there is an employee who observes travelers and stops those with a lot of baggage, as well as other suspects. The safest bet therefore is to have previously arranged with an official to go through customs without inspection. Over the years, the profession of contrabandist for this kind of goods became routine and reliable, contributing to a burgeoning informal sector catering to the transnational tastes of Brazilians.[5] But why the scams, why the illegality?

As readers may know, Brazil has had protectionist policies against imports, notably since the 1930s, when national industry was promoted through import substitution (Baer 1995). Only since the 1990s has the Brazilian government assumed a favorable position toward opening the market to foreign goods. Fernando Collor's presidential campaign in 1989 adopted a platform in favor of neoliberalism, including a promise to end protectionist policies for national products, but few changes occurred during his presidency (1990–92). When radical policy change was finally effected in July 1994 with the Plano Real (i.e., Fernando Henrique Cardoso's plan as finance minister; see chapter 8), popular sentiment was very favorable to reducing or ending tax on imports, given the more than competitive international prices and the expanded consumption opportunities afforded. Yet even then the change was incomplete and contested. An opinion poll by the *Estado de São Paulo* in 1995 (4/1/95) found most Brazilians were against restrictions on imports, yet industrialists and unions exerted pressures against this change. The metallurgical workers' union of São Paulo staged a protest against car imports in July 1995 (*Estado de São Paulo* 7/31/95); and indeed, tax on car imports, which had been decreased to 32 percent, was reincreased to 70 percent in 1995.[6] In October 1995, front-page headlines reported that products from the "Asiatic tigers," including domestic appliances, textiles, shoes, and rubber, were being withheld from the domestic market (which produces all these items) unless their prices were equal to or higher than domestic ones (*Estado de São Paulo* 10/2/95). With their characteristically satirical bent, the Brazilian newspapers called this practice "Operation (Back) Drawer."

Popular sentiment is that Brazilian businesses have forever been shielded by the government from foreign competition, and therefore can extract exorbitant profit rates. The nationally protected businesses were called "artificial industries" as early as the 1890s. A century later, middle-class consumers opposed government policy and national industry and as a result, labor. If the June 26, 1996 issue of *Veja* is reliable, sentiment against national businesses grew even more after inflation ended and the market opened. Speaking about perishable goods, Carlos criticized the government's attempts to curb consumption just after inflation was halted with the Plano Real in July 1994: "Let the people consume," he said, "and bring in imports."

Before and during my fieldwork, thus after 1990 and official government support of globalization of the market, imports of goods produced locally remained liable to such heavy duties at customs (e.g., an 85 percent tax on stereos and beer in 1990, *Veja* 8/1/92) as to effectively prohibit legal entry. Customs currently allows Brazilians to bring in, tax free, the equivalent of US$400 worth of goods (formerly $500). Beyond that, a tax is to be levied. Those returning with an excess of new goods may have recourse in the *jeitinho brasileiro*. Made famous by Roberto DaMatta (1990), this refers to the national, self-assigned knack for extricating oneself from difficult situations—in this case, the informal, illegal transactions of muambeiros, customs agents, and travelers.

Like the man with the microwave, Brazilians returning from U.S. travels typically have impressive amounts of baggage. And shopping does not even end with the trip home. Arriving at São Paulo's or Rio's international airport, one will spot many travelers who, remaining undaunted at this last phase (after nine hours in flight), enter the duty-free shop, later emerging with a case or more of scotch (the prestige drink in this sector), and/or other items, from toasters to perfumes to Pringles. (Although the duty-free shop is open to both arriving and departing passengers, it is far more heavily used by those returning to Brazil.)

Illegality at the airport borders has generally gone unchecked. Two incidents in recent years, however, have made front-page headlines. Brazil's soccer team returned in July 1994 triumphant winners of the World Cup; they also attempted to sneak in twelve tons of imported goods, and in fact filled five moving trucks with items including a refrigerator, washing machine, and gas barbecue range.[7] The president, Itamar Franco, wished to waive the duties (later estimated at $1 million) for the national heroes, an attitude that further disgusted the public.[8] In July 1995, the São Paulo newspapers reported that two sisters returning from shopping in the United States were pressured to pay R$930 (US$1,000) in order to receive their bags from customs. Ensuing investigations at São Paulo's and Rio's international airports estimated that the customs racket afforded US$1 million in profit per day (*Estado de São Paulo* 6/26/95 and 6/27/95).

This fairly elaborate system of obtaining imported goods at international prices has a long history, making it less troublesome or uncertain to succeed to those long familiar with it than it may seem to outsiders. However, there have been developments in terms of both scale and actors involved. Brazil's middle class has entered completely into consumption of transnationally offered goods, engaging in what had been an elite practice relating to Europe. And there is a twist: the means of appropriation has entailed what is technically white-collar crime. As we have seen, Brazilian travelers themselves become muambeiros, setting them at odds with the state. I have dwelt so long on customs in order to underscore that this is the site where the class-directed tactic, one conflicting with state policy, is exposed. Why all this trouble? Again, what is at stake?

We might well consider what goods and why. Observations from various trips to and from Brazil, photographic evidence at airports, visits to 47th Street Photo and downtown Miami, and fieldwork, including a (belated, and restricted) interview with a muambeira, reveal that the following items were the most coveted in the 1990s: large-screen TVs; cameras; VCRs; personal computers; camcorders; fax machines; cordless phones; cellular phones; microwaves; stereos; CD players and CDs; walkmans; tennis shoes; toys; beauty, hygiene, and health products from drugstores; and of course, clothes. These goods can be categorized as the latest in fashion for the body and the latest in hi-tech home appliances. As to the preference for novelty goods, one might recall McCracken's 1990 study of the rise of consumer society in Europe, especially England. Whereas the older elite families preferred heirlooms, the newly emerging middle classes, who lacked the option of old inherited goods, instead wanted novelty items from abroad. Campbell (1992) describes the current appeal of the new—the unused, improved, and novel—as having qualities that in turn correspond to the tastes of declassé groups for the

6. Paulistana teen at JFK airport displaying her purchase of a stereo system. *Photo courtesy of the author.*

"pristinian," "technophile," and/or "neophiliac." The difference between these two readings occurs on only one level: both consumption choices indicate responses to social mobility. The terms *positional* or *marker* goods are apt.[9]

The great and at times extralegal efforts of middle-class travelers and the increasing informal sector testify that imported goods and travel remain crucial to the local status hierarchy today, as in the past, in spite of the national constraints. Given the circumstances of their attainment and the national context, travel and imported items might well be called not just new but also luxury goods. Appadurai proposes that "we regard luxury goods not so much in contrast to necessity . . . but as goods whose principal use is *rhetorical* and *social,* goods that are simply *incarnated signs*" (1986, 38; emphasis his). It is interesting that the luxury/need distinction and the symbolic/material one collapse so perfectly with consumer durables. What is more practical than a phone? Yet, as Brazilian critics have scornfully pointed out to me, what is more superfluous at a friend's home, when that friend has a phone? I refer here to cellular phones, of course. There are those who quickly contest this criticism, declaring that the cell phone responds to a need—for security in this violence-laden society, or more simply, in order to have a phone (or second line) in a country greatly deficient in phone service. At a more popular level, tennis shoes have become obligatory and attainable, as are many brand-name clothes or theme-park T-shirts; at the other end of the spectrum are imported cars, an unrealizable desire for most, yet, as noted earlier, incessantly debated in the media. Extending Appadurai's suggestion, one would specify that these "incarnated signs," these "positional goods," signify modernity—symbolically glorified, practically justified.

Besides those items used publicly to support claims to distinction and modernity, there are others—quite possibly the majority of purchases—that remain in the home, a central arena for working out middle-class identity (see Frykman and Lofgren 1987; Rutz and Orlove 1989). Indeed, imports are not only arguments of status through modernity in public; they are also important in private home consumption. Analysis of the impact of foreign goods in Brazilian households is outside the scope of this chapter dedicated instead to their prehistory (but see Leal 1990 and Ardaillon 1997), yet I would like to touch on a few related matters.

Studies of consumption often emphasize the individual nature of the practices, yet imports and many of the goods discussed here are not for individual consumption. What Wilk noted for Belize applied to my study: "When incomes rise above a certain threshold, cash is reallocated to household luxuries and consumer goods; items like the house and furnishings that belong to the household as a corporate entity rather than to its individual members" (1989, 305). Recall the value of home goods as miniature investments in a period when real-estate investment was out of reach and car prices exorbitant (see chapter 1). Next, I would point out the very different function of such items in a Brazilian home in which a domestic servant works (see, e.g., Souza 1980 and Azeredo 1987). Issues arise since the items do not "replace" the maid, which might be the modernist aim, but coexist uneasily.[10] For instance, the middle-class owner of these appliances often fears the maid will lack the knowledge to operate them or be careless—and break them. This special attention foregrounds their preciousness.

Recall also the practice of keeping imported goods in their original packaging for an indefinite period (the examples were perfume and a coffee maker). Such care sacralizes the objects, in a way not usually associated with mass-produced goods. It may be that through this practice owners are somehow making the goods nonconsumables, turning them into quasi-permanent values.[11] For Miller, who encountered a similar practice in Trinidad, it "objectif[ies] transcendence" (1994, 217). The special value of the imported becomes even more obvious when the price is low and rarity lacking (such as the special purchase of Crest toothpaste; see Friedman 1989). Indeed, an informant recently remarked on a U.S. visit in 2000 that many of the goods formerly available only in the United States were by now available in Brazil. She was fed up with the compulsion to get a good deal (*fazer um bom negócio*), yet she remarked, while going up and down the aisles of a Walgreens, "Here the packaging is different, it's pretty, *this* attracts us." In short, the consumption and preservation of these goods is an index of the very strong desire to live with, or better, to incorporate, modernity and alterity on an intimate daily basis (see Needell 1987, 1988; Friedman 1991; and Burke 1996).[12] Thus I wish to underscore another motive for this consumption that includes but extends beyond individual status concerns, namely the way these goods themselves seem to make modernity intimate. Once again, recalling historical studies of bourgeois and middle-class predilections in Brazil and of middle classes cross-culturally, I do not claim this to be a novel practice or feeling, nor my perspective on status and modernity unique. To the contrary, I wish instead to register a continuity and commonality in middle-class desire and practice. Thus I would echo the concluding sentence of Burke's work on advertising in twentieth-century colonial Zimbabwe, where he suggests we "remember the resiliency and rootedness of desire" (1996, 216).

The provenance of the new, luxury/practical goods so highly desired is far from inconsequential. "Anyone" (that is, any Brazilian) can tell you that the brands available nationally are considered inferior, or the range too limited; or the specific item is not made; or if the imports are now available locally, their prices are prohibitive. (See Dean [1969] for comparison with the early twentieth century.) But, as one informant indicated, the desire for goods that are foreign, or have foreign features, reveals that alterity is a central aspect of their value. If this is so for foreign goods obtained locally, what of foreign travel, in particular to the U.S., which is in itself a consumption experience and a context for shopping?

Thus far the discussion has privileged the acquisition of transnational goods rather than transnational experiences, in part because so many more Brazilians engage in the former. But travel experiences are highly desired, and for some realizable, including for several of my informants. First let us consider the perspective of those who could not travel internationally. The following dialogue of a 1992 focus group session of women participants occurred after a long discussion about how middle-class people were having to do without because of the crisis. One woman noted how annoying it was that her husband came down on her over finances, another reported that they didn't have the means to set up a business and couldn't travel or go out to eat. A third, Speaker J, laid out a list of problems indicating how the middle class was being hit where it hurt the most: private schooling costs were prohibitive, rental prices or condominium fees were out of reach, middle-class people needed to really think before making purchases, and so on. The moderator then entered in: "What's your defense strategy now?" The transcription notes that all responded in chorus "Doing without!" followed moments later by the following exchange between Speaker J and another woman, Speaker L:

> J: Sometimes I get to thinking, "can all this be real?" Here we are thinking all this [about doing without], but if you go to the airport it's filled with people travelling, if you go to see *Beauty and the Beast* the line is enormous, in the international wing of the airport it's all full, you can't find a ticket to go to Miami. Really, I don't know what's going on. There are a lot of people doing really badly, but they won't allow themselves to lose their status. You go to the shopping center on Saturday, and it's filled with people.
>
> L: Oh, but there it's just people walking around, very few people are actually buying. My daughter complained, "Mom, all my friends are going to Disney, and I don't have anyone to talk to on the phone." . . . Since she turned 15 this year, that was the present she was going to get. (Standard, Ogilvy, & Mather, July 9, 1992)

As both speakers make clear, desires of consumption are both tangible and intangible—directed to goods and travel, or if that is not possible, to the "dream worlds" of window shopping (R. Williams 1982) and to conversations and musings about it. They are also multiple and linked. While I have thus far considered only transnational goods in the interest of analytical expediency, this is an artificial separation. The forms of transnational consumption (of goods, of foreign travel) are distinguishable, but, of course, they are also of a piece, linked together. In keeping with this sensibility, which joins rather than artificially isolates the different forms of consumption, the following fieldwork fragment addresses travel to the U.S. in order to briefly highlight the social desires surrounding it.

EPISODE 2: VELVET ROADS

After finishing high school, Marcos, son of Clarinha and José, and an engineering student at USP, went to the United States with his cousin, a travel agent. Recalling his trip for me, Marcos claimed they had driven from Miami to Orlando (a 230-mile drive) in just two and a half hours. Waving his arm out to span the horizon, Marcos said fondly, "The roads there are like velvet." After this warm recollection he remembered with annoyance that he had spent an entire day of his week-long trip looking for a twenty-seven-inch-screen TV. Including tax, it cost less than US$400 but in Brazil, Marcos said, it would have cost $1,200. His ticket was only US$400 because his cousin had found a last-minute charter deal. So, as Marcos put it, the trip was free.

As usual, the Rêde Globo TV satire "Cassetta e Planeta" had the first word about travel to the United States. In November 1994 it declared: "A trip to Miami—not even military service is as obligatory" [Viagem a Miami que nem serviço militar: é obrigatório]. Equally illuminating was the comment of an informant who came to the United States for the first time in January 1995. She said: "Well, now I will no longer have to put up with people saying, 'when I was in New York . . . ,' or 'when I was in. . . .'" It seems necessary to broaden the discussion begun in the previous chapter on Disney to encompass here most any foreign travel, since the experience serves as a genuine and irrefutable milestone for middle-class social identity. In public situations, the verbal display of international experience and knowledge is perhaps as operative as goods for claims to social distinction.

The desire to travel internationally is so great among Brazilians that Cancun has recently become a target vacation spot. Brazil itself has more than seventy-five hundred kilometers of coastline, most of it breathtaking and diversely so, and invites bathing and boating. Yet people often told me with indignation that a trip to the Northeast coast would run higher than an international package deal to Florida and/or Cancun. Airfares are comparable: a round trip to Northeast cities from São Paulo runs US$500, as do flights to Miami or Orlando. Brazilian tourists frequently rationalize travel expenses as absorbed by the low costs of items bought in the U.S. portion of a trip. By the time the Plano Real came into effect (again, among other things this was the plan that made real strides to end protectionist policies), domestic prices had reached an all-time high, and the dollar was set below the national currency, making travel to and shopping in the United States in the mid-1990s even more accessible and no less "necessary." Currency devaluations in the late 1990s reduced the real to half its value, thereby making such travel far more expensive again, and thus relatively prohibitive, for Brazilians.

Beyond economizing, however, it appears that what was desired by the Cancun travelers was not the "untouched beauty" of the deserted beaches of Ceará or Bahia, or even the noncamping, deluxe-hotel vacation, but the First World, out-of-Brazil experience. By going to Florida or Cancun, one had a respite from the crisis in whatever shape it has taken since 1980. Such was the interpretation of the news magazine *Veja*. *Veja* has done frequent feature articles on U.S. travel, emphasizing both the surprising fact that it has become cheaper to travel internationally than to the Northeast (4/11/90), and the popularity of Florida for Disney and goods (12/4/91). (This report stated that fifty flights a week were going to Miami.) *Veja* also remarked on the novel experience of stability on "firm land in a sunny First World, protected by a developed economy and free of bank confiscations" (1/2/91). Another article on (im)migrants to Florida gave a slight variation on this theme, stating that the object of Brazilians who travel abroad is "to have their feet on solid First World ground, [where it is] sunny, protected by a developed economy and safe from bank-deposit confiscations" (*Veja* 1/2/91). *Veja* expressly discouraged going to Argentina, precisely because it was "going through a more acute crisis than Brazil" so that it could not serve to "alleviate" the "economic hangover" of Brazil. Besides the advantage of a respite from the economic chaos in an economically viable state, by going to Florida or Cancun one could avoid the continually ineradicated poverty of the less developed parts of Northeast Brazil. One could also avoid acknowledging the inability to pay for a trip to the island of Fernando de Noronha, renowned for its Jacques Cousteau paradise, or the lack of a beach home in Angra dos Reis, for instance, which is one of Brazil's most exclusive beach and boating areas about three hours away from Rio or São Paulo.

In anticipation of a conclusion, I would like to point out that the quest for foreign goods and travel unifies the Brazilian middle class. This statement may seem innocuous. However, through it I disregard distinctions important to some Brazilians (the intellectual and sophisticates) who take pains to distinguish their more cultured consumption and travel from international bargain shopping. I emphasize this not to distance myself from a "native" (or "emic") distinction, but to register it.

There is a hierarchy of distinctions with respect to travel. Europe remains the irreproachable cultural experience; however, New York is now surpassing it in popularity. Ostensibly, one goes to these places for lofty cultural pursuits, and to Orlando-Miami for theme parks and shopping. An academic friend called those who travel to the United States for consumption rather than enlightening touristic purposes *sacoleiros do ar.* The translation I offer, international bargain shoppers, loses two important referents. First, there are the government-subsidized discount warehouses for fresh fruits and vegetables called Sacolão (Big Bag), where shoppers fill their bags and buy according to total weight, obtaining a much better bargain than in the supermarkets for selected items. *Sacoleiros* (big baggers), then, are those who come with bags to these discount houses. The phrase *do ar,* by air, recalls lower-middle-class people and informal-sector merchants who travel by bus to buy duty-free goods in Paraguay. This expression teases the upper middle class and nouveaux riches by likening their air travel to these cruder images. Such ribbing (some of it self-directed) has become a favorite pastime of certain Brazilians—but not all.[13] When I reported this joke to Maricarmen (herself cosmopolitan, being a Spanish immigrant and well traveled), she scoffed back at the "snobs." One could easily argue that even if the trip is largely or unabashedly devoted to buying, one does not come away with only that, for, of course, even commercial transactions abroad are "cultural" experiences. By the same token, even if one is anticonsumerist and culture is the main objective for travel, one cannot return home to Brazil solely with intangibles—relatives and friends will surely make requests for purchases.

Finally, to reflect further on the meaning of the U.S. travel experience for Brazilians it is helpful to listen to youth. Marcos touched on the magical realm once in relation to Florida roads, and again when we were watching an episode of the TV series *Beverly Hills, 90210*. As the scenes moved from one luxurious home to another, including the apartments of the former high-school kids then experimenting with adulthood, he remarked, "Of course, it's obvious that anyone would want that life." Indeed, from this perspective Disney seems to extend well beyond Orlando.

Once, I was able to spend some time with an entire family from my study who came to the United States. José Luis, Maricarmen, and their three teenaged girls made a trip to New York City during a particularly cold period of winter 1995. One night the parents had a date to hear jazz at the Blue Note, and I went with the girls to the Hard Rock Café (or it might have been Planet Hollywood). Their almost unbounded excitement throughout the entire experience was utterly charming. Excitement reached a pitch when one of the girls finally mustered the courage to ask the waiter to be in a photograph together with them. He readily obliged, and the night came to a perfect conclusion.

The preceding chapter took as a starting point for analysis of middle-class involvement in transnational consumption a call by Campbell to look beyond immediate, calculating intentions to a broader subjectivity. This directive was helpful in preventing us from arriving prematurely at a conclusion regarding the motive for Disney, and it encouraged us to consider motives as multiple. We saw that involvement in the more recent teenage rite renewed the entire family's social standing. Advantageously positioning the travelers in the First World arena, the Disney trip holds its own against the traditional/revived rite of passage, the debutante ball. Thus a second motive for the Disney trip concerns the quest for distinction through association with "modernity," globally conferred and locally defined in reference to another transnational "tradition." This chapter makes similar arguments. One major reason for the consumption of foreign goods and travel is the social distinction conferred. The bona fide travel experiences and possession of desired goods make for indisputable arguments, and hence strong claims to distinction.

Heightened status preoccupations have long been associated with deepening disparities of income distribution (see Luckman and Berger 1964 and Belk 1988). The uncertainties of position and identity in societies undergoing rapid changes in class and mobility exacerbate these very concerns. Not incidentally, recent works on expanding middle classes in Asia and South Asia (Breckenridge 1995; Lakha 1999; Pinches 1999), far from eschewing motives of status or cultural capital as part of consumption goals, emphasize them. Such efforts remind us that middle classes depend highly on symbolic groundings for social and economic claims. Appropriation of certain things is clearly central for claims to a class identity at or above the level of the individual or family in question. While working within a restricted communicative code, material goods in fashion can offer compelling symbolic/material grounding for these claims (McCracken 1990). As Dittmar puts it, "material possessions may constitute particularly powerful symbols precisely because they circumvent explicit messages about status, wealth and power differences, while depicting and thus reinforcing these differences in a visible and compelling way" (1992, 186). Consumption provides a fairly comprehensive, stable, and flexible means of renewing, ameliorating, proving, and challenging one's standing materially and symbolically. We have seen that even in a context of downward mobility transnational consumer goods and practices received intense interest, revealing themselves to be essential to the construction of identities and social hierarchies.

My perspective thereby partly concurs with and partly counters theorists who criticize interpretations of status-seeking as the reason behind fashionable consumption. As noted in the introduction, incitements to go beyond viewing consumption solely (and judgmentally) as a status-seeking venture have produced numerous interesting studies looking at consumption in much broader and deeper ways. However, to do so does not mean that issues of inequality are cancelled out. As cited earlier, Fine duly points out that "consumption . . . can itself be used as a means of stratification" (1995, 140). I would reiterate that to proclaim freedom from class and status feels suspiciously like a view from the standpoint position of a large First World middle class. This brings us to the question of the globalization of consumption.

Some years ago Featherstone presented a hunch that there could be a blurring of social distinctions and a "deconstruction of symbolic hierarchies" (1991, 18) due to the great quantity and worldwide circulation of goods and consumption experiences. Figuring that status-marking, or positional, goods work best in "stable, closed and integrated societies" (19), Featherstone speculated that "it may be that there are different modes of identity and habitus formation and deformation emerging which make the significance of taste and lifestyle choices more blurred— if not throughout the social structure, at least within certain sectors, for instance the young and fractions of the new middle class" (13). Featherstone is often cited for espousing a view that globalized consumption is leading to a breakdown of socially agreed-on status markers. However, I would point out the tentative nature of his discussion. Furthermore, later in this work (see 1991, 84 ff.), Featherstone rejects the idea of a breakup of hierarchies through the complications of global consumption, suggesting instead "new moves within" the social hierarchies.

Far from blurring distinctions with more goods and experiences, Brazilians, from both older and newer middle classes, have long been adept at adjusting things international to local classifications. Both the young and the old readily update intraclass distinctions. Thus I reject the speculation that class distinctions and symbolic hierarchies become dysfunctional in the expanding global market. In sum, to reject or avoid the explanation of social distinction as one motive for this involvement in consumption would be a blatant mistake. This rationale, one continually offered by the actors in question, is significant and cannot be discarded. However, I agree that the interpretation of status-seeking is overly narrow. And it is insufficient. The goal of modernity is also highly significant, inspiring desires and conflicts.

An interesting chapter in McCracken's (1990) work on consumption talks about how goods can reestablish access to ideals and meanings that have been unattainable. When there is a gap, a failure to realize a desire, one may find a displacement of the ideal—it could be relegated to the future and/or the local scene could be blamed. But this lack can be (somehow) regained via goods, which offer the advantages of symbolic value and either enduring or renewable variants. In McCracken's view, this compensatory function is a motivating force of consumption in modern society. He finds goods to be synecdoches—parts for the whole. I find this view illuminating of middle-class practice. However, based on a psychological analogy, it may overstate the capability of compensation and underestimate cultural variation and social, economic, and political conflicts. The problems of consumption (and lack thereof) gave middle-class Brazilians cause for complaint. The local shopping described in chapter 2 provided a jarring contrast to prior experience and to knowledge of transnational opportunities. Informants' critical analysis of the local conditions fed a growing criticism of their government for not leading them in the direction of the First World and its modernity. In short, to appreciate one realm of shopping, one must compare it to another. Each experience is informed by the context of the other: local household shopping (consumption as nightmare) and international sprees (consumption as dream).

From Hannerz (1987) to Miller (1994), we have considered the creativity in "native" incorporations and transformations of foreign goods. My prolonged discussion of the peculiarities of the means of appropriation of these goods is not at all intended to render these Brazilians "exotic," nor even to emphasize the creative and transformative ways of acquiring goods and appropriating Disney, although I believe their practices fully attest to this. Without wishing to diminish or minimize these aspects, my greater interest is in putting these forms of consumption in the context of class and nation.

Despite the lack of explicit communication from these mute goods, their provenance and the complicated means of their procurement indicate that modernity is located—in a place, a hemisphere, a nation-state—elsewhere. These valued foreign things come not from any old global context, but from one that compares quite specifically to the local context. The meanings associated with the goods and experiences reinforce not just local social differences, but invidious comparisons among nation-states, themselves viewed in a linear and hierarchical manner. The lack of such goods, and by the same token, their difficult or even illegal possession, refers to the Brazilian context. Hence my brief mention of contact with "velvet roads," with Disney's world of order and magic, with American TV, with Planet Hollywood suggests that such global "summons" to engage in the "new" transnational consumption serves to update old classifications among nation-states.

The motives for these middle-class Brazilians to engage in transnational consumption are plural and far-ranging: they seek to distinguish themselves socially and to take part in a modern world, captured momentarily in travels and/or in miniature, but more permanently and intimately in and through consumer durables smuggled back home. These experiences and goods provide, renew, and sanctify a spirit of modernity.

In a nation lacking stability, where Brazilians lost faith in an increasingly infernalized daily life and, specifically, were blocked from consumption practices central to the realization of their class identity, one means of bypassing or surpassing the national blockages has been through the circuitous, informal attainment of international goods. García Canclini's statement bears repeating: "To consume is to participate in a field of disputes over goods that the society produces and over the ways of using them" (1995a, 45)—and over goods the society does not produce or does not provide access to. Arguing, therefore, what some deem passé, I have emphasized that class distinctions are far from over, and instead may well be reinvigorated through transnational consumption. Second, I have emphasized the national-international division rather than the fluid notion of transnationalism for the simple reason that the nation-state has remained pivotal, precisely with respect to the means of appropriation of these goods and confrontations thereof. Furthermore, I find the intensity of significance attached to these goods and experiences has related to the nation, as have the tactics involved, both before and after the opening of the market. For again, it seems to me that middle-class Brazilians have become especially attached to things international in part to compensate for or even to surpass the nation in crisis. The decade-long crisis kept them grimly facing a continuing or aggravated Third World at home and constrained their ability to have, but fanned their desires for, First World modernity. This statement presents the First World/Third World hierarchy as validated by middle-class Brazilians. Indeed, international goods and experiences prompt the Brazilians who have them to reinscribe these terms.

6

DELIVERING THE CRISIS

The Media and the Middle

Class through the Collor Years

One may argue about the nature and the extent of the media's involvement in popular culture, but few question that the middle class is a privileged subject. This chapter concerns the role of Brazil's media in the construction of middle-class identity.[1] Events during the Collor presidency in particular have raised questions about the power of Brazil's media in the postauthoritarian, postcensorship democratic era. Some have claimed that the media got Fernando Collor de Mello elected in 1989 and impeached in 1992. This first direct election since 1959 featured universal suffrage (previously only literate adults could vote) and the central role of television in the campaign. Collor proved to be the white knight of the media, representing worldly beauty and sophistication. Regarding the impeachment, I refer first to the news magazine *Veja's* printing of Fernando Collor's brother Pedro's interview accusing the president's campaign manager, Paulo César Farias, of corruption, and second, to the TV miniseries *Anos Rebeldes* [Rebel years], which featured the U.S. hippie movement and aired soon after the scandal broke in May 1992. These "spectacular" media productions have been deemed responsible for inciting the impeachment movement led by middle-class youth. Yet the draw of television was soon said to account for the public's apparent indifference to Collor's forced resignation in 1992, as it coincided with but was superseded by interest in the tragic and sensationalized murder of telenovela actress Daniella Perez. Media analysts (e.g., Castro 1993; Rubim 1993; and Fausto Neto 1994) have found the Collor election campaign and his impeachment to represent not the triumphant return of democracy, but the media's power over the masses and middle classes.

I argue for a broader reading of the media's involvement in middle-class life and political culture than can be shown in analyses of the Collor campaign or the impeachment alone. Following Ang (1996), I wish to look at how people in everyday life are inscribed into larger relations of power through the media. Extending the period of inquiry to encompass the crisis era overall, I examine the relationship the press forged with the middle class as it engaged in constructing the economic crisis of the 1980s and 1990s for its targeted readers. In this chapter, I propose a reading of print news articles in order to sort out the kinds of involvement this media has developed in relation to this audience, and how this might help account for the reconstitution of middle-class political and economic positions in the 1990s. I indicate several ways this media made itself an indispensable ally of readers regarding their home life, employment, and politics. I then take a prolonged look at two "scandalous" events—the Plano Collor and the impeachment—joining into debates regarding the relative agency of the media and its public in Brazil. By broadening the time period to one encompassing everyday news (extraordinary in their own right as news of the crisis), one can better appreciate the intensifying media involvement with the middle class in and through the crisis, both in the private realm of home and work and in the public sphere of direct political action. Thus the spectacular media activities are a manifestation of a much larger process in the constitution of social "reality," "politics," and the "moral order" (Glasser and Ettema 1991). Why the news and not avenues of involvement and influence via the entertainment media? Analyses of the political implications immanent in telenovelas are extremely important, and genres like these are arguably more influential than directly political messages. My scope is limited in part because that literature is already rich (see, e.g., Miceli 1972; Leal 1986; Hamburger 1999 and forthcoming) and in part in recognition of the centrality of the middle class and consumption in the news.

Although one can readily see diverse positions assumed in the news, as well as assorted styles of address to readers, my reading focuses on two positions. In the first section, I characterize the media as a kind of self-assigned guardian angel for the middle classes, one who guided them through the tumultuous economic changes and in the process redefined their class. At the same time, the media's constant reports about the effect of the crisis on the middle class serve to identify this class as a singular unity and, more significantly still, as the targeted victim of the crisis. This myopic reading ignores the majority of the population and its diversity. Yet it fanned the fire of middle-class resentment at the government, which came to be seen as directly responsible for the economic chaos affecting this class. Hence the drama of the government acting against the middle class. With this framing of the context in mind, we can better appreciate the Collor years.

In the second section, looking at the Collor presidency through the feature articles of *Veja,* I see a complex mix of news, editorials, and scandal stories as taking on subject positions paralleling a range of readers. Through its "democratic" airing of debates, its outspoken views, and its insistent, increasingly irritated criticism of the government and society, the news media did speak on behalf of the middle class, becoming (besides guardian angel) a self-assigned proxy for middle classes. Its style of speaking to, at, and for the middle class in the public sphere and its unusual agency in the Collor presidency support the claim that the media stands in for and replaces the population in politics (see Garnham 1993b).

Varied in content, genre, literary conventions, and voice, the media's messages are of course open to interpretation. In the final section, I compare my own and other media analyses of the historical evidence of the middle-class movement against Collor, arguing first that we must qualify our sense of media agency and give due credit for this middle-class movement. Finally, I present how my informants viewed their role and the media's in Brazilian politics. Although they should not be taken as "self-evident facts" (see Ang 1996, 47), the commentaries of my informants and the mass movement itself offer the advantage of hindsight and caution against our own ethnographic practice as storytellers (Ang 1996).

THE MEDIA AS GUARDIAN ANGEL

Dramatizing the Middle-Class State of Being

Let us begin by reviewing what we have already seen of the print media. In chapter 1 we saw headlines blaring "For the middle class the dream is over" (*Folha de São Paulo* 10/13/87) and "The middle class was expelled from paradise" (*Jornal da Tarde* 12/28/91). The headlines and articles themselves constantly and invariably linked the middle class with consumption, indeed, so much so that we might apply Althusser's (1972) concept and say that in the news the Brazilian middle classes are interpellated as consuming subjects, and then as consuming subjects denied. In chapter 3, we saw the middle-class liberal professional represented as a doomed species, and the field of petty commerce (in high or low versions) presented as the inevitable course. Discussion of the obligatory nature of Disney and the latest imported goods in chapters 4 and 5 register the media's contributions to the realization and meaning of these goods and practices.

Besides the media's insistent identifications of flexible workers/dedicated consumers, let us take note of how the crisis offered new possibilities for the news media to insert, or better, to insinuate itself into middle-class households and minds. Middle-class Brazilians did not read or watch the news to find out what was happening in the world, but what was happening to them. The seemingly paranoid comments of an ad-agency focus-group participant compared government officials to little elves or mice: "While you're sleeping, they are up, tracing out their plans. The following day, you turn on the news, the TV, at seven in the morning, and you find out everything they planned and did during the night—against you" (Standard, Ogilvy, and Mather 2/26/87). People learned of each jarring change in the economy and in government policy from the TV and newspapers, which "delivered" the crisis with every nightly news, with every edition of the "Folha," "Estadão," and "Jota-Be." Of course it was the news that announced the mini and maxi currency devaluations; its reports of impending petroleum hikes sent people racing to the gas station; it proclaimed the price freeze, provoking consumer jubilees, and spread stories of Sarney officials closing down stores, as chapter 2 discussed. The news also told, most significantly, about the latest government plan—what this plan would do to one's salary, to the marketplace, and after the Plano Collor of 1990, whether it would "mess with savings accounts" (*mexer na poupança*), as people put it, referring to the savings-account freeze that paralyzed the national economy (to be discussed at length in the second section of this chapter).

With each disruptive stabilization plan, the news broadened and deepened its means for insinuating itself into middle-class private life.

Not limited to offering gloomy statistics and depictions of middle-class decline, it added vital how-to reports on the ways that this and that government plan would alter the rules of the game. With the Plano Cruzado, there was a new currency (the cruzado), new bases for salary calculations, and most importantly, new ways to shop, as the people were empowered by the president to confront business prices. Through such news reports, Brazilians could learn of new ways to act in the marketplace. The enormous changes provoked by the first price freeze, the novel contest between empowered consumers and black-marketeers—all produced a kind of action drama and novel protocol for social action of the middle classes, who could choose to act accordingly or not.

The media made itself indispensable to its readership during the crisis in myriad ways, growing further involved in "home economics." Newspapers published time-saving price comparisons of basic-basket items in several supermarkets, thereby assisting economizing households; their financial sections advised the best bet of the week not only for big-time investors, but for those with more modest investment potentials as well, citing for instance, the pros and cons of the markets in dollars, CDBs, savings, and the going price on consumer goods such as phone lines. The range of tips catered to middle-class readers of varying means, at times attaining a rather unexpected level of detail. For instance, reporting on the kinds of defensive responses to the Plano Cruzado price freeze by the business sector, *Veja* (8 / 13 / 86) told readers that the *jeitinho* of one toilet-paper producer was to continue to offer his product at the same price, thereby adhering to the freeze, but rolls became one-ply instead of two!

Nor did the media limit itself to the pragmatic. The print media excelled at personal counseling. One article told of the psychological impact of the crisis on the middle class: "The middle class is experiencing a hellish phase, marked by the fall in buying power, hopelessness, and fear of the future," reported a São Paulo newspaper (*Folha de São Paulo* 8 / 18 / 91), itself quoting from focus-group and survey reports published in the magazine *The Listening Post* prepared by the advertising multinational Standard, Ogilvy and Mather. Then, taking a therapeutic turn, another article reported on the kinds of spiritual intervention middle and upper classes were seeking to improve their lives: "Upper middle class seeks light in mysticism" (*Estado de São Paulo* 12 / 8 / 91).

Through this steady stream of articles offering everything from home ec to personal advice, the print media told readers how to save their shirts, how to mend their souls, even how their bathroom tissue was going to feel. Does what Baudrillard said of opinion polls apply? In his view, these media texts "exhibit this redundancy of the social, this continual voyeurism of the group in relation to itself: it must at all times know what it wants, know what it thinks, be told its least needs, its least quivers, see itself continually in the videoscreen of statistics, constantly watch its own temperature chart." For him, this constitutes "a sort of hypochondriacal madness . . . [a] real obscenity" (1985, 580). In my mind, again, the Brazilian media took on the metaphorical role of guardian angel, a protector and guiding light directly involved in the redefinition of middle-class identity. Or rather, that is one role it took on in its growing relationship to the middle class.

The news media had a whole other repertory of stories and styles of outreach to middle-class readers, including one I will characterize as a goading, mocking voice. As I am sure readers have detected, this voice is discernible in the almost apocalyptic articles on middle-class professionals becoming garbagemen or car watchers. It is most blatant in snide reports on nouveau-riche lifestyles—for example, the cellular maniacs—but it is also clear in the tongue-in-cheek laments of the lost paradise of consumption. For instance, the *Jornal da Tarde* painted this pseudo-sad picture: "Poor middle class. The dream ended. And the long nightmare begins. Days now are of few purchases, of only eating at home—rice bought from COBAL—of children without Danoninho (miniyogurt, a luxury item), ballet, or swimming lessons." The article provided a docudrama of photos of entire families in sparse living rooms, watching TV. Another report announced a 40 percent loss of salaries in five years, but then stated in (mock?) dismay that middle-class people were becoming *forofeiros* (manioc eaters) at the beach "without fear [receio] or embarrassment, sunbathing beside a styrofoam fridge, with beer, pop, and snacks." *Forofeiros* is a class-biased term used to denigrate poor people who travel far to the beach and bring their lunch. This distancing style appears to conflict with the role of guardian angel I am highlighting. How to reconcile this? It may not be necessary to do so, but it is possible to see the mocking style as guidance through a negative register.

Identifying the Middle Class as Victim

Thus far we have seen the media providing material "upon which groups and classes construct an 'image' of the lives, meanings, practices and values of other groups and classes" (Hall 1979, 340)—and their own class. The media also, according to Hall, assists people in "mak[ing] sense of it [the world] with preferred and excluded explanations and rationales." The Brazilian print media was, of course, an integral, constitutive part of the crisis and resource for the development of a vocabulary and interpretation of it. A 1983 *Estado de São Paulo* article states that "the Brazilian middle class has been hit the hardest by the economic crisis [a mais atingida pela crise econômica] (8/23/83).

From the earliest moment of the crisis, the media identified the middle class as the target of the crisis, as its major victim. Although there are distinctions among the newspapers, they all shared this perspective. The argument gained its coherence because of the constantly presented, never contested assertion that the middle class is defined through consumption, basically and existentially. Affirmed via consumption, the class was thereby negated by the crisis. This "common sense" understanding of the crisis was reciprocally shared between the media and the middle class. That the middle class was targeted in certain and important ways is not a problematic assertion. (For instance, suffering a loss of income that then required removing one's child from private school was specific to this class; the poor never had that advantage, and the rich did not lose it.) However, the idea that the crisis hurt the middle class the most depends on the erroneous reasoning that because poor people were by definition almost penniless, the crisis did not affect them, and/or that poor people cannot become more impoverished. In contrast to the view that the crisis especially prejudiced the middle class, as well as to stories exhibiting intimate concern with analyzing middle-class meanings, existence, and threats, news of poor people, such as the violence surrounding the drug trade in Rio, seemed to be presented unadorned, without explanation, thereby representing violence as if it were an essential and timeless quality of the working class.

My contact with informants and the media repeatedly brought me up against a seemingly remarkable coincidence: the same vocabulary regarding the middle class, consumption, the crisis, and the political state of the nation—and more generally, reciprocally shared views and frameworks.[2] The onslaught of news regarding the impact of the crisis on the middle class presented a perspective that could both unify the class and isolate it from other classes. In Hall's view, the media performs one last major function, namely, the "production of consensus, the construction of legitimacy" (1979, 340–341)—in this case, middle-class righteousness and victimization against the government's mishandling of the national economy, as well as middle-class activism.

Media analysts have argued that media production of a spectacle induces, or should induce, passivity in the audience, rather than create a critical public (see, e.g., Raboy and Dagenais 1992). Similarly, analyses of daily news in stable First World societies such as the United States (Jensen 1992) find audiences (and middle-class audiences are presumably the referent) to be fairly disinterested. Dahlgren (1992, 215) goes further in arguing that the news has a deterring effect, so that the viewer does not "locate her/himself as a political subject in an historical setting." Some studies emphasize a social distancing created in and through the news; others, as presented by Ellis (1982; cited in Ang 1996), argue that the rhetorical strategies create a "complicity of viewing" between the media and the audience, and further, that the media takes on the role of looking into world issues "on behalf of" the viewers (Ang 1996, 23).

During the crisis era (1980–94) the Brazilian news presented an ongoing dramatic saga in which the middle class was constructed as unified through consumption, and with consumption its raison d'être, as the major subject/object of the crisis. The government became its main opponent, especially in the person of President Collor. Although I have underscored that the economic crisis did not target the middle classes alone, it did affect them directly and generally during the Collor presidency owing to the bank-account freeze (see below). Thus by watching or reading the news about these matters, middle-class Brazilians were seeing or reading about a spectacle, or better, a drama, in which they were players, in which their own family context (Morley 1986) was directly implicated. That being the case, the question of agency takes center stage: in these circumstances, and through its rhetorical strategies, did the media texts incite, inhibit, or stand in for social agency?

Let us turn to the irritated voice of critique that began with reports on the Sarney government's mishandling of the economy, and culminated with the even deeper economic and then political crisis of the Collor presidency.

THE COLLOR PLANS: FROM "BIODEGRADABLE MONEY" TO "MONEY BUYS LITERALLY NOTHING"

The Collor Plan Is "Lowered"

The Plano Collor, announced March 17, 1990, had many measures, but the one of overriding and enduring interest was this: "*Withdrawals* from checking and savings accounts of deposits made until March 13 of this year [when a bank holiday was declared until March 17] *will be limited to Cr$50,000.* Values beyond this will be sent back to the Central Bank and converted into cruzeiros eighteen months hence—that is, after September 16, 1991" (*O Globo* 3/17/90; emphasis added). Unlike other plans noted for price freezes and currency changes, this one added the freezing of monies.[3] In fact, $US74 billion were blocked out of a GNP of $US350 billion, or $US26 billion from savings and checking and $US48 billion from the overnight (*Folha de São Paulo* 3/17/90). The intention of the drastic reduction of currency in circulation was precisely to curb spending—and speculation. Brazil's problem was glaring: $US120 billion, or nearly a third of the GNP, was in the financial market. Planners reasoned that a major oversight of previous plans had been the consumer sprees following price freezes. They assumed Congress would approve this plan, arguing that it did not adversely affect workers, but rather penalized speculators. Congress did approve the Plano Collor with all its austerity measures. With this first presidential act, Collor outmatched the spectacle of his presidential campaign.

Informants vividly remembered the stunning effect when suddenly, from that day forward, they had a very finite sum of savings. No one I asked came close to gauging the equivalent of Cr$50,000, which was about US$1,200.[4] More than three years after the Plano Collor, Esther, a journalist herself, described the plan this way (with interjections made by her husband, Gil):

Esther: The intention was to stop money from circulating and start a new economy. The fact was that the plan was designed in a very closed way, it required absolute secrecy of the economic team, the story couldn't leak, because the idea of the plan was the impact. In his inauguration speech on television, with the whole population watching, he [Collor] had already said—one of his campaign slogans was that he was going to kill inflation with just one shot. This was the most curious because he—

Gil: He almost killed everyone.

Esther: The slogan became famous. So panic was generalized. Because suddenly there was a finance ministr*a*—the first woman minister—saying, "From now on you have fifty thousand cruzados, each."

Gil: No, it was cruzeiros. Cruzados was—

Esther: So everyone had debts in cruzados novos [the old currency]. So we negotiated on the basis of an exchange of debts. The old currency continued circulating, but not in the circulating realm [meio circulante].

Gil: This was the first big surprise. The second big surprise, we discovered that with this plan the market ended [acabou]. I will never forget, one day, a Wednesday, there were no cars on the streets. It seemed like Sunday. A few days later, the stores were closed, everything had stopped. I went to the office, [but] I didn't know what to do . . .

Esther: There was the highest incidence of bankruptcy.

Gil: I went to the club to clear my head. On the way, I heard the daily quote of the volume of São Paulo's stock market. It was what I had in my bank account, understand, this the stock market of São Paulo! I live off building projects. [Gil is an architect.] So it was over. Works stopped, there was nothing to do. The third big surprise, the price of buildings fell.

Esther: No one had money. No one could buy, no one knew what would happen. All markets stopped.

Removed in time and having recovered from the Plano Collor, this couple presented the lowering of the plan with both humor and drama.

As reported in chapter 1, José Claudio and Maria do Carmo were able to keep up payment on their apartment, yet most of their neighbors were not, thereby losing all prior investment. Running out of freelance work during this time, Aninha attempted to be a salesclerk. Ricardo lost his job, and only regained it with a huge salary loss. His wife, Maria Regina doubled her teaching hours. To these accounts, one could add others for many families in the study. For instance, Miriam and Marquinhos shook their heads over those years, debating which was worse, 1989, 1990, or 1991. Struggling with two toddlers and caring for an elderly parent, Miriam has worked sixty hours per week teaching English classes. Sociologist Marquinhos took on a series of jobs, including bartending, before finding permanent (low-paying) union work. School teacher Lisete soon recalled the Collor years in our first meeting:

> So then came the Plano Collor, plan such and such, plan, plan, plan. We told our little boy, "When you were little, your grandparents opened up a savings account for when you grow up." They said it's for a trip to Europe, or to buy a car, or for anything he needs. Now he's growing up and the money in the savings won't be enough for absolutely anything. So you see how real the crisis is. How much we stop being able to do certain things. I don't see a light at the end of the tunnel. I think it's ever more reduced, the space for this light to appear.

Three other couples, all in public and low-salaried positions (like teaching), made a point of saying that they take care not to convey their pessimism to their children, so as not to raise a defeated child (*um filho derrotado*).

One couple, Maurício and Elisa, experienced a tragedy. In 1986, Maurício, in his early thirties, was gunned down by an assailant and became severely disabled. In a terrible way, their life story reflects recent tendencies of Brazil and the middle class of the crisis years. I report their story here with some reticence, as I fear trivializing or demeaning their circumstances by referring to them in the context of social analysis. But the couple told the story readily, with apparent interest in providing the details.

At the time of the assault Maurício had his own business related to marketing. He had a secretary, architect, and office boy; the business was his alone. Maurício said with pride that his family had three cars, a country home, a beach house, and an apartment in São Paulo. The three years of this business, from 1983 to 1986 were the best of his life. It was then, when he was at the top, that the assault occurred. At the time, he had some financial investments earning interest legally, Maurício emphasized, but paying higher than the market. Soon after Maurício got out of the hospital, the lawyer who had been handling his investments went bust, disappeared, and was never seen again. He left with everyone's money, but Maurício had been the biggest investor. Maurício's company folded.

After recovering from the shooting, Maurício sold cars—it was something he could do by phone. Elisa began selling frozen prepared foods, and she helped Maurício with the administration of car sales by doing the banking. This sounds like a viable recourse; however, in 1990, precisely when Collor froze the nation's savings accounts and changed the currency, Maurício was in for another surgery and the check Elisa had received from a car sale was suddenly worthless. During the Collor administration, no one had any liquidity. Cars were more sellable than houses, though. Still in 1987 they sold their house in São Paulo—of all their property, the easiest to dispose of at that time—and went to live in their country home, which had a pool and sauna. "Anyone who'd look at us would have thought . . . but we had no work. We sold what we had in order to . . ." Elisa said, trailing off. They lived there from 1987 to 1993.

In 1990, during the Collor administration's first year, Elisa opened up a luncheonette at the school her oldest son attended; this paid for the boy's schooling. For this venture, Maurício did the bookkeeping, while Elisa prepared the food. In late 1992, they returned to São Paulo, where Maurício obtained professional work in his field through a family connection. Since 1993 Elisa has worked at an NGO advocating for disabled people.

Newspapers wasted no time in supplementing information about the plan with vignettes of how it was wreaking havoc in the lives of Brazilian people. *Veja*'s first major commentary article (3/21/90), headed "Week without end: Rumors, bank holiday, and a plan with drastic measures made last week one of the most hallucinating that the country has lived through," recounted the confusions peculiar to this plan. What if one had more than one bank account? What would happen with older checks yet to be deposited? Would stores accept old money? Even though the 50,000 rule may appear clear, problems arose: checks with the old currency were not always recognized (despite official rulings), banks did not allow withdrawals for employee paychecks beyond the 50,000 amount, and banks improvised various other blockages. At some banks the disruption turned violent.

The newspaper *O Globo* reported a near riot outside the Rio Citibank, when people learned after a three-hour wait in line that they were not to receive their unemployment compensation (despite the exemption of the FGTS funds from the ruling).[5] The situation calmed down only with the shock forces of the military police and word from Citibank that the FGTS payments would be made (*O Globo* 3/21/90). In Mato Grosso do Sul, *O Globo* reported a one-man battle by a forty-one-year-old farmer who had, on March 12, sold his ranch, including buildings, cattle, tractors, and home, and then invested in the open market. A few days into the plan, desperate, he rammed his car through the glass doors of the bank and shouted: "I'm poor, miserable! This government took everything I had. It stole my money." *O Globo* deftly added, "Security responded quickly" (3/21/90). The injuries sustained as a result of the plan were varied: heart clinics in Rio received twice as many cases after the measure; a twelve-year-old Paulista girl could no longer go to Disney World that year (*O Globo* 3/24/90). The media managed to offer some relief. Leftist economist Maria da Conceição Tavares was interviewed by the late-night talk-show comedian Jô Soares. Tavares said, "Now isn't the time for joking." Ever quick, Jô responded, "What?! They're even going to confiscate *that* from me?!"

Misfortune came in many guises. In one "typical" case, an individual had just sold an old car and put the money in the "open" when the bank holiday was decreed. The Plano Collor left him with no money and no car. A couple who had sold an apartment, also making an open-market investment prior to buying a new home, found themselves in an even graver situation: with no money and the prospect of no place to live. Such adversity, in which insult added to injury, was quintessential to the Collor plan.[6] While *Veja* also offered stories, its forte was in creative forms of editorializing. I turn now to *Veja,* mainly because of its singular feat of printing the breaking story of the presidential corruption scandal of 1992 but first because of its stylistic peculiarities.

The Plano Collor, According to *Veja*

With a circulation close to one million, *Veja* (owned by Brazil's largest publishing house, the Editora Abril) is by far the nation's most widely read serious weekly magazine. It has no pretensions of being popular in the sense of being of the people. Feature articles provide information for privileged groups, such as on foreign vacations and international credit cards. Its advertising regularly features cars, jewelry, major-brand stores, Varig airlines, car insurance, tennis shoes, and, since the Collor presidency, imported goods available nationally. In a word, *Veja* targets those who can afford such things and the middle classes. Its price has steadily risen. A year's subscription was US$150 in 1993. In 1995, a single issue of *Veja* cost three reais, or about $3.30. My informant pool was evenly split between the two main São Paulo newspapers, the *Folha de São Paulo* and the *Estado de São Paulo*, but *Veja* was a common referent (and more than half subscribed). Sources vary on the number of newspapers circulating daily in the major cities, from three million (Straubhaar, Olsen, and Nunes 1993) to six million. A former journalist for *Veja* estimated three readers per newspaper, and six for every *Veja* issue. In the journalist's view, one might occasionally miss reading the newspaper, but not *Veja*. A common news source, it brings readers together for its highly elaborated narrative reworking of the news (Bell 1991), or "cultural discourse" (Dahlgren 1992, 204).

During the campaign period the major media positively pursued Collor. He rose out of obscurity when *Veja* made his alleged war of "decadent" maharajas its cover story in 1988, in virtual advertisement for the white knight's candidacy.[7] Collor was known during the campaign for his adeptness on TV; certainly his glamourous style matched his platform to modernize Brazil into a First World country. It has been convincingly argued (see V. A. Lima 1993) that Collor was created by the media, particularly through the TV station Rêde Globo, whose owner openly supported Collor. President José Sarney's departure was jeered by *Veja* writers, who remarked: "With the interest on the overnight up to 100 percent last week, the third currency used by Sarney in five years, the cruzado novo, followed the same path as the cruzeiro and the cruzado, into disuse. All over the country, accounts were being done in dollars, in BTNs, LTNs, and even a currency used exclusively by taxi drivers, the UT (taximetric unit).[8] Even the UT is less exotic than the cruzado novo, that biodegradable money: suffice it to stay in your pocket one day for it to lose 2 percent of its value. By making money a lie, Sarney transformed it literally into the expression 'time is money'" (*Veja* 2/14/90). After offering support integral to Collor's rise to power, *Veja* was immediately skeptical of the mediamade president; it turned a satirical eye on him and proved itself to be quite versatile in the role of public defender against the Plano Collor.

Reporting that the government circulated a memorandum stating in late April that retirees had two days to present the necessary documents to obtain their blocked money, *Veja* wondered sarcastically, but at the same time charitably vis-à-vis the elderly, why the government alone had not been able to predict what a cruel problem this presented for the thirteen million elderly and disabled who had to spend hours in line (5/9/90). Another area of mismanagement again involved the unemployment compensation fund (FGTS). Within a two-month period, *Veja* reported, the FGTS accounts were frozen; freed for one week; freed in general, except for withdrawals related to buying a home; freed for a certain unemployed group; blocked in general; unblocked. This was Finance Minister Zélia Cardoso's "handiwork," *Veja* (5/16/90) sneered.

Collor himself was soon ridiculed for incessantly needing to fix the plan. As *Veja* (3/27/90) dryly reported, he signed 348 acts regarding the financial sector alone, many of which rectified errors in preceding ones, and in the year 1990, he instituted no fewer than 146 (provisional) measures, prompting political scientist Francisco Weffort to calculate an average of one emergency measure every two days. The worst result was that the heterodox measures did not stop inflation. After the plan, the money in circulation dropped from $120 billion to $40 billion. Within a month, lacking financial means for production or salaries, businesses registered a slow down or halt (*paralização*). Production dropped 25 percent, moving the country deeper into recession, *Veja* announced dolefully a week into the plan (4/18/90).

Unencumbered by stylistic restrictions and preferring excess over sobriety, Collor's "bullet" became a "bomb," or an atomic bomb, or even an earthquake in the hyperbolic words of its journalists. Said *Veja*: "*One fears that the package has the virtues and defects of the neutron bomb, that which leaves people alive but destroys everything around them*"

(4/4/90; emphasis added). *Veja* writers reported that the First World was apprehensive of a president who "wakes up one day with the idea of confiscating 80 percent of financial activity and presents this as a non-negotiable fact." Such an act, they continued in ironic tones, is not surprising from a country moving into socialism, but it is when used by a politician with a liberal discourse. At times indignant rather than sarcastic, the magazine proclaimed that besides breaking a campaign promise, "in confiscating money from the checking account, Collor intervened in an unheard-of way in private property, leaving *people* to think that nothing is really safe from the government" (3/21/90; emphasis added). *Veja* variously spoke for—on behalf of—all Brazilians (one, people), and for a vast number of others (the First World). Such speech illustrates what has been called the "fictive 'we' " (Allan 1998) or "ventriloquiz[ing]" of views (Fairclough 1998).

In the following citation, *Veja* speaks directly on behalf of the middle class. The magazine first presented the rationale of the freeze on bank accounts according to its designers. Ninety percent of savings accounts held less than the Cr$50,000 limit, declared the president of the Central Bank, Ibrahim Eris; as Finance Minister Zélia Cardoso de Mello put it, just 10 percent of the population was affected. The 10 percent targeted by the measure included not only speculators, but, *Veja* reasoned, those twelve million of the middle class earning between Cr$18,000 and Cr$120,000 (that is, from US$425 to US$2,900 per month)—a group described by *Veja* as one whose "children go to private school, [who] go to restaurants, buy cars once in a while, and even travel internationally on occasion, and who put 17 out of 100 cruzados novos in savings" (3/28/90). (This descriptive definition minus the last empirical excess matches several in my informant pool, as we saw in chapter 1.) *Veja* righteously argued that it was all very well to curb speculators, but this group of small savers hardly warranted the same treatment.

Depicting Middle-Class Resistance and Paralysis

As early as one week into the plan, *Veja* announced (not without pomp) that the middle class "abandoned their customary silence and began to complain" (3/21/90); a week later *Veja* cited a middle-class person arguing that "the confiscation is not only theft, it is a violation of our constitutional rights" (3/28/90).[9] The magazine went on to inform readers that by the end of May 1990, twenty-seven thousand cases were initiated against the blocking of bank accounts. Even if such passive language described rather than prescribed actions, the television, radio, and print media's dissemination of information worked. Indeed, legal suits represented the first major political expression of the middle class versus the Collor administration.

Bank administrator Carlos said: "I only woke up with Collor. That was a coup. Besides taking everything, he pushed [us into] hyperinflation. Even I have filed a claim to recover the money. Inflation had been 80 percent and he hadn't paid the difference between inflation increases and salary [the *dissídio*]. So far, I've recovered 20 percent." Carlos's wife, Sandra, added indignantly, "He says recover, [but] do you know how he has to do this? Taking legal action. Although it is his right, he had to demand it, in an action against the government. He had to pay a lawyer to get this money back, this money which is his right." I asked: "Did you win?" Sandra: "We won." Carlos: "I won 20 percent. Now I'm in another suit to get the rest."

The legal issue concerns the *dissídio,* which is the difference between the salary corrections given in a period (e.g., a quarter) and the de facto inflation. One method adopted by the Sarney and Collor governments was to ignore the inflation of the time just preceding a plan. Given that devaluation is high at such times, salary losses could be significant. Legal claims were also made regarding monetary correction of FGTS funds at lower than inflation. Sandra was quick to point out that the news media played a part in catalyzing these legal actions. She claimed that "everyone complains but no one here goes to fight for their rights. . . . In the beginning, people got really, really mad (*bravas*) at the government, criticizing, but no one had the courage to do anything. With jurists who came on TV and the radio, some well-known ones, they said that by the constitution he [Collor] could never have done this with the money of the people. But people here don't fight for their rights. . . . They always wait for someone to do things for them. . . . Some got brave and went and won. Then people thought it was worth it and started too."[10] Significantly, in her rendering, the television and radio were educator-catalysts. *Veja* also printed the jurist evaluation of the plan.

We saw earlier that the print media engaged in showing and telling readers about the middle class's changing state of being and activities. Here too *Veja* offered a kind of how-to—showing them how to argue against the government and explaining how to take action—or not—and telling readers how they felt. A month into the plan, *Veja* (4/18/90) dedicated a long article to the psychological impact of the economic shock, described as provoking a "paradoxical confluence of extreme nervousness with paralyzing apathy." The most angered Brazilians, said a psychologist, were those who voted for Collor. They felt both "cheated and accomplices."

Resorting again to the favored style of irony, three months into the presidency, *Veja* deemed the president's image "cinematographic." Collor's first months in office were, we learn, a study in motion. He was photographed jet skiing and on a submarine; piloting a supermarket cart to research prices; and otherwise constantly jogging or training with Brazil's World Cup soccer team (Seleção Brasileira de Futebol). *Veja* reported (tongue-in-cheek), "Since assuming the presidency, Collor has publicly practiced a dozen sports, traveled more than 50,000 km., and worn nine uniforms" (6/20/90). In other words, while Brazil and Brazilians were "paralyzed"—a term *Veja* reiterated regarding the middle-class state of being in reaction to the Plano Collor—the president, literally and figuratively, was exuberantly hyperactive.

From the moment the first Collor plan was lowered, *Veja* adopted a critical position toward the government's plans—and the person of the president. But *Veja* was not a unitary voice speaking consistently and solely on behalf of the middle classes against the government. Just as the press could take on a mocking position as well as one of sympathetic solidarity with the middle class, so too could *Veja* turn a critical eye on middle-class acts.

Interpretive *Veja*: The Culture of Inflation

In June 1990, *Veja* crisply informed readers that with salaries at 35 percent of the GNP, the attempted repression of the dissídio was of anti-inflationary, and not simply antipopulist, intent. The sum of inflation in February and March 1990 (said to be an outrageous 166 percent) would raise the salary amount to $27 billion. *Veja* noted that "in the opinion of economists, there is no way to produce additional monies for these readjustments—other than by putting the Printing House [Casa da Moeda] to work eight shifts a day. But then there would be hyperinflation the following day—one calculates a jump of 40 percent in the first month, and higher thereafter. Another consequence of this increase would be to throw close to 30 million workers into the street. In this case, the Brazilian economy wouldn't enter into the realm of recession or depression—it would return to a tribal state similar to the Yanomami Indians" (6/13/90).

Interestingly, through this argument and a wild (and eventually offensive) narrative of hyperinflation, *Veja* sided with the government against legal suits. It chastised its middle-class readers, who might imagine they were losing 166 percent of their purchasing power in the absence of monetary correction in the months just prior to the plan. That was "obviously" not so, *Veja* retorted. If that were the case, people would not be able to buy even a match (to calculate currency devaluations in terms of this specific purchasing power was "classic" in *Veja*). The plan would not have the support of 75 percent of the population. *Veja* did not point out that *all* plans had received initial positive compliance despite personal hardship. Instead, *Veja* explained that salary corrections, albeit below the full amount, had been made, such that the real loss for January was "just" 13 percent and then in February another 10 percent before the plan. Readers could add for themselves.[11] In short, without knowing why, we can only surmise that *Veja* had its own agenda, one that changed with the times, at times speaking for, other times in critique of, middle-class Brazilians. And it went further, expanding its criticism to Brazilian society in general.

By July 1990, the theory of the culture of inflation had been launched, and *Veja* embraced it. By this theory, "after decades of living with inflation, a good part of Brazilians developed an almost accomplice behavior with the regime of rising prices" (7/11/90). Guilty players included merchants who chose to raise their retail prices (*remarcar os preços*), or to raise them once gross prices were raised (*repassar os preços*), to go beyond the inflation level (*preços absurdos*), or to adjust prices without due calculation. Also guilty were shoppers who bought needlessly (thus *Veja* ignored the understanding that goods are a safekeeping measure when money is devalued). In this same article, the magazine did present a counter opinion. The second of two main finance ministers of the military regime, famed economist and representative Delfim Neto, was quoted as saying: "Don't delude yourselves. Inflation is a mechanism that transfers wealth from the worker's pocket into the government's. If the government stopped producing inflation, all this culture of inflation would vanish in the air" (7/11/90). Although this voice of authority was included, the culturalist explanation nonetheless prevailed in *Veja*'s analysis. It went on to represent the cultural bent as a pervasive historical pattern (citing high inflation in 1577, 1690, 1808, 1822, 1890, 1937, 1945, 1964, 1985, 1986, 1989, and 1990). Although it ended by calling inflation the "worst tax that there is," since it lets no one off, attacks the poor more than the rich, and cited the government as the motive force, *Veja*'s last word was that the government operated within a society that moved in an inflationary direction.

In the second semester of 1990, reports focused on the plan's adverse impact on the economy, which put the country into the worst recession since World War II. Bankruptcies increased 233 percent in September and October (10/31/90). State accounts were wiped out, employees paid late, works interrupted; exports were the lowest in three years. Just before Christmas, an article about *favela* (shantytown) settlements reported that 60 million citizens had no homes or schools for their children. By then, 100,000 people were living in the streets in São Paulo (population 17 million), and a shocking 120,000 in Recife (population then 1.3 million).

Even while reporting these discouraging trends, *Veja* still maintained the culturalist explanation, saying that "the difference between Brazil and other countries that managed to deal with the recession has a cultural basis. [In Europe] the automatic remedy for rising prices is recession. The society accepts it as a routine fact. 'Here recession is an ugly word,'" a foreign researcher of the Fernand Braudel International Economy Institute was cited saying (12/5/90), thereby offering support from a foreign expert for *Veja*'s position. Elsewhere, *Veja* continued, businesses did not depend on banks so much, and thus suffered less with interest rates; furthermore, they did not lower production and raise the profit margin. These "sins" were Brazilian "habits."

Chapter 7 deals with the culture of inflation theory further; there I discuss how it appeared in informants' discourse. Since the origin of this culturalist explanation for Brazil's problems seems impossible to deter-

mine, I merely point out here that the media and my middle-class informants shared this theory that naturalizes Brazil's economic problems.

Plano Collor II, or *Salve-se Quem Puder*

Although the Plano Collor of 1990 was the most notorious of all
government plans, and it received huge criticism, *Veja's* pronounced
reservations on public opposition to the government and its espousing of
the cause of inflation as societal rather than governmental showed some
measure of acceptance of the government's policy. With the Plano Collor
II (1991), *Veja* dropped the culture of inflation view entirely and focused
instead solely on the government's responsibility for the unending crisis.

Indeed, it lost its patience, giving brittle commentaries. Regarding
the price freeze, *Veja* decided: "This is not going to work, as the previous
ones have shown." The next measure of readjusting salaries with an
average of the last twelve months of inflation, plus freezing, prompted the
judgment "This *is* going to work; every time they freeze the salaries, they
stay frozen." Regarding higher public-utility prices, *Veja* commented:
"This will also work; in fact, it has since last Friday." In response to a
measure replacing long-lived indexation measures (the BTN and BTNF
indexes) with something called *taxa referencial de juros,* referential interest
rate,[12] *Veja* snapped "This is illusion: to exchange the [inflation] indexation of the past to that of the future." The press, *Veja* summed up, spared
no sympathy for Zélia, who defended her price controls by insulting
businessmen. In her words, they had shown they could not "behave
themselves with the liberty" (of lack of indexation). The magazine's
response was curt: "Price freezes don't work because they discourage
production and stimulate consumption."

Surpassing even itself in irony, *Veja* (2/6/91) noted that Plano Collor II had managed to go beyond all other plans in complexity. For
instance, the method of calculation for the readjustment of salaries was
different for those who received their wage once a month from those
who received it twice. It differed for those who received the first of the
month from those received the tenth and in turn the fifteenth. The employee who received payment once a month had to make fourteen mathematical calculations to know the month's adjustment. For those who
received biweekly, twenty-six operations were necessary. Those paying

monthly installments needed to check to see if the amount was listed in BTNs or cruzeiros. If in the now extinct BTN, the value would be exactly what it was the month before. If in cruzeiros, the calculation depended on a "little table" used to annul the interest exacted by commerce, which in a price-freeze period should not exist. Biannual school readjustments would allow a 30 percent increase for inflation but also one of 70 percent relating to the staff salaries. Rent contracts signed in October would be readjusted in April. To calculate a new rent, the BTN between October and February was to be used. If the contract was in indexes of FIPE (Fundação Instituto de Pesquísus Econômicas, Foundation Institute of Economic Research), then all months of inflation would be incorporated into the new rent.[13] As readers can see, elucidating the plan was clearly secondary to *Veja*'s rhetorical goals. *Veja* strongly reclaimed an irritated, condemning position, one unambiguously blaming the government for the crisis and not the populace. As well it might.

With Plano Collor II, the country entered into the worst recession of its history. The number of people laid off was higher than in the 1982 recession and twice that of 1988: one million people in São Paulo alone. After fourteen months, Zélia left the ministry (*Veja* 5/15/91). And in late 1991, when fears of hyperinflation resurfaced with a stock-market tremor, *Veja* offered this delirious speculation: "Last Tuesday the country tried to reinvent the end of the world, with a version that its GNP of 400 billion dollars would disappear in plain day in the exchange speculation, which averages (in the better or worse hypotheses) 20 million dollars per day. This black hole would then be eaten by ants" (11/6/91). The same issue offered its very first sober definition of hyperinflation. According to the USP economist quoted, it is "that moment when you try to buy something with money and no one accepts it. At this point no one wants to sell since at this moment any price charged won't be enough to cover the producer and factory or the merchant to replenish stocks." Reverting again to baroque style, an article had the headline "Salve-se quem puder," with a subheading of "Money buys literally nothing." The expression *salve-se quem puder* can be translated as "each one for him/herself" or, better, "dog-eat-dog society," for the situation envisioned to be the nightmarish result of hyperinflation. The popular expression brings out the image of moral chaos in a civil society destroyed by economic crisis.

A series of depressing reports ensued without relief between November 1991 and May 1992: middle-class children whose parents could no longer afford private education going to public schools, engineers bartending, a wave of supermarket sackings (twenty-nine in May in Rio), and, horribly, 424 children murdered in Rio in 1992. All these occurrences were suddenly superseded by Pedro Collor's revelations. Indeed, the ultimate critique and goad occurred with *Veja's* exclusive interview with the president's brother.

Before moving into this, the biggest scandal story, we must think over how or whether *Veja's* position "balanced out." *Veja's* reporting gave a never understated and sometimes apocalyptic perspective on the crisis and the Plano Collor. Its voices seemed "plural" (see Anselm and Goulianis 1994); it not only accessed experts, politicians, middle-class people, and more, whom it cited; it also presumed to speak in "everyone's" place. *Veja* was outspoken in its criticism of the government—sarcasm and irony permeated the pages—but its messages were conflicting: criticisms of the plan and reports of dire straits in the economy were countered by defense of austerity measures and the culturalist explanation for the inflation crisis. Its rethematization of issues specifically about and for the middle class at times sounded like a middle-class or upper-middle-class person thinking aloud, and at other times like an authority talking down to this social group. Thus at times *Veja* spoke for and other times against the middle-class readership. As the next chapter considers in detail, middle-class people themselves criticized Brazilian society for being a culture of inflation. The diversity of attitudes presented in *Veja* might therefore be perfectly congruent with its ambivalent readership. Thus I argue that even when the media's criticism, sarcasm, and irony were aimed at the middle class, perhaps in part precisely through its very criticism of this "mainstream," it succeeded in modeling a position members of this social sector could itself adopt—against the government and against themselves.

Exaggerated in style, *Veja* aired critical ideas, conjured up wild imaginings, vented indignation, at times urging and at other times discouraging positions—indeed, stopping short of recommending certain acts with economic and political impact. That a mainstream magazine should be ambivalent, contradictory, and conservative "underneath" is hardly surprising, nor entirely the point. Rather, registering what this media produced, the question becomes how it was received—and, vice versa, how the media received and responded to the middle class. Did this media (regardless of intentions) provide a kind of vent for readers' feelings, an exacerbation of them, *or* a replacement for them? Notice how the print media recounted people's anger and frustration, characterizing their state as one of impotent rage. Notice its indignation at the Plano Collor's unconstitutionality versus its cautions against taking legal action against it. Let us now reconsider the media's role in constructing a middle-class identity in light of political actions in response to news reports of the Collor corruption scandal and then in light of middle-class views on their own and the media's "activism."

THE MEDIA, THE MIDDLE CLASS, AND THE IMPEACHMENT MOVEMENT

From Corruption Scandal to Social Movement

Interrupting and superseding all other news were the accusations leveled by Fernando Collor's youngest brother, Pedro, in May 1992 against Paulo César "PC" Farias. Farias was Collor's campaign treasurer and known to have been an unofficial but central figure in the first year of government. Pedro Collor claimed that PC had pocketed 15 million of the 100 million campaign dollars, engaged in election fraud in Alagoas, and handled business with politicians through extortion. For instance, for ensuring that a paper company won a government contract, PC was said to be receiving 3.3 billion cruzeiros per month since late 1990; for solving a debt problem sugar-cane industrialists of Alagoas had with a British bank, he was being compensated one million cruzeiros per month. Pedro also said PC had presented pearls and fine clothing to former finance minister Zélia Cardoso in return for answering his requests. For a man of so many gifts and possessions, it was odd, noted *Veja,* that PC's tax returns showed his salary was just 5.5 million cruzeiros, or 2,100 dollars per month.

Everyone knew that since Collor's election, PC Farias circulated among politicians and businessmen, even naming state employees and doing business. Why expose these irregularities now, unless the idea was to shake up the democratic institutions? This was the jaded reasoning *Veja* presented initially. One hypothesis first advanced was that through

PC's dealings in Alagoas, Pedro's own branch of the family business (an Alagoas newspaper) suffered. Pedro also said PC had used state funds for personal speculation. *Veja* immediately supposed that the real target (despite Pedro's pleas to the contrary) was the president. For this it chastised Pedro, saying that ever since Cain and Abel such brotherly fighting had been deplorable, and added that given the country's grave difficulties, the fight acquired "a character of bold irresponsibility" (5/20/92).

It is interesting to note that several months prior to the exclusive interview that initiated the scandal, *Veja* had already ruminated over impeachment, warning conservatively: "Don't believe that an impeachment process can be contained within the limits of the president's person, without damaging faith in [sem desacreditar] the institutions" (10/9/91). Once the scandal broke, the magazine seemed reluctant, not to attack the president verbally, but to foster a proceeding against him. It did cover the corruption scheme of PC Farias exhaustively (reveling in the details), decried and derided the president, and *after* middle-class youth took massively to the streets, reported on the movement. Eventually, *Veja* followed the middle-class lead in demanding the president's resignation. This qualification notwithstanding, Veja's interview had major political repercussions. As Rubim said, "The bombastic declarations of Pedro Collor to *Veja* magazine in May ended up making the CPI [Congressional Investigating Committee] of June 1992 viable" (1993, 159). *Veja* can be credited this feat; its competitor magazine, *Isto E,* also had its own pivotal role.

Isto E exclusively covered the declarations of Francisco Eriberto Freire Franco. Former chauffeur at the Collor home, Eriberto provided the first material evidence that supported Pedro Collor's disturbing but still unsupported accusations. Eriberto's testimony to *Isto E,* later repeated to the CPI, was that he had delivered money from PC's business to the Collor family home (the Casa da Dinda), turning the money over to former secretary Ana Acioli, whose bank account had the unlikely average monthly deposit of the equivalent of $53,000. These monies paid for such things as the president's wife Rosane's toilette and utilities bills. Eriberto also deposited sums that the secretary gave him in bank accounts under another name. *Isto E* emphasized Eriberto's character. Not only was he consistent (and all facts later verified); this worker from the northeastern state of Rio Grande do Norte had an awe-inspiring courage, sincerity, and dignity. Collor sympathizers (congressmen of Collor's party and others) who tried to denigrate his position by insinuating motives of personal gain appeared almost cynical by comparison. The magazine printed the following exchange in bold: A congressman asked, "And *senhor,* you mean to say that you are acting only out of patriotism?" [O senhor quer dizer que está agindo só por patriotismo?]. Eriberto replied, "And *senhor,* you think that is little?" [E o senhor acha isso pouco?]. The front cover that week featured a portrait of the chauffeur and the headline "Eriberto, a Brazilian."

Ensuing investigations soon showed a direct connection between PC and the president's home, to the amount of $230 million. (Later estimates were at $1 billion.) The investigations of PC Farias revealed a series of crimes, including receiving payoffs by businessmen wanting funds from the federal bank loan institution (CEF); making a false declaration of campaign funds to the Justice Department; and accepting illegal contributions. PC cynically pointed out, as if in his own defense, that everybody does such things in campaigns. PC's illegal activities were said to extend to involvement with cocaine traffickers. In *Veja's* summary, "the 40,000 checks stored in the CPI safe form up to now the most impressive set of monetary connections between Collor and PC Farias. They document that the ex-treasurer of the president mounted a bank constellation with a team of [8] phantom bank-account owners to pay for the expenses of the Collor home"—and the expenses of other Collor relatives. In the end, more than one hundred cases were brought against Farias, many of which implicated the president. By July middle-class youth of Brazil had begun demonstrating.

Described as "beautiful, good humored, habituées of shopping centers and the beach," these young people, said *Veja* in a feature story a month later, "understood very well what was happening in the high spheres of power" (8/19/92). The youth who propelled the impeachment movement became famed for their exuberant, theatrical protest style. Called the *caras pintadas,* they painted their faces with verbal protests and jeers, using green and yellow, the colors of Brazil's flag.

If news magazines can be credited with prompting and furthering the CPI investigations, television has been linked with the youth movement. As noted by Rubim (1993), and highly emphasized by journalist Alma Guillermoprieto (1994), the miniseries airing that June and July on the Globo TV channel gave an object lesson in youth political activism. The series, *Anos Rebeldes*, depicted the radical youth of Brazil in the 1960s. The main characters were modeled after the guerrillas famed for kidnapping a U.S. ambassador in 1969.[14] It included clips from youth movements worldwide. One from the United States of flower children was seen as a model for the caras pintadas.

This series and its theme song, "Alegria, Alegria," are considered to have been inspirational for the youth street demonstrations (A. Albuquerque 1993). From the Tropicalism period, the song was a 1960s anthem and referred to Caetano Veloso's political exile more than twenty years earlier—when the demonstrators were not yet born.[15]

Insults added to injury. Investigations showed that several last-minute deposits and then withdrawals by the able secretary immediately prior to the bank holiday and the lowering of the plan allowed PC and Collor to escape the confiscation. As any lawyer knew, *Veja* pointed out, the use of privileged information should mark the end of any public official's career. Furthermore, most of the forty thousand checks between PC and Collor's secretary were dated between May and June 1990—exactly when most Brazilians were left empty-pocketed after the confiscation of the Plano Collor. Against terrible evidence and public protest, Collor tried to assume a bold cooptive stance by calling the people to "patriotically" take to the streets on an upcoming Sunday (August 16) in the Brazilian colors. Thousands and thousands *did* march on that day, wearing not green and yellow but black. (The wearing of black is uncommon in Brazil.) Demonstrations in several cities averaged 20,000 on that Sunday; in Rio, 50,000 (*Veja* 8/26/92). Becoming defiant after he was voted down in the preliminary CPI, Collor went on TV saying he refused to resign. The youth of the nation responded tenfold: 250,000 students marched on São Paulo's Avenida Paulista, shouting, "Thief, thief, thief." *Veja*'s opening editorial on September 2, 1992, read: "The president ought to step down."

Presidential investigations moved rapidly. They were set in motion by early September 1992, and the demand for the president to step down (authorized through articles 85 and 86 of the constitution) was presented to Ibsen Pinheiro, President of Congress, almost immediately thereafter. Jurists said the president had "lost all moral authority to govern the nation" (*Veja* 9/2/92). The third week of September brought 300,000 protestors to downtown São Paulo (Vale do Anhangabaú). September ended with a public vote: 441 representatives in favor of the Senate judgment, 38 against, 1 abstention, and 23 "cowards" who were absent. Only at the very end of the year did Collor resign. Evidently Collor's best bet was to be pushed out without due process, in which case he could be a victim with rights to exile.

At the time of his resignation in late December, what came to dominate news instead was the tragic, vile, and violent murder of young TV actress Daniella Perez by a male costar (possibly with his wife as accomplice). After a nuanced analysis of the intermingling of news and fiction on TV, Guillermoprieto (1994) presented this event as bizarrely more important to the nation than the impeachment. It might just as well be argued, as did anthropologist and media analyst Esther Império Hamburger (personal communication), that closure had come at the end of September, and Brazilians were already living their postimpeachment lives.

For his part, PC Farias was convicted in 1993, sentenced, and sent to a prison for the wealthy from which he escaped in August of that year. Authorities were unable to catch up with him, but a compatriot vacationing in Thailand who sighted Farias was instrumental in his reapprehension. PC's misadventures did not stop there: in June 1996, he and his girlfriend were found dead by gunshot wounds in bed in his luxurious beach home in Alagoas, where he was staying under police arrest. Immediately after the bodies were found, Alagoas police burned the bed and bedding. Although the placement of the bullets in the bodies rendered the story impossible, the press, including *Veja,* came to present it as a crime of passion: the girlfriend was said to have killed him and then herself. This stopped investigations.

The Middle Class and the Media, or Will the Real Agent Please Stand Up?

Let us return to the initial question of the media's relationship to the middle class and how the latter responded in word and deed. My reading of *Veja* shows that it stimulated and fed into anti-Collor sentiment, but lagged behind the public demand for impeachment. This reading both concurs with and counters that of Brazilianist media analysts. In "Voices of Impeachment," Fausto Neto well argues that *Veja* was in no way external to the facts or merely reporting them, but made itself the "center of the crisis" (1994, 172)—that is, of the corruption proceedings. It became a kind of "paper parliament" in which "the areas of media and politics constitute each other, meet each other [entrecruzam], not only by external forces of a representational order, but through injunctions coming from its own discursive strategies" (176).

I agree that the case is remarkable for the high political agency of the media. Yet, along with Rubim (1993) and Straubhaar, Olsen, and Nunes (1993), I find this particular reading of the media's influence goes too far. Aggravating the injury, worrying over challenges to the plan, criticizing the president, and most importantly spilling a corruption scandal (and then editorializing on any of these matters), the media was essential to middle-class responses to the crisis—indeed was a critical catalyst—but it was not sufficient to prompt the impeachment movement. No matter how influenced it was by the media, the movement was its own. Rubim points out that the news did not even cover the first protest marches, and I question how "vanguard" *Veja* was regarding impeachment, since it demanded it only in September.

It is tempting to speculate whether the print media's assumption of vicarious subject positions of the middle classes—the telling of their stories, the speaking "as if" it knew what the middle class was, what negated it, what it would become, what it should or should not think or do—was "intended" to incite social agency or to stand in for it (see A. Albuquerque 1993). One might imagine that it does not intend for people to act, but rather, through its drama and diverse voices, to stand in for social agency. Speculations aside, one knows that for all its significance, the media cannot control its effects. It could not produce flexible middle-class workers, but it could compellingly represent that story. Similarly, we know that the press promoted but could not actually produce the mass movement to impeach Collor.

The anti-Collor movement has such clear connections with the adverse economic position and instability middle- and upper-middle-class people were put in under Collor that it is almost useless to rehearse them.[16] It was not until Collor's plan "pickpocketed" the middle class en masse that middle-class resentment against the government channeled into action, first in the form of legal suits contesting the plan's constitutionality. The Collor corruption scandal, which showed the president to have directly benefited from the very austerity measures hurting the population, was the ultimate outrage prompting unusual middle-class public protest—or rather, protest by their youth. While in no way denying or lessening the ethical motives of those who participated in or supported the impeachment movement, I would argue that in forcing the resignation of the country's first democratically elected president in thirty years, middle-class Brazilians voiced their outrage not so much at Fernando Collor de Mello's corruption as at their own collapse after years of government failure to achieve economic reform. Although I call attention here to self-interested motives, it does not follow that they provided the means for mobilizing. Instead, the movement is noteworthy— and perhaps characteristically middle class (cf. Eder 1993)—in its basis on moral grounds. Again, I argue that the media's efforts in shaping middle-class politics, in producing and tapping into politicization, far predated the Collor period and extended in many more areas than have been discussed. Yes, it could and did catalyze; it could and did insist on representing the middle class as *the* victim of the crisis. Still, it could not have predicted the fact or kind of politicization that occurred, nor could it have produced the movement.

I was aware that the most important middle-class movement since restoration of democracy had been the Collor impeachment. (Immediately prior to this democratic transition, there was in 1983–84 a mass, cross-class and cross-generational movement, called *diretas já,* to demand direct elections). Yet, all informants who discussed it with me a year later insisted that it had been a youth movement and that they had not participated in it. Declaring themselves to be inactive politically, they gave the credit for the activism to their youth. One informant specified that upper-middle-class youth propelled the movement. According to Roberta:

> There is this evolution, even if you consider the economic aspect, you see that either certain values exist or they don't. I don't believe it was the economic crisis that led the upper-middle-class youth—it wasn't lower-class youth—to the streets to take out Collor. No, it wasn't the lower class. Because it's who has access to the press. Parents, schools in the periphery [poor outlying slums], don't even know from the television or newspapers. It was four of five of the top [private] schools who organized the marches on Avenida Paulista.

In her view (like Sandra's, reported earlier), the press was a key catalyst for middle-class action.

After identifying the political actors as youth, informants went on to explain their own lack of political activity: it was attributable to their having lived through the dictatorship, through which they learned to fear reprisal from the military authorities. Brazil has a history of military interventions in the government, since the beginning of the republic (1889), in fact, and has experienced long dictatorships. Though amnesty for political exiles was declared in 1979, the last dictatorship ended only in 1985 (with a civilian president elected indirectly by Congress). The numbers of tortured and killed citizens was small in Brazil compared to Argentina (125 officially recognized in Brazil, versus tens of thousands in Argentina [Arns 1995]); but the Brazilian authorities were exceedingly thorough. Even if one did not personally know anyone arrested, an incident (e.g., arrest for questioning) could well have involved a neighbor, or a neighbor might have been in the military. The thoroughness of investigations (thanks to advances in information systems); the many prohibitions, especially against freedom of speech and assembly (through Ato Institucional 5); the knowledge and rumor of torture and killings; the forced exile of many illustrious politicians, intellectuals, and artists; and the ubiquitous presence of the various police and military forces in the cities created a threatening and hopeless atmosphere. One São Paulo site for questioning—and torture and murder—was a military base located until today in the center of the south zone just off the well-traveled Rua Tutoia, that is, the area comprising the several neighborhoods where many of my informants lived. The height of the repression coincided exactly with the economic miracle: 1968–73. The youth of the impeachment movement were infants or unborn. Two-thirds of my informants were in their twenties during the dictatorship.

Maria Cecília explained that her generation had been "super quiet . . . I was twelve years old when the military took over. No one gave an opinion, no one talked about anything, you got accustomed to that sort of thing, my generation was very quiet." She added, "My oldest brother, who was in medical school, one of his friends was arrested, tortured, and killed. The whole med-school class went to the burial and there were people there taking pictures of all who had gone to the boy's funeral, and the next day, they were there on campus interrogating students. It was enough to make us real quiet. At eighteen or twenty, you wanted to do something, but when you saw that it was really ugly, you adapt to it, you stay in your own little space [você se acomoda num canto]. . . . Now the generation of my children, they caught another period." Maria Cecília told me proudly that her daughter had participated in the impeachment movement.

Besides their fearless youth, informants felt that the media stood in for them in the public sphere. While discussing the corruption investigations taking place in 1993 (see chapter 7), Maria Cecília mused over middle-class inactivity. She said, "We watch these things passively. I think deep down there is hope of seeing things improve. I don't think this brings emotional instability to people. . . . We want to see them punished, those who are doing the wrong things, this is a general feeling. For example, when there was the denunciation that Collor was stealing, was doing this and that, everyone armed themselves to go there, to see, let's uncover all this. I don't think this changed people's lives, everyone kept on with their little lives, but they were concerned with what was going to happen." Note here the distancing evident in the phrase *little lives* and the emphasis on passive reception.

Psychologist Marcos connected passivity to watching the news. Giving a much more negative appraisal, he said, "It's a pathology. You laugh at suffering. You use the suffering as a transfer [intercâmbio]. You always watch the news. 'I want to see the corruption investigations, the disgrace. . . . On TV there never was so much disgrace as today. The people's level of masochism is huge. They sell disgrace." Marcos was skeptical that real political interest motivated people to follow the news; rather he felt that the news was soap operatic and that, as viewers, people were paralyzed from acting. Without using the extreme psychological language of Marcos, Milton felt the media had taken over the middle-class voice, autonomy, and power. He said the middle class used to be the "shaper and leader of public opinion. Someone of the middle class would think 'this is wrong!' . . . and all would think that this was wrong. The middle class had this power, today it doesn't. It was the shaper of public opinion because in its midst were the intellectuals, the press, the educational system, teachers. . . . I think that today the great shaper is the major media, television, radio, newspaper, the large-scale media. They even command political economy and finance. In my opinion, it is the major media that directly influences all these questions." Thus an understood increase in the media's agency translates to an imagined decline in that of the people.

Others praised the press, but worried over how certain people could be swayed by television (see Skidmore 1993 and Flynn 1993). Brazil, Ricardo lamented, should not be like this; it had had a chance with direct elections, but voted for Collor. The population, said Ricardo, has a short memory. He feared a military takeover again and recalled how in the past "the press couldn't speak, now it can—not the TV, not the 'spoken' press but the 'written' one." He and his wife, Maria Regina, trusted the print media but mistrusted the TV news, which they felt was confusing for "the people," meaning working-class poor people. According to Maria Regina, "The people have no consciousness"; this left her anxious and anguished (*agoniada e angustiada*) because "the population doesn't know, we need to educate them." Informants tended to worry that "the people" were too ignorant to understand what was happening and could be easily duped. Something other than lack of education, perhaps, would be needed to explain why similar proportions of São Paulo's middle and working classes voted for Collor (see Pierucci and Lima 1991). This included both the "conservative" north zone of petite bourgeoisie and the "modern" south zone.

Quite often I heard views that simply praised the press for its critical reporting against the government. Lara was hopeful: "This is a very good thing, the position of the press. It is taking the lead [carro-chefe] and making demands [reivindicando]. If it hadn't been for the press, we wouldn't have gotten Collor out! . . . The same way it had a role in electing him, it did in removing him. And now this congressional investigation, the press isn't letting us forget it. The press is demanding responses, and I have the impression this is going to keep on. This is the hope that I think the Brazilian has." This sense of the press's role in democracy has clear parallels with Watergate.[17] Several informants were encouraged by the investigations of those in power (cf. Curran 1991); they did not seem troubled that the media was acting for them. The fact that the news lacked "objectivity" and coupled its authority as conveyor of information about the government with open criticism of it was taken by many as a good and necessary role of an independent media previously under government censorship.

In sum, informant attitudes toward the media varied from positive to negative; however, they shared a view that the media stood in for the population in the public sphere. Unlike my own "balanced" view on the media's influence, my informants (with or without ambivalence) felt the media was their representative in this postcensorship era. Informants did not appear to feel that they could influence the press "back"; rather they acknowledged their own inactivity, and that the media (for better or worse) was their proxy in politics.

The media's role in covering corruption scandals and producing pressure for the legislative proceedings was significant in the Brazilian political process; furthermore, these acts do not exhaust the media's involvement in middle-class identity and social change. It has been pointed out by many that it is just as important to dwell on what is unremarkable in the media's messages as on what is scandalous. We saw the development of a tight interdependency with the middle-class in the areas of work and private life. The definition of the middle class through consumption was unproblematically presented in the press and by informants. With this as the base definition, it was a small step to represent the crisis through what occurred to middle-class living standards, then another small step to indicate that the government targeted the middle class in its bungled interventions. And then the Collor scandal erupted.

However, while acknowledging middle-class agency, giving in particular full credit to those many who did participate in the impeachment movement, one needs to account for those who supported the movement yet stayed home, as well as their own sense of lacking agency. The newspapers' repeated argument that the middle class was victim of the crisis, and *Veja*'s reporting with heavy sarcasm, irony, and indignation certainly modeled a position many of the middle class could adopt versus the government in self-righteous, self-interested criticism, or, alternatively, in disinterested ethical conviction—without acting on it. One may accept my informants' explanation for their disinclination to go to the streets based on memory of the government's dictatorial power or not. One may instead imagine their stance to be a "choice" merely of passivity. Or one may note that to talk but not (have to) act publicly in a directly political way is consistent with the middle-class vision of its place in society: it should (be able to) stay off the streets, the popular sites.

Their youth could march in the streets, as by definition they did not have economic motives, but rather ethical ones. In the end, no matter which way one argues about middle-class politicization and agency, one still confronts a strong media. This media not only presented spectacle, and saturated by insinuating itself in daily and weekly installments into the deepest and highest reaches of middle-class public and private life; it became a story of itself, an enactment of its own voice of resistance, its own political agency. And it went further: it convinced even parents of the caras pintadas that this was so.

7

THE MIDDLE CLASS

VERSUS THE NATION

Discourses of Region / Race

and Morality

In July 1992, the advertising agency Standard, Ogilvy, and Mather held focus groups in São Paulo with middle-class male participants to discuss the state of their class. Well into a session the following exchange occurred:

> R.: Today you can't even plan your family life. There's no more plan-
> ning. This kept changing more and more, it started years ago. Today
> the parameters are totally unreal. You buy something today from
> within an unreality.
> W.: I think since '79 things took a violent turn.
> R.: Or more precisely in 1973 with Senhor Delfim Neto and his "Bra-
> zilian miracle."
> A.: I'm still waiting for this miracle.
> Moderator: Do you believe in the Brazilian miracle?
> W.: We see miracles every day.

Turning from the "unreal" to the "miraculous," the last speaker was evidently alluding to the Collor corruption investigation then under-way. This "miracle" would soon generate another: the impeachment movement.

A year later, in August 1993, when I arrived in São Paulo to do fieldwork on the middle class and the economic crisis, I expected at least some residual excitement over the popular victory against Collor. Instead I heard jokes about the latest maxi devaluation, which turned a 1,000 bill into a one note. Referring to the name change of the currency, from cruzeiro to cruzeiro real, some quickly scoffed: "É muita realeza para nossa moeda" [That's a lot of royalty for our currency]. Punning on the dual meaning of *real,* others said: "*Real* means now your money is *really* going to disappear."

The last week of July 1993, seven children spending the night by a church in downtown Rio (Candelária) were murdered. Two more massacres occurred within two months: close to forty Yanomami were killed by encroaching miners, and more than twenty were slaughtered in a Rio favela (Vigário Geral) in a terroristic revenge act of the police. However, a year after the Vigário Geral massacre, the police assassins remained free. Ex-president Collor's powerful associate PC Farias, recently convicted of myriad acts of political corruption, had just escaped from prison. After less than a decade of democracy, the country was plunged into recession, corruption, confusion, and violence. Inflation was breaking all previous records, yet President Itamar Franco (former vice-president) appeared incapable of choosing any direction. Among those informants hit most by the crisis, the mood ranged from angered frustration to hopelessness in the face of an unending economic, social, and political nightmare.

My wider interest in this chapter and the next is to examine how the middle class was positioning itself in the nation-state. To this end, I discuss two discourses that I identified in middle-class conversations: one attacking Brazilian society and state for being corrupt and/or bent on exploiting rather than working productively, and one attacking Brazilians of the Northeast region. These discourses were not necessarily held by one and the same person. I bring them together to show two ways middle-class Brazilians, through means particular both to their class and to their regional and ethnic/racial background, represented "other" Brazilians, thereby separating themselves off from them.

Earlier we saw that informants constructed their class identity in part on negative boundaries—"their" vulgar versus "our" cultured consumption and educational pursuits. But I detected another, more pernicious distinction, ostensibly based on culture and region. For some, the most radically distanced "other" was the poor, dark-skinned Northeasterner, blamed for many problems and for just being in the city. Against the background of recent European and Japanese immigration to São Paulo (and the extreme south of Brazil), this construction had specific characteristics. Thus I first examine a discourse that constructed a radically different identity of Northeasterners in contrast to Southeasterners. I argue that this "regional" identity scarcely hides racial and class oppositions, hence that it is built on classist and racist lines.

This discourse was prevalent during the crisis, perhaps even exacerbated by it. Yet I understood from the very casual, inconsequential nature of many remarks, shown in everyday cracks about Northeasterners, that the discourse had a far deeper time frame. The material I present was not representative of the people in my study; rather, it constituted a minority position within the group. I discuss it because I believe it to be a significant form of prejudice and because, based on experiences I have had overall in the region, I strongly suspect these views to have been fairly prevalent among a certain sector of the middle-class population.[1] I close this section by pointing to what was not discussed concerning these and other poor Brazilians—namely, the poverty, hardship, and violence facing them.

The second part of this chapter looks at a discourse often presented in quasi-academic terms, as a debate on Brazilian society and character. Whereas the comments in the opening paragraphs about inflation and Brazilian society were jokes, the comments I gathered from middle-class Paulistanos tended to be highly unamused. The discourse of my sources was markedly similar: whether the topic was the government, shopping, money, or business, it always included a kind of "moral economy" critique. I say "kind of" because to apply the concept of moral economy to capitalism and the middle class may seem a distortion, since it has mostly been used to describe resistance to capitalist dictates by working classes and peasantries (E. P. Thompson 1971; Scott 1976; Larson and León 1995). Recently, however, theorists have argued that "all economies are moral economies" (Booth 1994, 662; see also Wuthnow 1987; Schneider 1988; Bloch and Parry 1989; Dilley 1992); that is, all economies are socially instituted (Polanyi 1944) and subject to moral evaluations over production and exchange relations.

My intention is to take this suggestion and apply it to middle-class Brazilian commentaries on the political and economic crises. As we will see, the statements add up to a set of claims that many economic activities in the nation during the crisis violated middle-class principles. The grievances construct a political identity founded on an assertion of a moral code versus one depicted as opportunistic and corrupt in Brazilian government and society. Overall, the discourse delegitimates state and society. Having identified a position of moral superiority, I then look at the middle-class moral economy when applied to a concrete situation in the marketplace. Comments on the period of the Plano Cruzado provide a good case for studying consumer perspectives on the market under government-regulated price controls. Turning in the final section to reasons for the entrenchment of inflation in Brazil, we find the direction of the critique turning inward, into a culturalist explanation (known in the media and scholarly circles as the culture of inflation) blaming some or all Brazilian people for the economic crisis.

Again, although the two discourses were entirely separate in aim and content and arose in very different communicative contexts, I bring the two together because of the way they locate the speakers in the nation-state. Each critique—of Northeasterners and of nation and state—constructs a middle-class stance that is isolationist. Because the latter discourse condemns all of Brazilian society, it is markedly ambivalent.

I draw this discursive material from two sources: my informants and focus-group transcripts from Standard, Ogilvy, and Mather (see chapter 2). The latter material is deemed inadequate by classic anthropological methods that can situate discourse with reference to other understandings of the speaker. Notwithstanding, I found the material extraordinarily rich, as I believe the opening dialogue indicates. It also had the advantage of recording comments at the time of the events. Furthermore, as I met with informants, and compared their comments to those in the focus-group discussions, I found both discourses, and within them, a similarity in treatment. Hence another reason for my use of the singular: middle class.

REGION/RACE AND MIDDLE-CLASS PAULISTANOS

If in the United States ethnicity is a common idiom for identifications, among Brazilians the analog would be region. Many times people I met emphasized that they were Paulistas (from the state of São Paulo) or Paulistanos (from the capital city of the state), or more generally, that they were from the Southeast. (A few noted being from the South).[2] This regional identity came out in discussions of a political-economic order, in discussions of downtown São Paulo or the favelas, and in discussions of working-class people.

Perhaps the most readily offered, unself-conscious commentaries concerned domestic workers.[3] Ridicule and criticism of them were two variants. Twice with one family there was amused discussion of the maids' language. An informant's brother-in-law recalled laughingly how his maid said *forgo* for *fogo* and *bloco* for *broccoli*. Noting her domestic worker was from Bahia and tended to overuse cleaning agents, one woman said ironically, "Her strong point is not scrubbing." She also complained that the maid did not heat the oil before cooking. A common criticism was that domestic workers wasted things (e.g., overused oils, threw out leftovers). One woman told me indignantly that she had caught her worker, who had come practically straight from the interior of Ceará (the most drought-ridden Northeastern state), throwing garbage out onto the area behind the apartment (*quintal*).

These "cultural" commentaries are surely classist, but not solely. People did not fail to identify the region or state of the offending worker, as if this information explained the purported misbehavior. I have never heard anyone specifically complaining of a worker and noting that (s)he came from São Paulo.[4] In fact, the person who transcribed some tapes for me claimed that they had better critical powers than other workers. The discussion was sparked off when, aware of her annoyance with my informants for blaming "the people" for political problems, I noted that although middle-class individuals often say the people are not critical, in my experience they are. She responded that this might be true here in São Paulo, but not elsewhere, and proceeded to give the example of her cleaning woman from Bahia, who did not know the value of the new currency, the real. She told of another time when the cleaning woman wanted to buy cream for her hair at nine reais. The typist reminded her that her half-day's pay of five reais would need to be doubled in order to afford it, thus she would have to wait a month to buy it. Instead she should have her hair done at the hairdresser's for twelve reais, and it would last six months. The woman, said the typist, did not get it. Neither did I—why would it be easier to come up with twelve than nine reais? I was also surprised that difficulty with math, at a highly confusing moment of change in currency, was given as an example of lack of critical thinking. I told the typist that the laundress I employed did not know about the real currency either, yet she was from São Paulo. I was then informed that most of Brazil is rural. These incidents suggest that in discussions of poor Brazilians, these middle-class Paulistanos manage to assume a kind of naturalization through a more radical distancing involving "culture" to which class and region are associated. In order for readers to better appreciate the "difference" expressed through the regional idiom, a minimum of background information on the Northeast and Southeast regions in Brazil is necessary.

Brazil's first major export cycle was based on sugar production in the Northeast, produced through African slave labor in a latifundista, plantation economy. Although noted for being one of the earliest colonial centers, the Northeast in the late seventeenth century began a long decline owing to the competition of cane production in the Dutch Caribbean (Stein and Stein 1970; Furtado 1963, 1977; M. C. Andrade 1973; Eisenberg 1974). Before the nineteenth century, São Paulo had been characterized as a fringe area of pioneer smallholder settlements (Lockhart and Schwartz 1983). Then, after starting in Rio de Janeiro state in the mid-1800s, coffee production expanded enormously in São Paulo and inward into the frontier, first through slave labor, then, after abolition, through the labor of immigrants, actively recruited, often lured by free ocean passage and false promises, to work as tenant farmers (Viotti da Costa 1966; Dean 1976; Holloway 1980; Stolcke 1988). Subsidized passage in the early twentieth century brought two million Europeans to the state of São Paulo (Andrews 1991, 279). Huge fortunes were won by the coffee barons, whose mansions graced the Avenida Paulista, once an outlying uptown area of the state capital. The world depression had an enormous impact on coffee sales. However, by then São Paulo had become the leading industrial center (Dean 1976; Baer 1995; Font 1990). As Weinstein (1982) points out, decentralization, implemented with the first republic (1889–1930), served to the advantage of the state of São Paulo, which obtained a lion's share of federal revenues and economic policies—and to the exclusion and detriment of other states and regions, particularly the Northeast (see Levine 1978 and Love 1980). Thus for years coffee planters received government subsidies for their product, such that their gains could be transferred into industry. After World War II, Paulista industry experienced a great growth spurt when "import substitution" protecting the development of national industry became official policy (Dean 1976). European and Japanese immigrants moved from the interior of São Paulo to the capital (Saito 1980). Indeed, a massive rural exodus (Camargo 1968) occurred throughout Brazil in the 1950s. With a dense rural population, the severest poverty, and intermittent droughts, the Northeast sent people everywhere—to the Amazon at various times; to Brasília, for the construction of that city (Epstein 1973); and in large numbers to Rio de Janeiro and São Paulo, to engage in industry, construction, and the (informal) provision of services. Although migrations were not only out of the Northeast rural areas (the backlands of Minas Gerais has a comparable history of poverty and out-migration), the history of out-migration by Nordestinos is large, protracted, and socially visible.

In contemporary Brazil, from a romantic, nostalgic perspective, the Northeast region connotes opulent, graceful colonial days. Northeastern writers and themes are well represented among Brazil's literary classics, and much of Brazil's famous music is produced by Northeastern musicians, whose rhythms, melodies, and themes are distinctive. Yet, the Northeast may be viewed as the locus of seigneurial decadence, rural political corruption, illiteracy, poverty, backwardness. There is one final twist: although the states of Minas Gerais and São Paulo are famous for producing politicians, the Northeast has held considerable political clout in recent times.[5] In contrast, the Southeast region connotes European immigrants, *brava gente* (brave folk) who pioneered the territory, creating agricultural and later industrial wealth. Its past (grafted onto the idealization of trailblazing *bandeirantes*) may be narrated as a path of rags-to-riches through hard work and perseverance; its present a new world seen as utterly unlike the majority of Brazil to the north and inland. The concept of "two Brazils" captures this notion of separate realities. It was expanded in the 1950–60s studies of unequal development (see Furtado 1963); however, the dualist construct dates farther back with divisions of the "developed" coast versus the "uncivilized" hinterlands, such as is described in Euclides da Cunha's 1905 classic, *Rebellion in the Backlands.* In short, the old colonial center became the modern-day periphery (see Leff 1972), and the periphery became the core.

A certain Southeastern perspective unfolds as follows. The Southeast and the South are the breadwinners for the nation, while the Northeast is a (parasitical) drain on resources. Qualifications as to why there might be

such imbalances and redistributions of this kind are not offered. Rather
than discuss these possibilities, one might allude to the drought industry
(*indústria da seca*). After a feature story on this subject appeared in *Veja* in
1993, the diverting of these emergency funds "suddenly" became a matter of common knowledge—and outrage by those outside the Northeast.
The outrage was not on behalf of the Northeastern poor whose corrupt
politicians are the main beneficiaries of relief-funding during droughts.
Rather it was the indignation of the hardworking folk of the nation who
felt abused by such unchecked corruption. I am not suggesting that there
is no knowledge of the "victims" in the Northeast; I am merely reporting
that this unfortunate majority was left out of the discussion. Perhaps the
fact that the droughts, cyclical as they are, are so repeatedly depicted on
the news and in popular song has made the problem incapable of arousing
sympathy anymore. (The *retirantes* [migrants from the drought] are depicted in clay figures by regional artisans.) Some informants mentioned
coronéis—landowning political bosses of rural areas—with disgust. Anti-
corruption discourse was, however, less surprising to me than lack of
sympathy for or criticisms of poor Northeasterners.

A wealthy doctor's wife (interviewed once) noted that "we hear all
the time about poverty in the Northeast, but everyone there has *farofa-
farinha* [roasted manioc meal], pumpkin, *rapadura* [brown sugar block].
The farinha has starch; the pumpkin, glucose; the *rapadura,* glucose. Now
we might find this very poor, but this is relative, this is relative." As if
to prove the point in reverse, another informant (who also criticized
working-class men without naming their region) told me that he was not
convinced that there was all this poverty so often described of the Northeast. He said he had done a lot of traveling in Brazil, including a road trip
made from Maceió, the capital of Alagoas, to Recife, the capital of
Pernambuco, the neighboring state to the north. Speaking of the abundant seafood (shrimp and lobster) and of the fruit growing everywhere in
this coastal area, he affirmed that there was ample sustenance available—
of luxury foods, no less.

Those familiar with the Northeast can attest to the lush tropical coast
(described in Kottak's 1983 work, *Assault on Paradise*). They may recall
that in the 1970s most rural housing there was mud huts and schistoso-
miasis was rampant. From then until now in this densely populated rural
area, workers have done the rigorous work of cane-cutting for minimum

wages, or less. The Northeast is the poorest region of Brazil and one of the world's most depressed areas. Demographic data on infant mortality, life expectancy rates, education, and other living standards reveal the extent of regional imbalances. Wood and Carvalho (1988, 117) report infant mortality to have been 64/1000 in São Paulo at the end of the 1970s. Working from IBGE (Brazilian Institute of Geography and Statistics) figures published in 1986, Scheper-Hughes (1992, 279) reports the rate of 116/1000 for the Northeastern states. Life expectancy in São Paulo in 1980 was sixty-four years; in the Northeastern states, fifty-three years (Wood and Carvalho 1988, 73). Average literacy in the Southeastern states was 79 percent in 1980, yet just under 48 percent in Northeastern states (73). In the Southeast in 1980, 81 percent of households had electricity, 56 percent had sewage or septic tanks, and 70 percent had piped water. In the Northeast, in contrast, 42 percent of households had electricity, 16 percent had sewage or septic tanks, and 30 percent had piped water (73). São Paulo shares the highest living standards of Brazil with certain other cities of its region, the South, and Brasília. Large numbers of poor Northeasterners now reside in slums and favelas in these centers of urban modernity.

Two terms are often used in these parts to identify Northeasterners besides *Nordestinos,* which is used by the people themselves. One, *Bahianos*—those from the state of Bahia—is used to refer to people from all Northeastern states (besides Bahia, these include eight other states: Sergipe, Alagoas, Pernambuco, Paraíba, Rio Grande do Norte, Ceará, Piauí, and Maranhão. Bahia is the most populous Northeastern state. It is also the state with the highest proportion of Brazilians of African descent (see Hasenbalg, Silva, and Barcelos 1989). The stereotypical Bahiano is a carefree black, always ready for the beach and Carnaval, but never for work (a regional embodiment of the mock national character *Macunaíma,* created by Mário de Andrade in 1928). The other term, *Nortistas* (Northerners), is also used to refer to Northeasterners, who, however, know that Nortistas live instead in the Amazonian region. Perhaps to a Paulista (like New Yorkers in relation to the rest of the United States), the term includes anywhere from Rio to Belém do Pará. Although I admit to having a sensitive ear in this regard, I believe *Nortista* is used in a dismissive or even derogatory way.

The main point, however, is that the regional terms and identifications scarcely mask racial and class oppositions. Compared to the South-east and South regions (São Paulo and parts to the south), the Northeast has had a much higher population of Brazilians of African background, and a high rate of intermixture (including of Native Brazilians). As noted, the South and Southeast had significant recent immigration of Europeans and Japanese.[6] The regional identity not only pits the worthy immigrants against the decadent colonial natives; alternatively, these same good folk are overridden by the Northeastern lumpen proletariat. Oftentimes, I had the impression that the reference to Northeasterners was an indistinguishable amalgam of the two—as if the two groups, so worlds apart, were one homogeneous mass of undesirable Brazilians—indiscriminately poor and black *and* rich, corrupt, and decadent.

During the three years I spent in Recife, I would continually hear that São Paulo was the richest and most advanced (most First World–like) region. On a first brief visit there in 1985 from Recife, I attested to its modernity and abundance. It therefore came as a surprise to me that Paulistas felt so nationally downtrodden.[7] For some the presence of Northeasterners living in São Paulo was disagreeable. From this regional perspective, the main objection about Northeasterners was, as an infor-mant showed, that they come to São Paulo to cash in. Roberta told me how she had teased a friend who had moved from the interior: "I said to him, you're just like a Northeasterner, you came here after money." Evidently, from such a standpoint, these migrants are not comparable to the European and Japanese immigrants to Brazil who later migrated from the rural areas to the capital. Some voiced resentment that "these people" have come to São Paulo without there being work for them, becoming burdens on the natives and making the city impossibly overcrowded. If an explanation was offered, it was the lure of money, not the "push" factor of rural landlessness nor the "pull" factor of the urban demand for cheap labor in production and services, much less an analysis that might ques-tion the rationality of these equilibrium models and consider, instead, broader and deeper systemic imbalances. A Portuguese immigrant in-formed me that 90 percent of all workers in São Paulo are Northeast-erners, but "they don't like to work, don't remember what you tell them." His wife (from a Southern state) said they just like parties, adding that in the South people do work. Interestingly, outside his parents' presence, their college-aged son later made a point of explaining to me that the minimum wage was so low as to scarcely offset transportation costs. This ethnic/racial construction makes the region and especially São Paulo's middle class (uncorrupt, upwardly mobile workers) economically and morally more worthy in the national hierarchy (B. Williams 1989). One could surmise that the poverty of these others was an affront to some middle-class South(east)erners.

The commentaries thus far convey an array in views from amusement to antagonism. In two instances, I experienced what seemed to be an intense reaction against Northeasterners. A Paulistana of Italian background, whose family was exactly median in financial terms in my study, was often led to bring up Northeasterners. On my first visit this woman, whom I will call Paola, wondered what I knew of São Paulo, noting that she and her husband liked downtown. The center of the city has suffered a decline commercially; its many pedestrian walkways, however, are always thronged with people. Paola said that although her friends wonder how she can stand going downtown, she and her husband enjoy going to the municipal market there. When I mentioned having been to the Pinacoteca Museum (located alongside the train station and in the vicinity of the market), Paola warned me that I should be careful, not because it is traditionally a red-light district, but because there were lots of Northeasterners around there.[8] Noting the many street vendors in the area, she was led to ask whether street vendors in New York City were New Yorkers. Yes, I said (although certainly I was wrong in part). Paola informed me sharply that this was not true of São Paulo, and that furthermore, during Mayor Erundina's term, lots of Northeasterners had migrated here. (Erundina, the first female mayor of São Paulo, is from the Northeastern state of Paraíba.) Since this was our first meeting, I was not sure whether these last comments were neutral or negative. At any rate, her point on migration was not confirmed. Raquel Rolnik of the City Planning Department told me in 1991, thus still during Erundina's administration, that São Paulo's population growth was by then native, not through migration. By now, however, 25 percent of São Paulo's population is of Northeastern background. Mere contact with Northeasterners was, I came to see, problematic in Paola's eyes. Talking on the phone during the World Cup, she asked where I had seen the previous game.

When I reported having seen it downtown (at Anhangabaú) with a friend, she objected, exclaiming, "But it's full of Nortistas—Bahianos, Pernambucanos!"

I therefore became especially interested in seeing how the family dealt with downtown visits. I went one Saturday to the municipal market, a huge indoor emporium, with Paola, her husband, and her daughter, whom I will call Pedro and Maria. Driving through the streets of this older rundown section of downtown, Paola noted it was full of dirty people. Maria said she would not want to live downtown. As they compared products and prices of specialty items (olives, cheeses, Japanese peanuts, capers, dried fruits, spices), Paola pointed out to me the sun-dried/salt-preserved beef (called *carne de sol*), explaining that poor Nortistas without refrigerators have to eat this. A few minutes later, seeing some again, mother and daughter indicated that they would not eat this food "nem sonhando"—that is, they would not dream of eating it. Although carne de sol does preserve meat without refrigeration, it would now be more accurate to say that it is traditional, not poor people's food in the Northeast. Because meat is so expensive, this premium beef is considered a delicacy (and some São Paulo restaurants serve it as a specialty). After leaving the market, we stopped by the Praça Dom Pedro momentarily. A street some distance ahead was filled with people. These were the *camelô* (street vendors), I was told. These were the "Nortistas, Erundina's people," said Paola derisively. "Don't speak badly of Erundina," Maria retorted. "Will she win [the election for senator]?" I asked. No one responded.

Granted, the comments were aimless. But it definitely seemed that Paola was preoccupied with the subject of Northeasterners; it seemed their presence disturbed her. I did not at any moment question her attitude, nor did I ever again, after my first meeting, mention my acquaintance with the Northeast. In another case, when the contrary had occurred, a heated debate ensued.

An intellectual acquaintance who brought me to a party presented me to a friend of hers by saying we both had been married to Northeasterners. This woman had been married twice and divorced twice. "So you must like Northeasterners," I badly joked. She said, "Not at all," and pointed out how violent they were. The discussion turned to how Nordestinos were prejudiced against Paulistas, and how they came here to live but then spent their money back in Bahia. Moments before, several people had been telling me how well Paulistanos integrated. When I objected that I had heard São Paulo was stratified and segregated, my academic acquaintance informed me, somehow disregarding the vast stretches of slums in the east zone of the city where so many poor people of color live, that there were no ghettos in São Paulo. On the way home, I confided to the academic contact that I had been shocked by the discussion because in my mind it sounded like a racist discourse. The acquaintance immediately launched into a venomous diatribe against Northeasterners, repeating that "they" are prejudiced against "us," "they" do not like São Paulo, "they" talk up the Northeast, "they" have the wealth. I responded that São Paulo is their city by now as well, they are Brazilians, and after all Brazil is one country. (I said this fully aware of the "two Brazils" construct.) The woman laughed derisively, saying, "That's an old story." I repeated the point I had tried to make at the party, that in the United States, negative views such as these are often stated of poor minority ethnic groups. This attempt to draw parallels was "too theoretical," said the acquaintance, who added, as the evening reached a grand finale of heated argument, that I knew nothing of Brazil, its history, and in particular, nothing of the realities of São Paulo and having to live with "those people" on an everyday basis. Incidentally, after recounting this story to my former sister- and brother-in-law, visiting from Alagoas, Zélia recalled the well-known fact that Nordestinos literally built São Paulo (from the 1950s forward, being heavily in construction). Zé said a taxi driver had asked him the other day where he was from. Hearing he was from the Northeast, the driver said in surprise: "But you don't have a flat head [cabeça chata]."

It was startling to me that Nordestinos were treated in the evening's discussion as foreigners. Similarly, while speaking of how development eventually exacerbated the problems of the rich and poor, banker João remarked: "At the moment when they look at themselves, the real truth is this difference between the rich and poor is what creates the movement [fluxo]. Just like the movement from country to city, like the Northeast to São Paulo, he goes from the poor country to the rich one. The Mexican enters the United States, the Arab, the African goes to Europe for a better life. . . . Like the Northeasterner, who left the sertão and came to live in a favela here, here he has food, there he hadn't had food for days." Note how João compared Northeasterners to foreigners.

As these everyday comments suggest, the "idiom" of region is important and versatile in representations differentiating identities. That the identification of the poor as Nordestinos, Bahianos, or Nortistas omits race from overt discussion is not exceptional, but rather the rule, and in no way can be taken to mean race does not matter. In fact, the racial basis may well be assumed given the racialized construction of the region; it may even be taken for granted in a group for whom racism (given certain "qualifying" factors) is acceptable. To use this idiom of region serves, I argue, to widen even more radically the oppositions that are already great owing to other forms of racism and classism. It is not that the other regions lack racist and racialist discourse. Rather, this material reveals a discriminating distancing constructed in this region, which conflates region, race, and class.

Guimarães (1997) points out that although one cannot accurately compare incidents of racism, since so much goes unreported, there appears to be greater racism in the South and Southeast regions due to greater publicity of such occurrences. He hypothesizes that this more overt racism relates to the higher wealth and literacy in these regions, where the "traditional" (paternalistic, hierarchical) forms have given way to a less disguised discrimination. Accordingly, I should clarify two points. First, by focusing here on a racist dimension to the Southeastern discourse on region, I do not claim that Northeasterners are free of racial prejudice. They share in this problem greatly. In fact, Northeasterners are also capable of making or at least enjoying caricatures made of Northeasterners, which, as both telenovelas and comedy programs show, are a seemingly sure way to get laughs. Second, it is worth reiterating that most of my informants did not make comments of this kind. A few informants distinguished themselves for their condemnation of racism. José Luis was outraged to report discrimination in social clubs against Northeasterners. Workers' party (Partido dos Trabalhadores) supporter Sumiko reported a Brazilian saying that deeply shocked her: "Branco pode mais que Deus," that is, the white man can do more than God.

Having discussed what comments surfaced here and there in conversations I heard and in focus-group transcripts, I would like to close this section by noting what I did not hear readily discussed. References to the increasing impoverishment of poor Brazilians were very infrequent during discussions I had with informants of the crisis and problems in Brazil. I am unable to respond with any certainty why this was so. Some must have accepted the interpretation that the crisis targeted only or mainly the middle class. But there are other possible explanations. One might argue that because informants knew that the focus of my study was the middle class in the crisis they refrained from broadening the discussion, or perhaps they did not wish to speak of such things to a foreigner. But other issues and classes beyond the specific focus did arise, even during our initial, most formal meetings. The investigation of corruption in Congress was constantly brought up in the second semester of 1993, but not the massacres of the children at Candelária, the Yanomami, or in Vigário Geral, which occurred just a bit earlier that same semester.

I trust that for many informants the silence on the three recent tragedies was indicative of their horror, rather than indifference or worse. Brazilians often seem reluctant to name very negative things directly. Of course, I came across examples to the contrary. The first woman I interviewed whispered to me in horror of the vastly growing poverty. But in my study, most often if people spoke about class inequalities, they did so indirectly by, characteristically enough, noting with indignation the gravely inadequate educational system. Among my informants, a few alluded to violence, but in a particular way. Adalberto said, "I don't live in this country, as far as Rio de Janeiro is concerned." A couple of others said, "Rio de Janeiro doesn't exist." This kind of statement can be interpreted to mean that the problems in Rio had reached impossibly unacceptable, horrifying extremes. Yet the phrasing rejects rather than confronts the problem as one's own.

In the song "Haiti," composers Caetano Veloso and Gilberto Gil charge the population with indifference over the 1992 murder of 111 prisoners in a São Paulo prison. Thus: "And when you hear the smiling silence of São Paulo on the massacre / 111 defenseless prisoners, but prisoners are almost always black / or almost black—or almost white, almost black, they're so poor" (on the CD *Tropicália 2,* released August 1993). Active workers' party member Marquinhos reported to me in shock that at the time of the prison massacre, he had heard several times "Only 111?" These incidents and commentaries may call to mind how in other contexts of extreme economic recession and hyperinflation, racism and fascism developed. Being careful not to overdraw the comparison, one could point to the racialized scapegoating of Northeasterners prevalent in the South and Southeast; the middle-class silence regarding police brutality and death squads targeting poor people of color; and for some, a nostalgia for authoritarianism. (For an in-depth analysis of elites and violence, see Caldeira 2001.) One need not call to mind the extremes to register the importance of everyday forms of racism in middle-class discourse, and the need for further analysis (see Sheriff 2000 and, for comparison with South Africa, Crapanzano 1986). But again, given the impossibilities of interpreting informants' silence in my presence, I can only say that I did not hear people talk about the terrible things happening to poor Brazilians.

THE MIDDLE-CLASS MORAL ECONOMY AND THE BRAZILIAN CRISIS

My first interviews took place during the 1993 CPI on corruption, which lasted from October through December. Although I did not bring up these congressional proceedings investigating embezzlement of public funds by members of the Congress, many informants did, usually starting with metaphorical allusion to "all that dirt" (*essa lama toda*) or "dirty laundry" (*roupa suja*). Informants were indignant at corruption in the Brazilian government.

Bank employee Edilson (soon to separate from his wife, Bruna, a homemaker) had much to say of corruption and the government: "You have a CPI on corruption, it's going to get one-quarter of Congress. It's going to get one-quarter that was there, because if everyone had been there, they all would have done it. . . . The country is like this: the president robs, his assistants rob, everyone robs, everyone wants to get into government. Why? For love of the country? No!" As if this were not enough, he added bitterly:

> It's very hard to be genuine in a country like this, in a country in which the people are always suspicious about something. You can't be nice to anyone, because if you are, this person is going to think you want to get something out of it, you see, that you want *to take advantage of something,*

that there is something behind it. There is a saying that goes "When the alms are too great, the saint gets suspicious." . . . Here in Brazil, to be honest is to be a fool, to be honest is to be naive, credulous. Imagine a guy who worked on the budget committee and didn't steal money?! He would be famous for being stupid, naive (emphasis added).

Informants reported and censured opportunistic and shady dealings they had witnessed in the workplace and society. Edilson also complained of people obtaining their unemployment compensation, or FGTS funds, by making a deal with a boss to fire and later rehire them. The boss would receive a cut! Another bank employee, Milton, of the Caixa Econômica Federal, reported how banks themselves took advantage of the easy profits accrued from FGTS funds. Roberta, a public employee in educational administration and divorced mother of two, pointed out that at her "socioeconomic level, I can't build a house with a swimming pool." Yet other directors where she worked "are all finishing houses with pools and they earn my [same] salary." Roberta lived in a modestly sized, older apartment in Vila Mariana and earned less than the equivalent of US$1,000 per month. She argued that those who pilfered public office supplies such as pens, pencils, and paper were just as reprehensible as PC Farias. No, they were worse, she self-corrected, since PC knew he was committing a crime. She explained that the person who had confessed this pilfering had done so for her children's school supplies. Such a reason was not justified, in Roberta's mind.

I often heard censuring expressions for opportunism—*ser esperto, tirar vantagem,* and especially, the *lei do Gerson,* which mean, respectively, to be shrewd, to take advantage of, and (to apply) Gerson's law.[9] Gerson was a soccer player famous for always managing to turn a bad situation into one to his advantage. In the 1970s, he did an advertisement for cigarettes that incorporated this idea. Interestingly, it was a failure, as people did not accept this tactic. A man in a focus group during the Collor presidency said this: "Independent of social class, the moral concepts of our time were of one kind. Today they are totally inapplicable. So it gets complicated, because you get to thinking, what should I pass on to my child? In the past, the more honest the better. Today it isn't like that, it's the shrewder the better, it's Gerson's law" (Standard, Ogilvy, and Mather 7/1/92). While the terms *shrewd* and *opportunist* probably ring negatively in U.S. culture, certainly *to take advantage of* is capable of either a positive or a negative interpretation, where it could mean either to cheat someone or to make a profit. Such distinctions are absent from informant statements: each expression has a negative connotation.

Discussion of Gerson's law often led into expression of concern for the moral upbringing and futures of informants' children. Several times informants reported that other middle-class people were teaching their children to cheat (*passar a mão*), to be *malandro* (cunning, deceitful). Without resorting to hearsay, psychology professor Reinaldo reported an improper business involving his teenaged son, whom he was shocked to hear recount with innocent satisfaction that he was to receive a cut (*bola*) from a supplier for recommending him to a client.

Homemaker Lourdes explained that although most people were simply trying to get by during the crisis, there was a type of person who was "trying to see whether he could find a way for the inflation to even help him make more money." Her husband, Selmo, an engineer, exclaimed, "It's incredible how people win with the inflation," and later added, "In the end I think this business leads to despair, because it really doesn't do any good to work"—that is to say, to work honestly, for he then emphasized how some people were making it through illicit deals and tax evasion rather than through productive work. This couple reported having taught their children to pay taxes and not accept under-the-table commissions, but why they did so was not clear to their teenagers, who saw that this was how people made out better. I asked, "Do your children actually say this?" The mother answered, "They do." Similarly, Alice said of her teenaged children: "They could think, 'My mom works so much, studies so much, and to earn only this salary? . . . To work like a maniac and earn nothing? So is that it? Why should I study? It's not worth it.' . . . They see that your semi-illiterate politicians steal like hell, so they don't need to study. 'I'll be a politician and I'll steal.' "

A kind of moral critique of Brazil's economy seems to have been awakened in the middle class during Brazil's crisis. These statements decried violations in government and business in moral terms, underscoring that the government and society were becoming increasingly contaminated by unethical practices.[10] The Collor scandal was just a year old, and the congressional one was found to involve even one of the most highly honored politicians, Ibsen Pinheiro. This very statesman who had headed the investigation against Collor was among those found guilty of embezzlement—receiving at least one million dollars illicitly. People censured many things: petty or gross embezzlement of public funds—and the impunity of public officials; illicit private-sector deals; the way that inflation and corruption discouraged education and productive work. Taking the liberty of restating these criticisms of state and society as idealized prescriptions, we might say that in the middle-class representation, an acceptable capitalist economy would be one in which corruption (large or small) and opportunism (of an unclear magnitude) would have no place. It would be unwise, however, to read in an overly literal way statements that evidently had a rhetorical purpose. That is to say, one should neither disregard nor overestimate the immediate communicative context created by my presence as interlocutor. (Hence the comments might be seen as *para inglês ver,* in this case for the ears of a foreigner from a nation presumed to be ultraconcerned with moral standards in government and society.) Either way, middle-class people were at pains to emphasize their morality in contradistinction to an unjust state and society: they devalued and mistrusted both.[11]

What then would base their moral economy? Alice pointed to the violation of middle-class ways and means. The honorable road to upward mobility, a good job, and rewards should be through the merit system of education; this principle has been inverted, in an economic environment fostering unproductive speculation and outright cheating, and a political one in which thieves were holding the positions of models for and leaders of the nation. Alice argued for her worthiness to enjoy middle-class living standards; again her measure based itself on educational achievements to be duly rewarded by well-compensated work, in turn exchanged for consumer opportunities. However, given Brazil's abysmal public education, the middle-class trajectory to this advantageous situation is already one of privilege.

The connections are clear between the crisis conditions threatening to middle-class social and economic maintenance and their outrage expressed in a discourse of ressentiment. Rather than suggest a deterministic relation between economic crises and politics in Brazil, I intend, rather, to follow the well-chosen words of Markoff and Baretta: "We want to suggest . . . that the linkage [between economic crisis and regime change] lies in the ways actors conceive of crises, in what they hold to be their causes and solutions, more than in the economic circumstances as such" (1990, 423). One still needs therefore to take note of the striking similarity in my sources' strategy of protesting for absolute moral standards of business conduct. The very stringency of their discourse proves a moral authority independent of, uncontaminated by, the rest. In what ways did this group further construct the rest, that is, other Brazilians within and outside their social milieu?

An argument of how consumer-driven middle-class society could become perverse was put forcefully by a focus-group participant in 1986, after the Plano Cruzado price freeze had led to artificial as well as real shortages. That is, to black-marketeering. Interestingly, focus-group participants were less concerned with the wrongs of the black-marketeering retailers, whom they saw as victims of their suppliers, preferring instead to censure the willingness of middle-class people to accept the increases. Thus one woman said, regarding those who accepted illegal price hikes: "It's a [group of] people for whom it does not occur that buying [at the black-market price] will automatically make it impossible for those other people who cannot pay the excess charge to ever have the item" (Standard, Ogilvy, and Mather 2/25/87). The item in question was often meat.

This statement is striking, recalling as it does the debate over price controls versus inflationary hikes of the period in E. P. Thompson's original study (1971) on the moral economy of the English crowd, hence to conflicts over exchange. In the period Thompson studied, when a "moral economy" was pitted against a "political economy," positions clashed over whether, in periods of scarcity, regulatory protections should be extended to consumers, namely, the working poor of eighteenth-century England, or whether market forces should "ration" out the goods through price fluctuations, that is to say, price hikes (1993, chap. 5).

A broader criticism of violations of the Plano Cruzado price controls censures both parties, merchants and consumers, for participating in antisocial practice. Yet I noted in focus-group transcripts and found repeated in contacts with informants that while some criticized merchants for their "absurd prices," many pointed negatively to consumers for complying. In 1993 Bia criticized middle-class people for an oblivious consumer tendency. She said, "Instead of complaining, 'This is expensive, I'm not going to take it!' the person says, 'Oh well, it's expensive, but who cares.'" Underlying their criticism was an understanding that the way out of the inflation crisis was through a collective agreement. Over and over, informants criticized the tactic of "each one for him/herself," salve-se quem puder. Noncompliance (with a price freeze or other measure of a plan) was seen as being to the detriment of the common good and the good of the economy. The latter was held to be in need of external means to restrain inflation, here through a government decree and community adherence. Such a heterodox economic measure was indeed a classic moral economy position in the sense of favoring extra-economic (social and political) means and values to control the economy; the twist is that both businesses and consumers needed to abide by the obligations to do their part to halt inflation. Slater (1997) points out that the split between the acts of consumers and social consequences makes it difficult to discern responsibility. The Brazilian crisis might be one of the exceptions proving this rule, as the conditions exposed the clash between individual acts of purchase and societal detriment.

Such attitudes alert us to consider continuities in middle-class political consciousness and behavior across different time periods. Circumstances of worsened living conditions and high prices have prompted their activism over the marketplace rather than the workplace. The efforts of "Sarney's inspectors" may be compared to a cross-class consumers' movement, such as Meade (1997) documents for the early twentieth century. I found, however, as much evidence suggesting a lack of cross-class alliance and solidarity as an affirmation of it (see also Owensby 1999, chap. 7). This lack of solidarity surfaced particularly in a discourse of regional identity. In middle-class discussions, solidarity was identified as key to solving the crisis. Yet, as the focus-group dialogue below shows, community solidarity in the middle class was not assured. After the Plano Cruzado strategy to stop inflation by decree had backfired, a 1987 focus group recalled the initial solidarity and lamented the ensuing loss of it. One woman recalled the following supermarket conflict she had witnessed.

> Storyteller: The other day I watched a ridiculous scene. A woman was imploring another, who had six liters of milk, to let her take just one. Well, she didn't give it. "I have children." "But I want just one liter. I have a child and need to nurse." "No." There was plenty of type B milk, but no more of the special.
>
> First listener: Mean woman, huh?!

Storyteller: People nearby were disgusted.

Second listener: She wasn't Brazilian?

Storyteller: I don't know, I didn't ask.

Second listener: I think if she were, she would have given the milk.

Third listener: I don't think so, actually.

First listener: It would depend on your upbringing.

Third listener: That's right.

Storyteller: She must have been a Northerner (Nortista) or something
like that, from her appearance.

Although one might attribute the women's judgment against the
ungenerous woman to an ideology of motherhood, it is interesting that
national identity is the explicit referent. The consensus emerged that
Brazilians would normally share and be generous with respect to children's needs, until one person questioned this assumption. As the dialogue indicates, some found the antisocial behavior to be an inversion of
national identity, but at least one found it to be typical. Then the con-
sternation this moral dilemma provoked in the group appears to have
prompted the storyteller to quell doubts as to the character of the culprit
hoarding milk: being "Nortista" (literally Northern but meaning Northeasterner), a conclusion she says was drawn from appearance.[12] To these
Brazilians, the Northeasterner is of a lower class ("cruder") and of a lesser
"appearance" (darker color). For the witness of the event, as for most of
the others, such an act could not have been committed by a Brazilian, or
at least not one of their kind.

Having seen examples of what middle-class people variously denounce or lament, we need to ask what their moral economy might be
predicated on. To what values or tradition, if any, might it refer? Regarding the distribution of goods, in the aftermath of the Plano Cruzado
there appear to have been two distinct views on the question of price
controls: one that argued for government and community controls over
the savage inflation, hence for the common good; another that would go
along with inflation, based on the ability to pay. With lower-income
wage increases and price controls, the Plano Cruzado initially expanded
the greater effective consumer market to lower-income people, besetting
the more comfortable middle class with shopping hassles and inconve-
nient shortages. The recollections of the informants cited in chapter 2
suggest that they were among those of the middle class who would have

preferred to pay more (and save time) in order to have more, rather than be subjected to this unpleasantness. (Indeed, some middle- and upper-middle-class people sent maids to wait in supermarket lines crowded—for some, disagreeably—with people of various social classes.) In sum, two positions emerge, one in favor of price controls and condemning of all who disregard them, and one frustrated with the disruption of shopping-as-usual.

At issue is not a form of consumers' dispute for quality control, but more basically a political one of social conflict over the distribution of and access to goods in the society (see Singer 1988 and Barbosa 1993). The appeal to solidarity is an appeal to a morality "above" the marketplace, to values interjected from a spirit of goodwill by those not strapped by the crisis. We have seen an ideal of a communitarian solution, yet, as the resolution to the supermarket exchange above suggests, for some there is an underside to middle-class moralism, namely, one in which there are class and racial limits to solidarity. For others, ideals of solidarity may conflict with consumer goals. The latter harks back to an earlier moment in time for middle-class Brazilians, when upward mobility was wide open for them and when consumer opportunities were expanding, that is, the period in and surrounding the so-called Brazilian miracle of 1968–73. The tradition on which the generation of my informants rested claims would be those years, when many began their careers. Although few informants favored the military regime, most had experienced its material benefits. Our discussion of work and consumption already identified their adherence to a merit system based on education; however, given the grave educational inequality, this system relies on and furthers privilege. Thus, my reading of a middle-class vision of economic reform necessarily encounters class privilege. At the same time, these middle-class people might look instead to their parents' generation, first- or second-generation immigrants, in many cases, whose labor and long suffering led their families upward. By the 1990s, however, in the face of a corrupt Brazilian state and apparently accommodating society, there seemed to be no way to restore the track of economic progress and prosperity afforded these Brazilians.

THE CULTURE OF INFLATION AND ITS ROOTS

Since my research took place after more than a decade of economic crisis, when high inflation seemed impervious to remedy, it is not surprising that negative evaluations tended to be more generalized. In fact, a discourse developed against Brazilians as a whole. Just as criticism of corruption was aimed high and low, so too was responsibility for the inflation crisis. Ultimately, people blamed the government for the crisis; however, they also came to believe that some or all Brazilians were part of what became known in the media, as we have seen, and in scholarly circles as the culture of inflation (see *Veja* 7/11/90 and 12/5/90; Vieira et al. 1993). The reason for the endemic economic and political problems was thereby understood to be a kind of cultural determinism, in which people found the fatal flaw, as it were, to be in the Brazilian character.

Let us review some of the ideas advanced on the culture of inflation. As noted earlier (see chapter 2), economists underscore the government's fiscal policy as responsible for inflation, and rather than blame, understand the public's defensive responses as triggered by the poor handling of the economic crisis by those in power. In contrast, the media's conception of the culture of inflation is that Brazilian society aids and abets inflation through an unwillingness to "tough it out." Pointing out that inflation has recurred throughout the country's history, the media intimates that the soft or weak tendency is inherent. The discourse of my informants expands on the latter view.

During fieldwork, informants' explanations for the country's economic woes came in short- and long-term time frames. Regarding the crisis, informants would explain why Brazilians had a limitless ability to adapt to the chronic inflation and economic instability. One frequent explanation for the endurance of the crisis was that Brazilians are too *pacatos*—calm, accepting, perhaps docile—and/or too *acomodados*—accommodating, conforming, resigned. In some versions, the quality of being pacato referred to poor Brazilians, seen as being easily duped by the dominant group or having a dependent (*assistencialista*) attitude. (In this rendering, such behavior would characterize the Northeast region as a whole.) But very often the referent was clearly the middle class instead. The traits are not directly malevolent, but by identifying a disinclination to fight for or against some problem with inflation, or to act out of individualistic acquisitiveness over the common good, the arguments indicated that passive submissiveness could have ill consequences. In other formulations, Brazilians were characterized as exploitative or opportunistic—this would be an active immorality. Thus as to the apparently bizarre claim on the part of some that many Brazilians preferred high inflation, I was told by one that the gambling aspect of the financial market had become an attractive habit, and by several that a minority took advantage of unique business opportunities for gain.

Taking a longer-term perspective to explain Brazil's problems, some informants found, from the very first moment of colonization, a sort of ineradicable tendency to exploit rather than to develop. I would hear near perfect renditions of Turner's thesis, which unfavorably contrasts Brazil's "extractive" colonization to an idealized vision of homesteading pioneers in the United States.[13] Thus one woman said: "Our colonization was to take possession. We didn't colonize. People didn't come here to develop the country, as was the case of the United States. This was an exploitative colonization. I see this as a characteristic of ours. This lack of love [desamor], this disrespect for everything. It runs in Brazilian blood, in mine too." This informant said she had confirmed this on a recent trip to Portugal. Another noted that the United States had been colonized by very different people—the English and Dutch were the examples given—whereas Brazil had been colonized by the Portuguese.[14] In this light an informant said similarly, "I think the structure of the country is sort of immutable. We are a colony-nation in which the idea was to grab [sugar] all that there was here and take it away. Today it's the same thing, grab to the maximum what the country has for oneself." Another informant, after mentioning U.S. pioneer settlements favorably, said: "The first civilization in Brazil was predatory." Still another said, "The country started being corrupt the day it was discovered." This was an old joke, explained yet another.

Although one might be tempted to further explore psychological aspects of the harsh moral condemnations and the ambivalent representations of Brazilian character, I would once again keep attention focused on how it fits into their readings of the economic crisis. Let us consider Roberto DaMatta's sanguine view: "If the Brazilian crisis has something positive in it, it would be our lack of confidence in certain remedies and doctors. In fact, one could read the current Brazilian crisis as being a symptom of the collapse of some of our instruments of comprehension" (1993, 17). He adds, "There is a crisis in the paradigms that orient our self-understanding [compreensão de nós mesmos]" (18).

An economic crisis, especially a novel strain such as this one, is far beyond the ken of most people. Its causes and solutions have been the object of complex research and debate among specialists. However, it was also obvious to any visitor to Brazil during the crisis years that Brazilians had, by force of circumstance, developed a sophisticated understanding of the economic and political dimensions of the crisis, by virtue of practice and the dire necessity of having to keep up to date on the economy and its financial twists and turns. Yet this complex understanding could be reduced to a culturalist explanation. That is, like the culture of poverty theory, this one attributed (blamed) national problems of a structural order to ingrained or inborn character traits. We saw earlier that racism and class privilege fomented in a particular way. Here the understanding was one of cultural determinism of the national character. These discourses indicate that in this "collapse" of their instruments of "self-comprehension," middle-class "lay analysts" fell back on time-worn paradigms. Wilk points out a problem with the "thesis that each culture has a unique historical identity that determines its development and change. This can lead us back to a frustrating particularism (culture is the cause, and every culture develops from a unique past) or to a very dangerous kind of *blaming the victim*. If culture is the ultimate cause, when some group or country *fails* in some way, then culture is the culprit" (1996, 125; emphasis his).

It is, of course, possible to interpret the reasons for Brazilians' behaviors otherwise: the accommodation might attest, as Reinaldo claimed, to an assessment of insurmountable difficulty in effecting change. Said Reinaldo: "People end up resigning themselves [se acomodando] in the face of the impossibility of seeing their intentions, their ideologies of the world, concretized." (Maria Cecília associated *acomodismo* with the dictatorship.) Significantly, a dissenting view on the culture of inflation/culture of underdevelopment theory also came from Reinaldo. After he and his wife, Ursula, had recalled the commonplace notion that Brazilians were untrainable and lazy, he commented: "I don't think it [the problem of Brazilian development] is the national character of the people; the problem is historical moments." Similarly Lara said in defense of illegal business dealings (as cited in chapter 3), "The Brazilian has good character [tem boa índole]. If you had a dignified, decent government, everyone would collaborate. I have no doubt of this. But the way things are, nobody feels like obeying the law. There isn't much law in this country. . . . It's a misgovernment [desgoverno]." These defenses stood out among the many global censures of the Brazilian people.

As readers may have noted, when most other informants spoke against Brazilians, it was often not clear whether they included themselves in the criticisms or not. Many times the speaker criticized the government, another social group, another region (making the latter another Brazil), or Brazilians overall. In fact, two informants pointed this tendency out to me. Sandra's comments first criticized the (initial) inactivity of people during the Collor presidency, and then expanded to a general assessment: "In the beginning people just got very, very mad at the government. They talked badly about it, but no one had the courage to do anything. People here don't fight for their rights. They always take a paternalistic attitude and wait acceptingly [esperam acomodados]. They always expect that someone is going to do something for them. . . . *People always talk as if Brazilians were those other people and as if I weren't Brazilian myself*" (emphasis added). Maricarmen gave the most elaborated interpretation of this tendency. She said "*Deep down, they manage to not be Brazilians,* they scold/rail at the Brazilian as if the Brazilian weren't he; this irritates me a lot. They criticize the Brazilian, as if the Brazilian were a neighbor, they don't put themselves in [não se inserem], but if you don't put yourself into the problem, you don't solve it. You have to become aware—'I am Brazilian,' look in the mirror—'I am ugly, I am beautiful, I am poor,' that is better" (emphasis added). She added that Lula, not Collor, was the Brazilian who represented the people more.

A cultural and moral superiority claimed for their own social sector can only be offset or undermined by the negative appraisals about the Brazilian character and the nation. Negatively formulated discursive boundaries may have supported a middle-class standpoint in isolation from "others" threatening to it. As Alice said, there is a "disbelief in the nation, a disbelief in the people, and even in themselves." Yet from this position of ambivalence and isolation, what are the implications for their commitments to the community and nation-state? This location does not lend itself readily to a way out—beyond the very route of salve-se quem puder that this same group firmly rejected.

These commentaries were recorded in late 1993 and early 1994, when the crisis had become chronic. No vision of a way out for Brazil was forthcoming in the year before the Plano Real; rather, after making criticisms of the Brazilian people, informants would go on to express the same lament. The frustrating thing was that Brazil was so rich in resources, had such great potential. Their statements strongly recalled the 1950–60s view of Brazil (big Brazil, country of the future) within the developmentalist framework. Interestingly, these Paulistanos referred not to the promise of industry but to the land. Beyond this, they felt that the crises could be positive if major political and economic reform ensued. But though heartened by the impeachment and the congressional investigations of corruption, they gloomily deemed reform unlikely. Rather than hope for a solution through a government economic stabilization plan, several pointed to bottom-up changes in the economy as positive moves, in the form of the growth of new small businesses (microempresas). As a rule, informants presented views strongly rejecting government and firm skepticism, declaring they had no faith either in politicians or in "Plans"; in fact that term provoked raised eyebrows. In July 1994, a new plan was launched, designed by Finance Minister Fernando Henrique Cardoso. By looking at the stakes these middle-class Brazilians came to place in the course their country should take and their chosen leader, we can view their political identity in the nation in a positive formulation.

8

An End to Inflation and

the Promise of Neoliberalism

The 2222 express train started to operate
From Central Station
Departing directly from Bom Sucesso
Headed for the year 2000 and beyond.
—From the song "Expresso 2222" by Gilberto Gil, 1972

THE PLANO REAL

The Plano Real began with an announcement, toward the end of 1993 while Fernando Henrique Cardoso (FHC) was finance minister under President Itamar Franco, that there was to be a plan. The plan would involve "anchoring" the next new currency to the dollar. The conversion was not to be, as in the past, a matter of lopping off zeros, but rather was a relationship of the dollar to the cruzeiro real. To achieve the new value of the upcoming currency, to be called the real, a financial indicator was created. Called the Unidade Real de Valor, or Royal/Real Unit of Value (*real* in Portuguese is a homonym with *royal*), its value fluctuated daily more or less in sync with the dollar, but also in relation to other indexes or anchors. By April, stores had started to use the pompous and clumsy term URV. Prior to this final determination, the URV values, as yet not readily translatable to any existing currency, were perplexing symbols. One would be quoted a price in URV and remain none the wiser. By May, many window displays gave two prices, one in the currency in use, cruzeiros reais, and one in URVs. Again, this did not seem to clarify values but act as a mysterious futuristic allusion. (See figs. 7 and 8.) Illustrations of the new currency, the denominations and change, were shown on TV and in banks for the public-awareness campaign. At the end of June 1994, the conversion was determined by the dollar exchange rate.

On the great day of the change, July 1, 1994, armored trucks and guards lined the Avenida Paulista, São Paulo's banking center. The atmosphere was quiet, the changeover deemed tranquil in the press, one of whose headlines read: "The real is born worth CR$2,750" (*Estado de São Paulo* 7/1/94). Conversion tables were displayed in banks and distributed to retailers and consumers, to assist in making what would otherwise be hundreds of calculations. As in previous plans, on the first days the public response was to avoid commercial interactions. Supermarket sales, for instance, dropped 13 percent in July (*Estado de São Paulo* 7/30/94); shopping-center sales went down 25 percent the first ten days (TV channel Rêde Globo, Jornal Nacional, 7/12/94). Many informants noted, "I'm only buying absolute necessities." Gradually people confronted commerce and the complications of dealing with two forms of currency. For two weeks, soon extended to six, one could still use the old currency or the new, and one could request either as change. In the end the most difficult areas were, as usual, the little exchanges—at the bakery, newsstand, food stand, and so on (thus informal-sector vendors must have suffered during currency changeovers). The wait at checkout counters was extensive, as people negotiated change, had questions or explanations to give, or had difficulties in determining or finding the right change. A minor but nonetheless curious problem was the size of some of the change: 0.50 reais was approximately 50 cents, and a one real coin about a dollar, yet the two coins were almost the same size, requiring one to scrutinize change. This created delays, for instance, on crowded buses. Usage of checks was advised to allow people to avoid the hang-ups with change during the transitional period. However, when confronted with difficulties in making change, middle-class people shrugged off the losses (which could run much higher than pennies). Although the government had repeatedly advised that the new coins were going to matter, for middle-class people (as I confirmed with informants), making a fuss over change, which normally had been of very small value, would be ridiculous (and undignified).

Overall the changeover was called well planned and carried out, but

7. Window display a few months before the Plano Real was implemented. The price listed above is in cruzeiros reais; the price below is in Unidade Real de Valor (URV). Note the confusing lack of correspondence between the two values. *Photo courtesy of the author.*

8. Window display a few months before the Plano Real was implemented. *Photo courtesy of the author.*

daily hang-ups occurred for the first weeks. It soon became clear that there was not enough small currency in circulation. Such an oversight seemed odd. How could the government have underestimated the need for this low level of money, given the fact that—as was true of all moments of devaluation—the largest bill in circulation came to have a very low value? Just prior to the change to the real (when devaluation was extremely high), the largest bill in circulation (CR$5,000 cruzeiros reais) had a value of the equivalent of US$3. Despite this low value, bills with "large" denominations were invariably hard to change on the street. Once at a popular market in old downtown São Paulo, I gave the equivalent of $20 to buy ten audio tapes at $1 each. When the vendor asked a neighbor if he had a ten to make this change, the latter immediately retorted, "If I could do that, I'd have gone home by now!" [Se pudesse trocar vinte, já tinha voltado p'ra casa!]. Ten dollars in a day would have equaled more than three minimum wages. Thus even the preplanned and preannounced Plano Real was at the outset another wrench in the works.

One could well imagine skepticism—and there was, specifically that this plan was designed to get Cardoso elected (a *plano eleitoreiro*), but that it would not last. Indeed the timing of the plan's implementation could not have been more felicitous for the FHC campaign. No one doubts that Cardoso won the presidential elections of fall 1994 because of the Plano Real. However, a couple months into the plan, only 2 of my informants mentioned this—the 2 who decided to annul their votes. Most of my informants voted for Cardoso. (Of 43 asked, 34 cast votes for FHC, 5 for Lula, and 2 abstained. The remaining 2 were immigrants from Europe and not citizens.) What was there about this plan and Cardoso that lent them credibility?

Stabilizing the currency by anchoring it to the dollar lent credibility. In fact, the currency stabilization was not based solely on the dollar, but that was the most publicized and most easily comprehensible aspect. The Plano Real stabilized the currency through the exchange rate (Sola, Garman, and Marques, 1998). Unlike other plans, this one was not a shock measure involving price freezes. Rather, it was revealed slowly over several months. Ample time was given for different sectors of the economy to establish prices and salaries, rather than the government freezing them at some arbitrary moment, against which there might have been reactive behavior. Though the URV had been unfathomable to me as a consumer, its use was for merchants and employers to settle on prices they could keep, via a stable indicator.

Marquinhos, a workers' party supporter and major Cardoso critic, specifically attacked the assessment that the plan was the result of democratic negotiation, finding it instead "equivocal . . . there was no negotiation. It was done in a cabinet meeting of intellectuals." However, the mainstream perspective was that if the other plans failed to stop inflation "by decree" (i.e., imposed top down, with price freezes on goods and/or personal income), provoking agents to take defensive measures, this one was to succeed through negotiation, with the intended result that businesses and banks would comply. Furthermore, it promised to deindex, end monetary correction, and cut the budget deficit. New exchange-rate measures would allow it to maintain parity with the dollar.

This plan *was* successful in dramatically reducing inflation. Inflation went from 48 percent to about 2 percent per month and totaled 35 percent in the first year of the plan. Perhaps the most immediate novelty was reduced prices. A business-section headline giddily announced: "Supermarkets reprice goods downward!" (*Estado de São Paulo* 7/9/94). But it was not possible in 1994 to predict what would come of the plan.

Besides its promising differences from other plans, which garnered support, the Plano Real brought something less rational, and perhaps of equal or even overriding weight: the hope (against hope) for deliverance. It is worth repeating that Brazilians initially supported *all* stabilization plans, which did reduce inflation drastically for a short period of time, but then failed. Although it may sound melodramatic or presumptuous, I find that this change of heart, from extreme disillusionment to hope, has been characteristic of Brazilian people at such conjunctures, middle classes included.

Certainly, the consensus achieved among major businesses and banks was crucial for the plan's success. Yet during the preelection, early plan period, I was most impressed by the adamant willingness of the middle-class population to reject anything deemed inflationary and consequently antisocial. This population treated the Plano Real as the *plano sagrado* (so to speak), so fervently did they wish the crisis would end. To strike for higher wages was widely disapproved by middle classes, for this was associated with monetary correction, hence inflationary practices. From this initial period of implementation on, the platform of the workers' party and their candidate, Luís Inácio Lula da Silva, who ranked first in the opinion polls at least until April 1994, were deemed antithetical to Brazil's successful end to inflation. Although Lula could not logically be held responsible for the previous governmental problems, he and his party came to represent a continuation of centralized government and state monopolies and a controlled economy (which had failed dismally to stabilize or end inflation). Even informants who said they respected Lula's "honesty" and "integrity" criticized his outdated (*envelhecido, antigo*) discourse, especially for upholding state monopolies, and his corporativist party—seen as advocating for special-interest groups whose "inflationary" wage policies would not be for the welfare of the whole (see Owensby 1999, chap. 8, for a similar stand taken by middle classes earlier).

In the 1990 elections, the race narrowed to Collor versus Lula. With the choice in 1994 between Lula and FHC, those with center-left leanings (who may well have voted against conservative Collor) had a candidate closer to their interests and identifications. To the success of the plan, one could add other well-known reasons for Cardoso's support from middle-class Brazilians. Cardoso represents the intellectual, sophisticated, urbane Paulistano. These "collateral" reasons for preferring Cardoso over Lula were consistent with the idealized self-definition of middle-class informants. Furthermore, although well-to-do, he was an academic, not a businessman (hence not associated with corrupt circles). In short, Cardoso could be seen as a representative of and for this middle class. The only point sullying this profile was his questionable, pragmatic alliance during the campaign with the dictatorship party (Partido Frente Liberal). Yet with only a couple exceptions, informants made no mention of it.

Whatever other objections my informants had against the workers' party candidate (metalworker union leader and founder of the workers' party, self-taught, from a modest background, Nordestino), they commented on Lula's lack of "statesman" qualities. As if to emphasize just how problematic lack of formal education and social refinement was for a president, informants would imagine (with a cringe) Lula socializing in an international setting. Although few were enthusiastic supporters, Cardoso was deemed qualified (*preparado*), able to give continuity to the plan, hence stability, and he stood for modern deregulated capitalism. Lula accordingly lost votes not only due to his party's association with a controlled economy but from a perceived lack of preparation for statesmanship, or simply for being *sem cultura,* that is, uneducated/uncultured. Many said of Lula *jamais, nem pensar,* never, impossible. One informant said he refused to vote for a Nordestino.[1]

Let us compare the vision Cardoso projected for Brazil and informants' perspectives. While Lula's position suffered due to the promising start of the plan, the unpopularity of a government with excessive involvement in the economy, and the worsening image of the workers' party, Cardoso's discourse harkened to a brighter period of "development and progress," suggesting its potential return in an open economy. Listening to a campaign speech, I was struck by what seemed to be the same 1950s modernization discourse that I had heard from informants. Collor had promised that Brazil would join the First World; Cardoso reclaimed this promise. This middle-class position seems to have been worked out from what one would be and on what one would not be. The middle-class votes seemed to have been based on a position against the workers' party, for deliverance from a crisis perceived as adversely affecting the middle class, and for the dream of Brazil returning to the First World track, via an open competitive capitalism energized by small business and international competition—globalization.

THE PROMISE OF NEOLIBERALISM

After this period of national crisis, it is not surprising that a deus ex machina solution should have presented itself successfully. Or rather, the reform so desired by middle-class Brazilians would have to take place within, but the ideal itself and some healthy agents would be imported in the form of 1990s neoliberalism. With the Plano Real, support for a free-market economy regulated by fair competition from global businesses was reaffirmed.

Years of "absurd prices" and knowledge of more competitive ones in the First World gave informants a strong sense that the national businesses were overly protected and their profit margins too high.[2] They welcomed the opening of the national market to imports—both for the goods themselves (which as of July 1994 entered the market on a new scale and with new accessibility) and to exert pressures on national businesses to set reasonable prices. In this way, Brazilians joined others

around the world who oppose state protectionism, "now viewed as artificial and irrational" (Coronil 1996, 68). The particular form capitalism
has taken in Brazil, that is, of long-term protectionism, and the recent
crisis, in which government regulations to attenuate the effects of inflation led to an impasse, brought some on the left as well as the right
toward globalization, a term with wholly positive connotations: it is seen
as the antithesis of the "archaic" and corrupt "traditions" of Brazilian
business.

In sum, the fact that the crisis threatened social reproduction and
invaded the most banal areas of middle-class daily life for a seemingly
interminable period, coupled with proof of gross government incompe-
tence and corruption, offered countless experiences from which to draw
the conclusion that, after all, Brazil's problem was not capitalism, but bad
government, national businesses, and consumers. The Brazil of the crisis
had produced a travesty of productive capitalism, turned shopping into a
nightmare, and pitted individual citizens against each other. Capitalism
on the right track would reverse the situation in which honest-working,
qualified (i.e., educated) middle-class people were losing ground while a
minority of opportunists got ahead. Neither problems of wages and
employment security due to downsizing nor threats to middle-class employment troubled my informants at the time the Plano Real was implemented. Issues of equality, fairness, and even economic development
were not so much ignored as smoothly displaced onto another ground
for their resolution. These Brazilians put faith in the external market,
which through its First World competitive price-making markets would
ensure the fairest prices, and in some undisclosed fashion, promote Brazil's overall development. The problem was a government-regulated
economy, not one that responded to the imperatives of contemporary
capitalism. The position can persuade, not only from a "rational" review
of the economic performance in the nation-state. It is also consistent
with the culturalist view. If the cause of the problem was posited in the
national character and the cultural economy it produced, then the solution would be in external forces and cultural attributes.

Thus we see that the emerging middle-class position on the economy is one that found that extraeconomic forces were not just outdated
but faulty, relying as they had on the following: the Brazilian government—incompetent and corrupt; Brazilian businesses—profiteers rather

than fair competitors; organized labor—with restricted rather than generalized labor interests; and the Brazilian people—variously incapable of acting, of acting beyond individualism, or of simply toughing it out. The imagined moral economy would be one in which the controls and the morality itself would come from within the capitalist system and its dictates, globally controlled, locally enjoyed. Government reform and economic renewal—globalization—would return the world of consumption to the middle classes. If their disenchantment isolated these middle-class Brazilians from the nation-state during the crisis, the end to it allowed the resurgence of an ideal for the nation and their futures: neoliberalism as an economy both modern and moral.

POSTSCRIPT

Soon before the elections, Aninha picked me up along with her children at their school in Pinheiros, and drove us back to her home in faraway Jardim Bonfiglioli. With bright excitement, she told me her news: she and Milton were buying a house—not the one they lived in, though that would be fine, but one in the neighborhood. For the rest of our time together that day, we discussed the house, the deal in the process of going through, her moving and decorating plans. Aninha spoke with precocious nostalgia of the house they were living in, and with almost uncontained joy of the home-to-be. On the way to dropping me off at the bus stop, she drove me past the house and told me about the owner. Aninha said he was very, very rich—in fact, the father of the late Airton Senna (Formula I car racer) was to move into the same apartment complex as the owner selling them their house—yet he was, as she kept repeating appreciatively, "extremely simple" (unpretentious). Learning I was to leave at the end of November, she exclaimed, "Then you'll be able to see us in our new home!" Yet by the time I left, the closing still had not taken place, leading me to worry that they were encountering difficulty paying for the home, since it was not a new construction.

At the time of the 1994 elections, it remained to be seen whether middle classes and the majority would benefit from the Plano Real and globalization. My contact since fieldwork has been occasional reading of the news, one brief visit, and letters. Soon after my departure, Carla, whose quiet, content, stable family life led me not to write of her previously here, wrote twice about excessive consumption. She said: "The illusion that everything is cheap [because prices no longer go up] led people to spend in excess. People bought so much by credit card, over-draft checks, or through loans or financing, that they ended up in the red. The result—an unheard of defaulting." *Veja* reported that three million Brazilians traveled abroad in 1995 (this includes two families in my study). The percentage of investments in savings accounts dropped from 41 percent in February 1994 (pre–Plano Real) to 23 percent in June 1996. It seems that the fever to consume did return.

Globalization hit businesses, said the *Folha de São Paulo* in mid-1996; half of the ten most efficient businesses in Brazil ended 1995 with losses (7/11/96). The *Estado de São Paulo* (8/18/96) reported that 40 percent of new investments were foreign capital. In February 1996 Carla again wrote journalistically that "Many industries have cut personnel; any business not competitive enough to survive with the open market closed its doors." Many businesses filed chapter 11 bankruptcy, including the computer firm where her husband, Chico, was employed. Claiming this had nothing to do with the Plano Real, Carla continued: "But the situation is calm and stable, and Brazil once again has become a good market for foreign investment." I learned in June 1996 that Chico's company had laid off many of his close colleagues. Reduced to half-time employment after eighteen years of service as a systems analyst and owed years of FGTS payments, Chico began picking up moonlighting computer jobs. Once a supplement, Carla's modest salary of US$500 per month as a half-time librarian had become crucial. She told me, "If you were doing your research now, we'd have a very different story to tell." Workers' party supporter Miriam (married to Marquinhos) wrote in June 1995: "Well, dear, you should consider coming back to do some special research now on the impact of the real on those families you worked with while you were here. I am sure they are all even poorer." Perhaps not all. When letters I sent to Milton and Aninha and to Sandra and Carlos from the United States in 1997 were returned to me, I inferred it meant these couples did buy homes after all.

The media soon reverted to its habit of measuring the middle-class ups and downs: "The middle class lost more since the Plano Real" (*Estado de São Paulo* 6/19/95); "The middle class, the most prejudiced by the Plano Real even according to the president, tries to adapt to the new reality of the country" (*Jornal do Brasil* 7/9/95). The Plano Real was perhaps not a miracle: by the time of its onset, the cost of living had already soared.[3] The basic basket was 130 reais—or 30 percent above the minimum wage. The media continued to satirize. A comic strip in *Vejinha Rio* made a joke about the price of a mango at seven reais: the "little woman" is thrilled with her man's "extravagant" gift to her of a mango—one of Brazil's most commonplace fruits. And the media continued to criticize. Television commentator Joelmir Betting said the following of layaway plans in February 1995 (more than six months into the Plano Real): "Many stores are going to continue layaway payment schedules with interest rates of 15 percent per month or more. In twelve payments, therefore, the consumer buying a stove will have paid for it four times over. In a civilized country, this transaction is not a subject for the Central Bank, but for the Federal Police."

Another cost of the Plano Real since 1994 was recession and spiraling violence: 260,000 jobs were lost in São Paulo industry in the first two years after the plan began, making a 12 percent drop in employment (*Estado de São Paulo* 8/13/96). There were twenty-seven incidences of multiple killings (*chacinas*) in the greater metropolitan area in the first six months of 1996; one out of six people in the area was a victim of assault that year (*Estado de São Paulo* 8/25/96). But Cardoso announced at the end of 1996 that real salaries had risen 30 percent, and *Veja* (12/18/96) reported that the buying power of lower middle classes had soared, and that the poorest sector was moving upward.

I recently became friends with a thirty-year-old Paulistana. On a warm, sunny winter day in June 1996 just after I had returned to Brazil for a brief visit, we sat down in the backyard of her parents' home. She asked me about my research. I began by citing the title, which contained the word *crisis,* then suddenly added to it the dates 1980–94 to indicate the time frame of the work. The friend objected and in a very vehement way: "If you put that in your title, people will be very skeptical." Departing only four months after the Plano Real's commencement, I had encountered optimistic reports from economists that Brazil was out of danger of the inflation crisis and the economy was showing good signs. The news provided confusingly abbreviated reports of banking and political problems, but it too periodically noted the low inflation, so all seemed to be working out. But in my friend's view (and as others then

NOTES

Introduction

1 Without belaboring the issue of resistance to studying middle classes per se (but see Burris 1986), I would still note that Nader's (1969) call for anthropologists to "study up," rather than limit themselves to studying poor people, has seldom been interpreted to mean study middle classes.

2 G. Velho's (1980) landmark study of middle-class upward mobility in Rio registers a north to south zone move and subsequent severing of ties. Other studies of the "modern" middle class in Rio's south zone include Salem (1985a, 1985b); Rezende 1990; Coelho 1990; Fiuza 1990; and Heilborn 1992. See Romanelli (1986) for a comparison of "modern" and "traditional" families of São Paulo's south zone; and see Mafra (1993) for a nuanced analysis of businessmen in the state of São Paulo. Two finely detailed studies in what might be called "traditional" areas, yet which avoid the trap of reifying that concept, are Abreu Filho (1980 and 1982) on a small town in Minas Gerais and Carneiro (1986) on Rio's north zone. Carneiro examines rituals crosscutting social divisions through festival competitions (the Balão de São João). On the middle class and gender, see Barros's (1987) study of intergenerational familial relationships and Ardaillon's (1997) study of middle-class women professionals.

3 Campbell's targets are Veblen and Weber, but Bourdieu's work, which is more relevant for comparison with this study, has also been criticized for understanding consumption motivations as limited to status-seeking goals (see Frow 1987; Rutz and Orlove 1989; and Calhoun, LiPuma, and Postone 1993).

4 Miller 1995b provides an extensive review. Key works for Europe include Elias 1978; R. Williams 1982; McKendrick, Brewer, and Plumb 1982; Mukerji 1983; Frykman and Lofgren 1987; and McCracken 1990. For my interests in class and nation, I found Blumin 1989; Wilk 1989; Thomas 1991; Silverstone and Hirsch 1992; Friedman 1994; Breckenridge 1995; Howes 1996; Miller 1997; Burke 1997; Comaroff 1997; Dávila 1997 and 2000; and Chin 2001 provide pathbreaking works on historical developments in consumption cross-culturally.

5 My point is not to replace production with consumption as determinant of class, but to reopen the study on broader grounds. For a critical discussion, see Burrows and Butler 1989. For diverging views of the turn away from studies of social class, see Beck 1987; Wright 1989; and Frow 1993.

6 Beck 1987 and Shields 1992 exemplify the ellision of class. Arguments and studies countering this trend include A. Tomlinson 1990; Featherstone 1991; Lunt and Livingstone 1992; Warde 1992; Dittmar 1992; Fine 1995; Campbell 1995; Marsden and Wrigley 1995; Chin 2001; Carrier and Heyman 1997; and Pinches 1999. Campbell points out that what is called lifestyle, as if in opposition to class, devolves into occupation, income, and education.

7 The translation is mine. The Spanish reads: "Consumir es participar en un escenario de disputas por aquello que la sociedad produce y por las maneras de usarlo."

8 Meade (1997) shows for the early twentieth century that middle-class Brazilian direct political action concerned not work per se, but private sphere and consumption issues. On middle-class politics in Brazil, see also Weffort 1965; Pinheiro 1975; J. A. G. Albuquerque 1977; Saes 1985; Boschi 1986; Pierucci 1987; Pierucci and Lima 1991, 1993; Bonelli 1989; Farias 1991; Grun 1992; Simões 1992; and Owensby 1999.

9 In Brazil, formal socioeconomic divisions are often made with reference to the minimum salary. Middle classes are designated as earning between five and twenty minimum salaries, which in a less inflationary period could correspond to US$500 to US$2,000 per month. Demographers Wood and Carvalho (1988) estimated Brazil's middle class to constitute 20 percent of the population. Economist Belik (personal communication) estimated from 1991 income declarations that about 16 percent of Brazil's population of 150 million earned between $10,000 and $39,000, and that less than 2 percent earned more than $40,000 per year.

10 Although my focus in this work is class, that does not mean that I argue for its importance over race. As Sheriff (1997) demonstrates, to frame the debate in terms of class versus race is to miss the point; they act autonomously and together. This work attempts to contribute to the broadening of discussion of race and ethnicity in Brazil (see Lesser 1995, 1999).

1 The Dream Class Is Over
Home Ownership, Consumption, and (Re)definitions of Middle-Class Identity

1 My use of the term *discourse* implies not a dominant ideology, but instead an argument or position (see Asher 1994, 940).

2 Bianco-Feldman (1981) provides an ethnohistorical study of middle-class family mobility in the countryside of São Paulo. The family stories I gathered from informants produced similar trajectories across the sample. Most (57 percent) shared the recent immigrant background for which São Paulo and the south of Brazil are known, and which distinguish those regions from the rest of the country. Their immigrant grandparents worked in agriculture or in modest service occupations in the city (e.g., policeman, chauffeur). A move to the city of São Paulo occurred during their parents' or their generation; in many cases, informants themselves but not their parents achieved middle-class standing in terms of completing college education (often normal school for women) and obtaining white-collar employment (see Owensby 1999).

3 For political and economic discussions of Brazil's inflation, see Bunker 1986; Frieden 1986; Bruno 1988; Singer 1988; Dinsmoor 1990; Markoff and Baretta 1990; Cardoso 1992; Barbosa 1993; Earp 1993; Garcia 1995; and Baer 1995.

4 Such middle-class apartments in São Paulo contain a joint living-dining room, kitchen, service (i.e., maid's) area, two or three bedrooms, and bath, but no den or separate family room.

5 An estimated twenty-five hundred rental apartments in São Paulo lay empty in 1993, cutting the rental market down by more than 50 percent (*Estado de São Paulo* 9/12/93) and attesting to the fact that this phenomenon of unused real estate was widespread. The new renters' law of 1992 greatly favored renters during the crisis. Rental contracts would soon lag well behind inflation, creating what to the owners felt like squatter conditions for their rentees. In these circumstances, landlords also appeared to display distaste for strangers in their homes.

6 Representative for the state of São Paulo in 1994, Delfim Neto was one of two main finance ministers during the dictatorship, and is associated and largely credited with the Brazilian economic miracle. Delfim Neto has been the economist turned to most often for an authoritative opinion on whatever plan or problem is pressing at the time. He is eminently quot-

able, with a gift for sharp, brief, devastating barbs, and is not unwilling to criticize the Right.

7 Roughly comparable to FHA housing in the United States, the BNH was created in the 1960s during the dictatorship to offer subsidized housing to low-income individuals. As with the FHA, those who benefited from the subsidy and its low-interest housing payments were mainly middle-class white people (K. T. Jackson 1985).

8 To specify the middle class in terms of consumer durables has heavy precedents in the academic literature on the economic miracle and in marketing research. Since the late 1970s, Brazil's marketing research has assigned what might be called a metonymic definition of class, in which classes (A to E) are determined according to possession of durable goods and education. (See Almeida and Wickenhauser 1991.) An even more damning critique shared by many Brazilian critical theorists is that the rise of consumer society and, specifically, the dynamic growth of the domestic industry in consumer durables during the economic miracle was a means of "corrupting" middle-class sectors into supporting the military dictatorship. (See Saes 1985, 143–183, for a critical review.) I do not endorse a definition that makes the middle class no more than "Things 'R Us," but rather wish to register the definition among different sectors in Brazil.

9 The newspaper then asked, "How to understand this interminable package of increases that the government shoots at the middle-class head?" [Como entender este interminável pacote de aumentos que o Governo atira na cabeça da classe média?].

10 The Plano Cruzado was the first government stabilization plan. Put into effect in February 1986, under President José Sarney, it featured a surprise price freeze. See chapter 2.

11 I am indebted to Barbara Weinstein (personal communication) for this point.

12 According to budgets provided by eight families, tuition was the second or third biggest expenditure (following food and rent or house payments).

13 Informants often pointed out the irony of the fact that in order to get into the best universities—the best higher education being free-of-charge state institutions—students must have had to pay for education in primary and secondary schooling. The covert tracking in other countries where public education serves all classes is perhaps not immediately obvious (Bourdieu and Passeron 1977). The inequality of this system of inaccessi-

ble, elite primary and secondary education leading to a minuscule number of positions in the colleges is very openly recognized in Brazil, where the economic and educational divide occurs clearly and early between the public and private schools. Bourdieu notwithstanding, there was no misrecognition of the way economic advantages translate to "human capital." See McDonough 1981 and Plank 1996.

14 Because I found a nearly ascetic rejection of the material in the discourse of participants, I was interested to read Neuma Aguiar's (1993) application of Simmel's classification of attitudes and habits of consumption to her discussion of the Brazilian economic crisis. The attitudes Simmel outlined in relation to money are, besides asceticism, greed, extravagance, cynicism, and a blasé attitude.

15 Interestingly, Rodrigues (1989) had similar findings in her 1977 study of low-ranking government employees in São Paulo, whose level of schooling and earnings were lower than those in my study.

16 These gaúcho-inspired restaurants (where different barbecue-roasted meats are circulated and cut from the spit in unlimited quantity) are prized by some, but scorned by others, perhaps as much for the clientele as for the style of service or the food itself.

17 One must not forget to mention Bourdieu's important contribution regarding the naturalization of taste and its mundane connections with reproduction of classes. Yet I am uncomfortable with analyses that read into practices without regard for subjective motivations. These Brazilians were not only constituted through consumption; they were also plagued by it and readily able to discuss it.

18 Although home and car ownership were the criteria informants chose for defining middle-classness, the fact of living in a rented apartment could not be taken as proof of marginality below the class. Three families who rented (Lara and Rodolfo, Elisabete and Antônio, Simone and Roberto) owned property, and were living in very comfortable, large apartments in good neighborhoods. In contrast, other renters unable to buy a home had financial disadvantages. Neither Sandra nor Aninha produced income. Miriam and Marquinhos were burdened with family obligations, supporting her mother, his father, and Marquinhos's child by a previous marriage. Alice had rented since her divorce. Yet all but the playwright/actor couple of Nicole and Miguel considered themselves middle class.

19 There are striking similarities with this material and that described in Pinches (1999) and Young (1999) for the Philippines: the importance of positional goods, the divisions between refined and vulgar consumption,

the construction of the new and old rich as "cultural opposites" (Pinches, 291). Pinches (1996, 123) observes that "in the Philippines itself, the term 'middle class' is commonly associated with perceived incomes and consumption practices. Many of those called 'middle class,' who drive cars, own expensive electrical appliances and live in what are known as 'middle class' housing estates, are the families of overseas contract labourers." Young discusses the parental concern with education.

2   Shopping Nightmares, Banking Games, Government Packages
Local Shopping during Inflation

1   The minimum wage was established under President Vargas in 1938. The law also set a "basic basket" (*cesta básica*) of goods, which includes food, such as rice, beans, cooking oil, sugar, coffee, powdered milk; and household goods, like soap and detergent. The estimated cost of provisioning a household with a minimum of these goods has since been used for adjusting the minimum wage to cost-of-living increases. It is a standard reference for salaries, and relevant for most Brazilians, who earn less than five minimum wages. It is not usually used for middle- and high-income earners (for instance, those earning ten minimum wages, or US$1,000 and beyond); rather, the amount in currency would be given. In more stable eras from the 1960s to the 1990s, one minimum wage has been about US$100. During the crisis, it reached as low as US$50.

2   The literature on household economizing strategies (e.g., Schmink 1984) has not usually looked at the middle class, but see Selby, Murphy, and Lorenzen 1990; Winter 1991; and especially Lomnitz and Melnick 1991.

3   See Miller (1998), especially chapter 1, "Making Love in Supermarkets," for a study of grocery shopping in First World conditions.

4   These currency changes were from the cruzeiro (Cr$) to the cruzado (Cz$) in 1986; the cruzado to the cruzado novo (NCz$) in 1989, the cruzado novo back to the cruzeiro in 1990, the cruzeiro to the cruzeiro real (CR$) in 1993, and the cruzeiro real to the real (R$) in 1994.

5   Sixty hours of transcript material from twenty-four focus groups (140–150 participants) held between 1986 and 1992 were generously conceded to me for analysis by Clarice Herzog from the advertising agency Standard, Ogilvy, and Mather of São Paulo. Her department conducted focus groups, divided by sex and segment of the middle class (according to the marketing classification of A, B, C, or upper middle, middle, and middle

middle), in which the opening question in an unstructured discussion (of about two and a half hours in length) was either general—"What is life like these days for you?"—or more specific—"How has [government stabilization] plan X affected you?" The purpose of the focus groups was not to elicit a response to some specific product. Rather, it was to gauge people's attitudes toward shopping during the crisis. Since consumption issues were quick to emerge, at some point a more specific question such as "Do you buy by the brand or by the price?" or "Do you still stock-pile?" would be asked. Although the agency used only a fraction of the discussion-group material, they did assess the mood or frame of mind people were in (gloomy, optimistic, etc.) in relation to the government or country. The agency turned this material and additional information gained from phone interviews into periodic journal reports for major businesses, in a series called *The Listening Post* (title in English). I found the hours of discussion very useful material for comparison with my own (see especially chapter 7). It also provided commentary produced in the period prior to my fieldwork.

6 But for a remarkable study on mathematical thoughts, anthropology, psychology, and shopping in the United States, see Lave 1988.

7 Even pocket calculators per se were not up to the task of inflation, as the magazine *Veja* reported. Most often they allow for only ten digits. The company Sharp smartly responded to this acquired need, producing a fourteen-digit version (*Veja* 6/9/93, 60).

8 Prior to denationalization, to obtain a new line from the phone company took years and cost about US$2,500 in 1993. It was common practice for people to sell or lease their phone lines (and it was a specified item in divorce proceedings). Market rates for leasing varied tremendously across and within cities. In December 1996 I read that a phone-line rental cost US$150 per month. In the early 1990s, there were just 10.8 telephones per 100 people in Brazil, versus 50 phones per 100 individuals in the United States (*The Brazilians* 12/96, 12).

9 Hutchinson, Cunningham, and Moore (1976) offer a quantitative analysis of shopping centers, installment buying, discount stores, telephone use, and housing with material from the economic miracle. For another empirical study of the rise in acquisition of consumer durables by middle- and upper-class sectors during that era, see Wells (1977). He associates the increase with income differentials, that is, real wage gains on the part of middle-class sectors versus depressed wages of working classes, and layaway plans.

10 Brazilianist Jerry Lombardi (personal communication) pointed out that those buying on a layaway plan might be able to keep their money invested, hence partially offset the store's interest. For many buyers, however, the decision more often was based simply on how much money was available at the moment. Informants always emphasized that planning and predictions became impossible.

11 Economist Walter Belik informed me that usury laws limiting real interest rates to 12 percent per year were reinstated in the 1988 constitution, after having been dropped in 1964. Belik inquired rhetorically in May 1994: "What are they going to do, arrest the president of Bradesco [Brazil's largest private sector bank]?"

12 Although Brazilians were not allowed, by law, to convert their money into dollars, wealthy people opened bank accounts abroad, typically in Miami. In Brazil the informal, black, or what came to be called parallel, market became increasingly open and sanctioned after years of clandestine dealings. This means of savings was perhaps the most accessible to the common person. However, even though the dollar was a stable currency, it was also a market and therefore speculative, with vacillating values. Although prices for certain goods were quoted in dollars—airfare abroad and imported goods, for example—the extent of reference to the dollar was actually quite limited.

13 The Fundo de Investimento, or Fundão, was part of Plano Collor II (see chapter 6) and replaced other short-term investments. With this fund instated automatically into one's checking account, all banking citizens were really buying government bonds. Sachs and Zini (1995) explain that "banks were not required to hold central bank reserves (monetary base) against these accounts," rather short-term securities that worked something like money-market funds in the United States (5). Any account owner, however, had one. As a result, Sachs and Zini calculate that "the monetary base is only 7.5 percent of Brazilian transaction balances (checkable accounts plus currency). In the U.S., by contrast, the monetary base makes up for 33.7 percent of that aggregate."

14 Savings accounts and the Fundão entailed little risk, since they were based on government bonds. Savings accounts were undesirable protection, though, as they were inadequately corrected for inflation and earned negligible interest. Furthermore, after the Collor bank-account confiscation (see chapter 6), great suspicion surrounded them. And whereas in 1991, savings and Fundão returns fell below the rate of inflation, medium-term (sixty-day) investments like bank-deposit certificates

(CDBs, now defunct) earned 26 percent. Three-percent-per-month returns on the commodities market (*fundo de commodities,* requiring a minimum investment of US$100) meant a 50 percent rate of profit per year. Better yet, the stock-market rates were 331 percent (*Veja* 1/8/92, 34). Other applications required even higher initial investments: most brokers required a Cr$50 million minimum in 1991 (*Veja* 1/22/92, 96). The specific market investment was left to the banks' decision to play the money markets via speculation abroad (*carteira livre*) or via the stock markets (*fundo de ações* and *bolsa de valores*). The names used to refer to these markets are indicative: they were called the *overnight,* or simply *over,* and *open.* English words were used.

15 DIEESE stands for Departamento Intersindical de Estatística e Estudos Sócio-Econômicos, or Inter-Union Department of Statistics and Socioeconomic Studies. Its monthly bulletins provide quantitative reports of the cost of living, reports on the activities of different employment sectors, and brief editorials. There were several inflation indexes, geared to various sectors of the economy. DIEESE, the trade unions' research organ, focused on household costs and tended to report inflation as higher than the government would publicize.

16 In 1970 the financial sector held 7 percent of the nation's income; by the end of the 1980s that proportion had grown to 15 percent. In 1991 alone, at the height of the Collor recession, banks grew 26 percent. Brazilian bank profits in 1991 were almost double that of the United States, or 13.6 versus 7.4 percent profit (*Veja* 8/11/93, 50).

17 The price of beef in 1994, for instance, was the equivalent of $4 per kilo.

18 Social scientists adopting a political economy perspective (Kovarick 1985; Oliveira 1988; Singer 1988; Wood and Carvalho 1988; but see Pastoré 1986 for a dissenting view) have characterized inflation as a kind of distributive conflict leading to increasing income concentration. In Singer's view, inflation diverts or disguises class conflict, hence is a "perverted form" of class relations (133). The social, economic, and political implications of inflation are explored in Vieira et al. (1993). Earp similarly defines inflation as "a kind of social relation through which is expressed the conflict over the distribution of the product" (1993, 96). This conflict involves the whole society, yet most unfairly, the poorest citizens. According to economist Barbosa, "in fact, inflation is an aggression on citizenship, because it consists in a tribute paid fundamentally by the poorest sectors of the population, without there being a legal norm established for this taxation" (1993, 33). Wealthier sectors, he adds, "have

access to mechanisms which give them greater protection against the devaluations" (39).

19   One might not be surprised that, as public enterprises in Brazil, utilities prices were controlled centrally. But the government also determined, for instance, when and by what percent private schools could raise their tuitions. This was a highly regulated economy, with a long history of governmental controls on national development. Though denationalization has received middle-class support since the late 1980s, and was a key part of Collor's campaign platform, it did not occur during his presidency, nor with the vice-president who replaced Collor, Itamar Franco. Privatization, even of "strategic" companies such as telecommunications, began in the Cardoso presidency, from 1995 forward.

20   The word *cruzado* refers to an old Portuguese coin. It also means crusade, crossing, and cross, as in boxing.

21   Funaro's plan was populist in several senses. About five months into the plan, in an effort to contain spending, the Sarney government decreed a compulsory loan surcharge on the price of fuel and on car sales (loan, because in principle this would be repaid by the government after a year); a tax on international air and sea travel; and a sharp tax increase on short-term, less-than-sixty-day bank investments. These measures clearly left "the people" out of it and taxed the better-off (*Veja* 7/30/86). It also took the wind out of the sails of banks, which were making stupendous profits off the inflation (see *Veja* 7/2/86).

22   Sachs and Zini continue: "Since Brazil was relatively cut off from world markets, both because of structure and policy, imports did not generally relieve the shortages. Also very important, the controls tended to turn the terms-of-trade against the government sector. Private prices kept creeping up while state-enterprises were held in place. . . . In this way, the price controls themselves enlarged the public-sector deficits, and thereby further undermined the controls" (1995, 8). According to Cardoso (1992), "among the factors leading to the failure of the Cruzado Plan, the most prominent was the overheating of the economy through loose fiscal and monetary policies" (175). She elaborates: "On the fiscal side, tax revenues rose disappointingly little, revenues of state-owned companies were hurt by the price freeze, spending ran higher than anticipated and subsidies, cut during 1983–1984, staged a come back in 1986. The public sector wage bill also increased. Loose monetary policy produced very low interest rates that permitted firms lacking confidence in the program to build up speculative stocks. Furthermore, the increase in real wages . . . and the

fast-growing economy rapidly expanded wages and sustained a consumers' boom" (175). She summarizes that "with the budget deficit left
untouched and growing trade surpluses, all the plans amounted to attempts to stop inflation *by decree*" (176; emphasis added).

23 Of the twenty-three households queried, fifteen women did all the grocery shopping by themselves (this included two divorced women); four
couples did it together; four men did it alone. As if in exact symmetry,
fifteen men did the banking by themselves; four couples did it together;
four did it separately. There was thus a gender division of grocery shopping and banking. However, it does seem possible there was increased
male involvement in household operations and decisions during the
1980s and 1990s.

24 The Plano Cruzado and other plans triggered some distortions, such that
new cars were fixed at lower prices than used ones (*Veja* 7/3/86).

25 J. Tomlinson (1991, chap. 3) argues that to blame consumer goods or
even the consumer for the fact that the meanings and purpose of life,
one's identity, and so on are now associated with consumption is misguided. Instead, he directs attention to the "structural determinants and
boundaries of individual 'lifeworlds'" of capitalism and their effects on
society (134).

3   The Discrete Sales of the Middle Class
Gender and Generation in a Globalizing Economy

1 Other businesses in the study included English instruction, computer
work, car sales, personnel development, a luncheonette, a psychoanalytic
office, and an architecture firm. Two other informants also planned on
starting businesses.

2 Incidentally, Gilda confided a sense of affront that salespeople at the
shopping center (Iguatemi) were better dressed than she.

3 Regarding "humanizing" stories, see Bird and Dardenne (1988).

4 Since the early 1980s the news has reported an employment crisis for
engineers, attributing it first to the increase in number of college graduates and Brazil's dependence on technology, and later to the recession.
Three thousand engineers in Rio marched in protest of unemployment
in 1984 (*O Globo* 3/28/84). A 50 percent drop in jobs occurred during
the Collor presidency; by 1993, only 25 percent were reported as working in the field (*Jornal do Brasil* 5/30/93). See Bonelli (1989).

5 Religion is beyond the scope of this work; however, it would be fascinating to examine the belief systems of the Spiritists in my group of informants, namely Sandra and Carlos, Nicole and Miguel, Lara, Renato (and his daughter Luciana), and freelance English-language teacher/Marxist, Miriam, in relation to other beliefs. See Campbell (1987) for an ingenious argument of how, in their very quest for spirituality and individual growth, people corresponding to those of Weber's *Protestant Ethic* channeled those desires into ongoing consumer pursuits.

4 The International in Daily Life
Of Debutantes and Disney

1 After returning from Disney in early 1995 and talking to me about the actual expenses of sending Martha to Minnesota for a month, Euclides and Gilda decided to send her here in July 1995. Possibly the advantageous exchange rate of the new "strong" currency (the real) helped. This later development does not, however, alter the prioritizing of Disney during the inflation crisis, when it was quite likely that only one trip would have been feasible.

2 *World Press Review,* March 1997, 28. My initial efforts to obtain the number of Brazilians who have been to Disney were fruitless. I soon learned from two other individuals who had published studies of Disney that the company was not open to direct inquiries from researchers.

3 "Brega e Chique" [Corny and chic] was the name of a soap opera of the 1980s.

4 In contemporary New Orleans only a set circle of families are eligible to have debutante balls. Civic exposure is also a dimension, as only these families compete in Mardi Gras pageants (Kimberly Flynn, personal communication). Such public exposure and competition are emphatically not part of the Brazilian balls. A *New York Times Magazine* report on Cubans in Florida (2/26/95, pp. 42–45) states that the North American balls involve a pageant competition, in which a queen of debutantes is chosen. Regarding elite debutante balls in Texas, see Haynes 1998.

5 Urry (1988 and 1990) draws attention to the increasing democratization of travel for pleasure in the twentieth century, and to the ways its spatial distance and contemplative activities (e.g., gazing) mark its separation from the world of work.

6 I am indebted to Barbara Weinstein (personal communication) for this point.

7 I am indebted to Jane Schneider (personal communication) for this point.

8 One might envision that both events could be income levelers as Worsley (1981, 247) notes of rural social rituals.

9 Criticisms of Mauss's classic *The Gift* (1967 [1925]), e.g., Carrier 1995, do not contradict the argument that gift giving can be an assertion of unequal social ties.

10 Analyzing architecture among Ecuadorians of different occupations, Colloredo-Mansfeld (1994) points out that their housing forms appeal variously to modernity or tradition as well. He argues that their housing is more than a display of wealth; it also shows that "conspicuous display . . . initiate[s] new appraisals of socially appropriate activity" (862). Interestingly, though, Colloredo-Mansfeld finds that conspicuous consumption is not necessarily socially "effective" (854).

11 See Lewin 1979; Nazzari 1991; Nizza da Silva 1984; Dias 1984; Balmori and Oppenheimer 1984; Needell 1987; Lopes 1989; and Trigo 1993. For comparisons, see Schneider 1971 and Martinez-Alier 1974.

5 International Bargain Shopping and the Making of Modernity

1 The issue of irony and the anthropologist was first brought to my attention by a dear friend and colleague, Hélio Belik (deceased). Irony can have its place, perhaps more appropriately by a compatriot critical of a national consumption practice than by a foreigner, particularly one from the United States.

2 For remarkably detailed and in-depth transgenerational studies of the history of consumer goods and working-class Mexicans living near the U.S. border, see Heyman 1994 and 1997.

3 An important gauge of the impact of inflation on national commerce was Christmas sales, which received high media attention. On materialist aspects of Christmas in the United States, see Belk 1993.

4 Certain imports were in fact targets for assault: tennis shoes and cellular phones.

5 In São Paulo, and surely in other cities in Brazil, new forms of arcades, called *galerias,* developed. In what is essentially a large room with direct street-level access, makeshift stalls are set up in several narrow rows.

Generally the items sold are nationally produced, sold at a cheaper price because they come "direct from the manufacturer," but there are some stalls where international goods are sold. I could not ascertain whether the prices, high compared to the United States (for instance, a thirteen-ounce bottle of Vidal Sassoon shampoo, which sells for $4 in the United States, cost $10–12 there), were elevated because the merchant adhered to tax regulations or because the merchant took into account contraband fees plus his/her own considerable profit margin in this inflation period.

6 For comparison, the tax on electrodomestic products was lowered to 42 percent, having been 72 percent; that on foods varied from 2 percent to 12 percent (*Folha de São Paulo* 4/29/95).

7 The Brazilian consulate confirmed that there is no formula for calculating import duties for individuals; rather, according to the employee I asked, it depends entirely on the official and the situation. However, *Veja* (7/27/94) calculated taxes close to 100 percent with respect to goods brought in by Brazil's soccer players.

8 The fact that the goods were delivered immediately to the players' homes made it complicated for the Customs Bureau (Receita Federal) to later verify the goods in question and calculate taxes.

9 García Canclini ups the ante on this point: "Being cultured—including being cultured in the modern era—implies not so much associating oneself with a repertory of exclusively modern objects and messages, but rather knowing how to incorporate the art and literature of the vanguard, as well as technological advances, into traditional matrices of social privilege and symbolic distinction" (1995b, 46–47).

10 In this light, see Ardaillon (1997) for a fascinating study of how modern technology was called on to underwrite middle-class women's professional work. She exquisitely captures the gender and class ironies of the huge fad in "freezers." In an effort to reduce reliance on maids, individually contracted professional cooks catered as many as a month's worth of frozen dinners.

11 I thank Shirley Lindenbaum (personal communication) for suggesting this to me. See also the discussion in Belk, Wallendorf, and Sherry (1989) on sacralization. This response to new purchases contrasts with Hirschman (1982). His charmingly humorous perspective is that consumers become disappointed after purchase of long-desired durables.

12 Creatively elaborating on Marx's suggestive concept of commodity fetishism, Burke finds that "fetishism is more than (but includes) the meanings invested in goods; it is also the accumulated power of commodities

to actually constitute, organize, and relate to people, institutions, and discourses, to contain within themselves the forms of consciousness through which capitalism manufactures its subjects" (1996, 5).

13 The joking pastime has been raised to an art in the absolute treasure by Guadalupe Loaeza, *Compro, Luego Existo* (1992). In this acute social analysis in fictional form, international consumption-driven practices are satirized through a stream-of-consciousness presentation of wealthy—indeed millionaire—Mexicans. I thank Betina Zolkower for this reference.

6 Delivering the Crisis
The Media and the Middle Class through the Collor Years

1 Hall 1979, 1980, 1986, and 1991 were most useful for developing this chapter. Also illuminating were discussions of the productions of social knowledge, stories, realities, and publics (Kress 1986; Anderson 1983; Gerbner 1985; Dijk 1985; Dahlgren 1991; Blumler and Gurevitch 1982; Grossberg 1991; Bell 1991); debates regarding audience responses and autonomy (Fiske and Hartley 1978; Hall 1980; Morley 1980; Woolacott 1982; Hartley and Montgomery 1985; Newcomb 1991; Curran 1991; Mattelart and Mattelart 1992; Dowmunt 1993); counterdiscussions of power (Ang 1990, 1996; Curran and Gurevitch 1996; Curran, Morley, and Walkerdine 1996); and analyses of Brazil's media, especially during the crisis and the Collor years (A. Albuquerque 1993; Castro 1993; Straubhaar, Olsen, and Nunes 1993; V. A. Lima 1993; Fausto Neto 1994; and Rubim 1993). John Thompson's (1984) discussion of ideology was also helpful.

2 Without lapsing into essentialism, I would nonetheless recall that journalists themselves are most usually members of the middle class.

3 The other parts of the plan—cutting public deficit and opening the economy to imports—did not receive much immediate attention. The removal of restrictions on imports, intended to counter local inflationary prices, was gradual and partial; and though Collor threatened a drastic cutting of the public budget with employee dismissals, this orthodox anti-inflation measure was not accomplished.

4 The small sums that informants recalled indicated that Cr$50,000 was for them very little money.

5 FGTS stands for Fundo de Garantia pelo Tempo de Serviço, or Guarantee Funds per Time of Service. The money deposited monthly in this fund

by the employer (8 percent is obligatory; however, employers are not necessarily compliant) covers what counts as unemployment compensation in Brazil—a fraction of accumulated earnings. This fund serves other purposes as well: retirement, disability, death benefits, and down payment on a first home.

6 Surprisingly enough, the government did "open its coffers" and liberate the money confiscated, albeit in stages, primarily to avoid consumer sprees. But this return—as promised, eighteen months later—never sat right, being unconstitutional and outrageous, nor could the losses and lost opportunities—of a house, car, dream honeymoon, trip, new business venture—be compensated (*Veja* 8/21/91).

7 By obscurity, I refer to the fact that Collor's home state of Alagoas might be compared to a very poor, southern U.S. state. His family background is colorful. Fernando Collor's father, Arnon de Mello, rose in business, coming to own the main state newspaper, then adding on radio and a television affiliate station of Rêde Globo, and he rose in politics, first as governor. Later, in the capacity of state senator and on the senate floor, Arnon shot and accidentally killed a senator from the state of Acre— accidentally, because he had intended to kill a senator and rival from his home state. He lost his political mandate. Son Fernando entered into politics, first as mayor of the state capital of Maceió, and then as governor. Critics might call his performance mediocre or terrible. This family held clout in the state and through the media. It had not, however, been a millionaire family (Jorge L. Souto Silva, personal communication). See Flynn 1993.

8 Bonds and bills had fixed monthly interest rates with the aim of "mopping up liquidity," according to Flynn (1993:365). I thank Hugo Sales Teixeira and Ciro Biderman for assistance on banking terms and usages.

9 The constitutional basis for suits against this law (law 8,024 created the confiscation) was that no one can be deprived of his/her goods without due legal process.

10 Sandra's emphasis on individual initiative is consistent with her belief as a devout Spiritist that we are all responsible for our "vibrations" and ultimately for our life outcomes, and therefore should perform positive rather than negative or passive acts.

11 *Veja* did not delve further into the matter, other than reporting a year later that the number of citizens suing to receive their cruzados novos back reached 120,000 (4/24/91).

12 The word *referential* added to interest rates indicates that this rate was the reference for some contracts.

13 FIPE is responsible for the Index of Consumer Prices.

14 A book by one of the kidnappers, journalist Fernando Gabeira, was made into a movie called "Four Days in September."

15 Tropicalism refers to a musical movement of the 1960s and 1970s led mainly by Northeastern musicians Gal Costa, Gilberto Gil, Caetano Veloso, Maria Bethânia, Tom Zé, and others, that took off in Rio de Janeiro. Whereas bossa nova had sought inspiration from North American jazz, creating a sort of "intellectual samba," this movement (like Modernism of the 1920s) was pointedly rooted in and revolved around Brazilian rhythms, melodies, themes, and lyrics (Mary Ann O'Dougherty, personal communication). The song "Tropicália" by Caetano Veloso plays ironically with icons of Brazilian identity—bossa nova, mulatta, Carmen Miranda. The fact that the song was not overtly political may in part be owing to censorship, but also accords with tropicalists' preference for cultural critique. Tropicalists "depict the contradictions of modernization in a developing country where the archaic and the modern coexist and collide" (Perrone 1989, 63).

16 Flynn points out that "Collor, of course, was not the first Brazilian president or politician to be suspected or accused of corruption" (1993, 364). Flynn's detailed analysis puts the corruption scandal in light of the political and economic inadequacies of Collor's presidency.

17 Impeachment had no precedent in Brazil. Watergate was the referent, and the English word was imported.

7 The Middle Class versus the Nation
Discourses of Region / Race and Morality

1 My view stems from focus-group material, from the Southern separatist movement, and from commentaries I continually encountered. Derogatory or condemning comments seemed irrepressible for many.

2 I had very few exceptions: one Carioca, one Nordestina. Two claimed some Indian heritage; none claimed African heritage.

3 The literature on domestic servants in Latin America is large. For a review on the subject in Brazil, see Azeredo (1987).

4 The many workers from Minas Gerais, a large state with one area with

conditions similar to the *sertão* (backlands) of the Northeast and a high population of African descent, did not receive negative criticism. It is possible that the proximity of the area to São Paulo and the lack of reputation for decadence makes this group less of a target, but the reasons for differential attitudes remain unclear.

5 The vice-president-turned-president (1985–90) José Sarney is from Maranhão, and ex-president Fernando Collor de Mello (1990–92) is from Alagoas. The ultrawealthy, powerful conservative Antônio Carlos Magalhães is senator for the large state of Bahia, and the radical workers' party leader, Luís Inácio Lula da Silva, is from Pernambuco. Counterbalancing the conservative Northeastern politicians is Teotônio Villela, the senator from Alagoas who fought for amnesty for exiled Brazilians during the dictatorship and for direct elections of the president at the end of the military rule, in the movement called *diretas já!* (direct elections now!).

6 According to Hasenbalg's assessment of figures from censuses (by PNAD, the National Household Survey [Pesquísa Nacional por Amostragem de Domicílios]), the nonwhite population in São Paulo went from 5.9 percent in 1940 to 10.7 percent in 1976. In the Northeast, the nonwhite population was 53.6 percent in 1940 and 47.2 percent in 1976 (1985, 29). Hasenbalg notes that "there are reasons to think that the 1976 PNAD [census] overestimates the increase in the concentration of nonwhites in the Southeast . . . [however] the geographical polarization of the two racial groups is still considerable, with almost two-thirds of the white population living in the Southeast and a greater proportion of nonwhites in the rest of the country, particularly the Northeast (47.2 percent) and the Minas Gerais–Espírito Santo region (14.1 percent)" (28).

7 Paulistas told me that the Northeast is overrepresented in Congress. Representation is proportional by the constitution. However, there are floor and ceiling limits, which, as Alfred Stepan explains, mandates that "no state, no matter how small in terms of population, can have fewer than eight representatives in the Lower Chamber, and that no state, no matter how large the population, can have more than 70" (2000, 149). The states of the Northeast, North, and Central West have 43 percent of the population, but 74 percent of the seats in the Lower Chamber of Congress (157). To isolate the Northeast as the culprit is inaccurate. Indeed, one vote is extremely weighty in the Northern states of Roraima, Acre, and Tocantins. In contrast, the most underrepresented states—São Paulo, Rio de Janeiro, Minas Gerais, Rio Grande do Sul, Bahia, and Pernambuco—include two populous Northeastern states (Flynn 1993, 353). In

this context, it is worth noting that the Senate, with three senators per state, has far greater decision-making power than U.S. senators. I thank Stuart Schwartz for indicating sources pertaining to this question.

8 This struck me as particularly odd in a warning directed at me, for this was one of the families to whom I had recounted my prior experience in the Northeast. In fact, I most often found that people would self-censure once I noted I had lived in Recife or had been married to a Northeasterner. The typical practice would be for the person to immediately switch gears, saying, "It's very beautiful there." This happened so often that I stopped my frankness policy, thereby allowing such comments to flow uninhibited.

9 Of the three expressions, only the first can have a qualified positive acknowledgment of the wits involved. One opposite of *ser esperto* is *ser bobo,* to be a stupid (but honest) fool, which, as Edilson's comments show, might be considered ridiculous.

10 In *Na Corda Bamba* social scientists note that the era bred mistrust (*desconfiança*), doubt, and uncertainty, creating, as César Fernandes put it, "an ethical crisis, associated with the culture of inflation . . . [which] corrodes modernizing values, like those of citizenship, discipline, individual responsibility in the face of universal norms, etc., and also corrupts the traditional values that sustain the relational society" (1993, 46).

11 Dean (1969, 235) similarly suggests that in the early twentieth century, the middle class, fearing encroachment by lower classes, became "isolated and bitter in its sense of moral superiority."

12 Whether or not the storyteller's memory was accurate, the explanation produced (i.e., even if not recalled) would possibly have derived from a reasoning of "dark, therefore Northern." If this was a recollection, she would also have heard and recalled the distinctive accent, which would confirm the region (but not the class or color of the person). One of the many problems with focus-group transcripts is of course that we do not know much at all about the participants beyond simple socioeconomic designations and occupations, and in this case, we cannot ask, for instance, the question of accent, how the woman was dressed, and so on.

13 Turner's thesis (1986) is criticized in Otávio Velho (1979). See also Vianna Moog's (1954) work *Bandeirantes e Pioneiros,* which presents how São Paulo's "West" was won—by bandeirante explorers whose aim was extractive ("predatory") fortune-hunting in contrast to the pioneering homesteaders of the United States.

14 Anthropologist Patricia Tovar (personal communication) tells me that

in her country, Colombia, people regret not having been colonized by the English.

8   Deliverance
An End to Inflation and the Promise of Neoliberalism

1   An analytical view of Brazilian middle classes would see their downward mobility and await an alliance with working classes. To this, the majority of my informants would surely say, "Nem morta!"—over my dead body. Without reviving the old true and false consciousness debate, one might nevertheless recall that it hinges on theoretical grounds and rationalism. This leads to an unpromising situation in which one waits for people to act as theory would have them act. But would they do so? Even entertaining a rationalistic mode of decision making, it would make sense for middle-class people to place their chips with the system that has generally gone their way, rather than resign themselves to a lower position (see Wallerstein 1991). This does not necessarily mean that the middle class lacks autonomy, as has been argued (see Pinheiros 1975 and Saes 1985).

2   These views have a long history. Dean (1969) and Topik (1978) report that the middle class prior to World War II was critical of industrialists—both their protected products and their profits.

3   The inflation rate projected for 1994, based on the first semester—hence the period immediately preceding the Plano Real—was 7,350 percent, as reported by economist Márcio Garcia (1995).

BIBLIOGRAPHY

Abreu Filho, Ovídio de. 1980. "Raça, Sangue e Luta: Identidade e Parentesco em uma Cidade do Interior." Master's thesis, Universidade Federal do Rio de Janeiro.

———. 1982. "Parentesco e Identidade Social." *Anuário Antropológico* 80:95–118.

Abu-Lughod, Lila. 1990. "The Romance of Resistance: Tracing Transformation of Power through Bedouin Women." *American Ethnologist* 17 (1): 41–55.

Aguiar, Neuma. 1993. "Cultura Inflacionária: Vida Cotidiana e Relações de Gênero." In *Na Corda Bamba: Doze Estudos sobre a Cultura da Inflação,* ed. J. R. Vieira, L. Neves de Holanda Barbosa, L. C. Delorme Prado, M. A. P. Leopoldi, and M. C. D'Araujo, pp. 113–128. Rio de Janeiro: Relume Dumará.

Albuquerque, Afonso de. 1993. "O Espetáculo da Crise: Os Media e o Processo de *Impeachment* contra Collor." In *Comunicação e Cultura Contemporâneas,* ed. C. Pereira and A. Fausto Neto, pp. 144–148. Rio de Janeiro: Notrya Editora.

Albuquerque, J. A. Guillon. 1977. "Classe Média: Caráter, Posição e Consciência de Classe." In *Classes Médias e Política no Brasil,* pp. 11–31. Rio de Janeiro: Paz e Terra.

Allan, Stuart. 1998. "News from NowHere: Television News Discourse and the Construction of Hegemony." In *Approaches to Media Discourse,* ed. A. Bell and P. Garrett, pp. 105–141. Oxford: Blackwell.

Almeida, Pergentino Mendes de, and Hilda Wickenhauser. 1991. "Finding a Better Socio-Economic Status Classification System for Brazil." *Marketing and Research Today* 19 (4): 240–250.

Althusser, Louis. 1972. *Lenin and Philosophy, and Other Essays.* New York: Monthly Review Press.

Anderson, Benedict. 1983. *Imagined Communities.* London: Verso.

Andrade, Manuel Correia de. 1973. *A Terra e o Homem no Nordeste.* São Paulo: Brasiliense.

Andrade, Mário de. 1984. *Macunaíma.* Trans. E. A. Goodlund. 1925. Reprint, New York: Random House.

Andrews, George Reid. 1991. *Blacks and Whites in São Paulo, Brazil, 1888–1988*. Madison: University of Wisconsin Press.

Ang, Ien. 1990. "Culture and Communication: Towards an Ethnographic Critique of Media Consumption in the Transnational Media System." *European Journal of Communication* 5:239–260.

———. 1996. *Living Room Wars: Rethinking Media Audiences of a Postmodern World*. London: Routledge.

Anselm, William, and Kosta Goulianis. 1994. "Exclusionary Representation: A Hegemonic Mediation." In *Mediating Culture: The Politics of Representation*, pp. 119–132. Toronto: Guernica.

Appadurai, Arjun. 1988. "Putting Hierarchy in Its Place." *Cultural Anthropology* 3 (1): 36–49.

———. 1990. "Disjuncture and Difference in the Global Cultural Economy." *Public Culture* 2 (2): 1–24.

———. 1996. *Modernity at Large: Cultural Dimensions of Globalization*. Minneapolis: University of Minnesota Press.

———, ed. 1986. *The Social Life of Things: Commodities in Social Perspective*. Cambridge: Cambridge University Press.

Appadurai, Arjun, and Carol A. Breckenridge. 1995. "Public Modernity in India." In *Consuming Modernity: Public Culture in a South Asian World*, ed. C. A. Breckenridge, pp. 1–20. Minneapolis: University of Minnesota Press.

Ardaillon, Danielle. 1997. *O Salário da Liberdade: Profissão e Maternidade, Negociações para uma Igualdade na Diferença*. São Paulo: Anna Blume.

Arns, Paulo Evaristo, and Catholic Church, Archdiocese of São Paulo. 1995. *Brasil, Nunca Mais*. Petrópolis: Vozes.

Asher, R. E. 1994. "Discourse." In *The Encyclopedia of Language and Linguistics*, vol. 2, pp. 940–947. Oxford: Pergamon Press.

Azeredo, Sandra Maria da Mata. 1987. "Relações entre Empregadas e Patroas: Reflexões sobre o Feminismo em Países Multiraciais." In *Rebeldia e Submissão*, ed. A. Costa and C. Bruschini, pp. 195–220. São Paulo: Vértice.

Azevedo, Thales de. 1986. *As Regras do Namoro à Antiga*. São Paulo: Atica.

Baer, Warner. 1995. *The Brazilian Economy: Growth and Development*. 4th ed. Westport, CT: Praeger.

Balmori, Diana, and Robert Oppenheimer. 1984. *Notable Family Networks in Latin America*. Chicago: University of Chicago Press.

Barbosa, Fernando de Holanda. 1993. "Inflação e Cidadania." In *Na Corda Bamba: Doze Estudos sobre a Cultura da Inflação*, ed. J. R. Vieira, L. Neves de Holanda Barbosa, L. C. Delorme Prado, M. A. P. Leopoldi, and M. C. D'Araujo, pp. 33–42. Rio de Janeiro: Relume Dumará.

Barros, Myriam Lins de. 1987. *Autoridade e Afeto: Avós, Filhos e Netos na Família Brasileira*. Rio de Janeiro: Zahar.

Barthes, Roland. 1967. *Système de la Mode*. Paris: Seuil.

Baudrillard, Jean. 1981. *For a Critique of the Political Economy of the Sign*. St. Louis: Telos Press.

——. 1985. "The Masses: The Implosion of the Social in the Media." *New Literary History* 16 (3): 580–588.

Beck, Ulrich. 1987. "Beyond Status and Class: Will There Be an Individualized Class Society?" In *Modern German Sociology*, ed. V. Meja, D. Misgeld, and N. Stehr, pp. 340–356. New York: Columbia University Press.

Belk, Russell. 1988. "Third World Consumer Culture." In *Marketing and Development: Toward Broader Dimensions*, ed. E. Kumcu and A. Fuat Firat, pp. 103–127. Greenwich, CT: JAI Press.

——. 1993. "Materialism and the Making of the Modern American Christmas." In *Unwrapping Christmas*, ed. D. Miller, pp. 75–104. London: Routledge.

——. 1995. "Studies in the New Consumer Behavior." In *Acknowledging Consumption*, pp. 58–96. London: Routledge.

Belk, Russell, M. Wallendorf, and J. Sherry Jr. 1989. "The Sacred and the Profane in Consumer Behavior: Theodicy on the Odyssey." *Journal of Consumer Research* 16:1–33.

Bell, Allan. 1991. *The Language of News Media*. Oxford: Blackwell.

——. 1994. "Telling Stories." In *Media Texts: Authors and Readers*, ed. D. Graddol and O. Boyd-Barrett, pp. 100–118. Clevedon, UK: Open University.

Bell, Allan, and Peter Garrett. 1998. *Approaches to Media Discourse*. Oxford: Blackwell.

Bianco-Feldman, Bela. 1981. "The Petty Supporters of a Stratified Order: The Economic Entrepreneurs of Matriz, São Paulo, Brazil, 1877–1974." Ph.D. diss., Columbia University.

Bird, Elizabeth, and Robert W. Dardenne. 1988. "Myth, Chronicle, and Story: Exploring the Narrative Quality of News." *In Media, Myths, and Narratives: Television and the Press*, ed. J. W. Carey, pp. 67–87. Newbury Park, CA: Sage Publications.

Bloch, Maurice, and Jonathon Parry. 1989. *Money and the Morality of Exchange*. Cambridge: Cambridge University Press.

Blumin, Stuart. 1989. *The Emergence of the Middle Class: Social Experience in the American City, 1760–1900.* Cambridge: Cambridge University Press.

Blumler, J. G., and M. Gurevitch. 1982. "The Political Effects of Mass Communication." In *Culture, Society, and the Media,* ed. M. Gurevitch, T. Bennett, and J. Curran, pp. 236–267. London: Methuen.

Bonelli, Maria da Glória. 1989. *A Classe Média do "Milagre" à Recessão: Mobilidade Social, Expectativas e Identidade Coletiva.* São Paulo: IDESP.

Booth, William James. 1994. "On the Idea of the Moral Economy." *American Political Science Review* 88 (3): 653–667.

Boschi, Renato. 1986. "A Abertura e a Nova Classe Média na Política Brasileira: 1977–1982." *Dados* 29 (1): 5–24.

Bourdieu, Pierre. 1977. *Outline of a Theory of Practice.* Cambridge: Cambridge University Press.

———. 1980. *Le Sens Pratique.* Paris: Minuit.

———. 1984. *Distinction. A Social Critique of the Judgement of Taste.* Cambridge: Harvard University Press.

———. 1993. *The Field of Cultural Production: Essays on Art and Literature.* New York: Columbia University Press.

Bourdieu, Pierre, and Terry Eagleton. 1992. "Conversation: Pierre Bourdieu and Terry Eagleton on Doxa and Common Life." *New Left Review* 191:111–121.

Bourdieu, Pierre, and Jean-Claude Passeron. 1977. *Reproduction in Education, Society, and Culture.* Beverly Hills: Sage Publications.

Bowlby, Sophie. 1988. "From Corner Shop to Hypermarket: Women and Food Retailing." In *Women in Cities: Gender and the Urban Environment,* ed. J. Little, L. Pealce, and P. Richardson, pp. 61–83. New York: New York University Press.

Breckenridge, Carol A. 1995. *Consuming Modernity: Public Culture in a South Asian World.* Minneapolis: University of Minnesota Press.

Bresser Pereira, L. C. 1962. "The Rise of Middle Class and Middle Management in Brazil." *Journal of Inter-American Studies* 4 (3): 313–326.

Bruno, Michael, ed. 1988. *Inflation Stabilization: The Experience of Israel, Argentina, Brazil, Bolivia, and Mexico.* Cambridge: MIT Press.

Bunker, Stephen G. 1986. "Debt and Democratization: Changing Perspectives on the Brazilian State." *Latin American Research Review* 21 (3): 206–223.

Burke, Timothy. 1996. *Lifebuoy Men, Lux Women: Commodification, Consumption, and Cleanliness in Modern Zimbabwe.* Durham: Duke University Press.

Burris, Val. 1986. "The Discovery of the New Middle Class." *Theory and Society* 15:317–349.

Burrows, Roger, and Tim Butler. 1989. "A Review Article: Middle Mass and the Pitt: A Critical Review of Peter Saunder's Sociology of Consumption." *Sociological Review* 37 (2): 338–364.

Caldeira, Teresa. 1996. "Building Up Walls: The New Pattern of Spatial Segregation in São Paulo." *International Social Science Journal* (March): 55–66.

——. 2001. *City of Walls: Crime, Segregation, and Citizenship in São Paulo.* Berkeley: University of California Press.

Calhoun, Craig, E. LiPuma, and M. Postone, eds. 1993. *Bourdieu: Critical Perspectives.* Chicago: University of Chicago Press.

Camargo, José Francisco de. 1968. *A Cidade e o Campo: O Exôdo Rural no Brasil.* São Paulo: Editora da Universidade.

Campbell, Colin. 1987. *The Romantic Ethic and the Spirit of Modern Consumerism.* Oxford: Blackwell.

——. 1992. "The Desire for the New: Its Nature and Social Location as Presented in Theories of Fashion and Modern Consumerism." In *Consuming Technologies: Media and Information in Domestic Spaces,* ed. R. Silverstone and E. Hirsch, pp. 48–64. London: Routledge.

——. 1994. "Capitalism, Consumption, and the Problem of Motives: Some Issues in the Understanding of Conduct as Illustrated by an Examination of the Treatment of Motive and Meaning in the Works of Weber and Veblen." In *Consumption and Identity,* ed. J. Friedman, pp. 23–46. Chur, Switzerland: Harwood Academic Publishers.

——. 1995. "The Sociology of Consumption." In *Acknowledging Consumption,* pp. 96–126. London: Routledge.

——. 1997. "When the Meaning Is Not the Message: A Critique of the Consumption as Communication Thesis." In *Buy This Book: Studies in Advertising and Consumption,* ed. M. Nava, A. Blake, I. MacRury, and B. Richards, pp. 340–351. London: Routledge.

Cardoso, Eliana. 1992. "Deficit Finance and Monetary Dynamics in Brazil and Mexico." *Journal of Development Economics* 37:173–197.

Carey, James W., ed. 1988. *Media, Myths, and Narratives: Television and the Press.* Newbury Park, CA: Sage Publications.

Carneiro, Sandra Maria Correa de Sá. 1986. *Balão no Céu, Alegria na Terra: Estudo sobre as Representações e a Organização Social dos Baloeiros.* Rio de Janeiro: Funarte.

Carrier, James. 1995. *Gifts and Commodities: Exchange and Western Capitalism since 1700.* London: Routledge.

Carrier, James, and Josiah Heyman. 1997. "Consumption and Political Economy." *Journal of the Royal Anthropological Institute* 3 (2): 355–373.

Castro, Maria Ceres Pimenta Spinola. 1993. "Deveras, uma Fabulação do Real?" In *Comunicação e Cultura Contemporâneas,* ed. C. Pereira and A. Fausto Neto, pp. 129–143. Rio de Janeiro: Notrya Editora.

Chin, Elizabeth. 2001. *Purchasing Power: Black Kids and American Consumer Culture.* Minneapolis: University of Minnesota Press.

Coelho, Maria Claudia Pereira. 1990. "Jovens Atores e Jovens Católicos: Um Estudo sobre Metrópole e Diversidade." *Comunicação* 18 (Universidade Federal do Rio de Janeiro): 26–47.

Collins, Patricia Hill. 1990. *Black Feminist Thought: Knowledge, Consciousness, and the Politics of Empowerment.* London: Routledge.

Colloredo-Mansfeld, Rudolf. 1994. "Architectural Conspicuous Consumption and Economic Change in the Andes." *American Anthropologist* 96 (4): 845–865.

Comaroff, Jean. 1997. "The Empire's Old Clothes: Fashioning the Colonial Subject." Reprinted in *Situated Lives: Gender and Culture in Everyday Life,* ed. L. Lamphere, H. Ragoné, and P. Zavella, pp. 400–419. New York: Routledge.

Connell, Ian, and Adam Mills. 1985. "Text, Discourse, and Mass Communication." In *Discourse and Communication,* ed. T. A. Van Dijk, pp. 26–43. Berlin: de Gruyter.

Coronil, Fernando. 1996. "Beyond Occidentalism: Toward Nonimperial Geohistorical Categories." *Cultural Anthropology* 11 (1): 51–87.

Crapanzano, Vincent. 1986. *Waiting: The Whites of South Africa.* New York: Vintage.

Cross, Gary. 1997. "The Suburban Weekend: Perspectives on a Vanishing Twentieth-Century Dream." In *Visions of Suburbia,* ed. R. Silverstone, pp. 108–131. London: Routledge.

Curran, James. 1991. "Rethinking the Media as a Public Sphere." In *Communication and Citizenship: Journalism and the Public Sphere in the New Media Age,* ed. P. Dahlgren and C. Sparks, pp. 27–57. London: Routledge.

Curran, James, and Michael Gurevitch. 1996. *Mass Media and Society.* London: E. Arnold.

Curran, James, David Morley, and Valerie Walkerdine, eds. 1996. *Cultural Studies and Communications.* London: E. Arnold.

Dahlgren, Peter. 1991. Introduction to *Communication and Citizenship: Jour-*

nalism and the Public Sphere in the New Media Age, ed. P. Dahlgren and C. Sparks, pp. 1–26. London: Routledge.

———. 1992. "What's the Meaning of This? Viewers' Plural Sense-Making of TV News." In *Culture and Power: A Media, Culture, and Society Reader,* ed. P. Scannell, P. Schlesinger, and C. Sparks, pp. 201–217. London: Sage Publications.

DaMatta, Roberto. 1985. *A Casa e a Rua.* Rio de Janeiro: Guanabara/ Koogan.

———. 1990. *Carnavais, Malandros e Heróis: Para uma Sociologia do Dilema Brasileiro.* 5th ed. Rio de Janeiro: Guanabara.

———. 1993. "Para uma Sociologia da Inflação: Notas sobre Inflação, Sociedade e Cidadania." In *Na Corda Bamba: Doze Estudos sobre a Cultura da Inflação,* ed. J. R. Vieira, L. Neves de Holanda Barbosa, L. C. Delorme Prado, M. A. P. Leopoldi, and M. C. D'Araujo, pp. 15–32. Rio de Janeiro: Relume Dumará.

Dávila, Arlene M. 1997. *Sponsored Identities: Cultural Politics in Puerto Rico.* Philadelphia: Temple University Press.

———. 2001. *Latinos, Inc.: The Marketing and Making of a People.* Berkeley: University of California Press.

Davis, Fred. 1992. *Fashion, Culture, and Identity.* Chicago: University of Chicago Press.

Dean, Warren. 1969. *The Industrialization of São Paulo, 1880–1945.* Austin: University of Texas Press.

———. 1976. *Rio Claro: A Brazilian Plantation System, 1820–1920.* Stanford: Stanford University Press.

de Certeau, Michel. 1984. *The Practice of Everyday Life.* Berkeley: University of California Press.

de Lauretis, Teresa. 1986. "Issues, Terms, and Contexts." In *Feminist Studies/ Critical Studies,* pp. 4–25. Bloomington: Indiana University Press.

Dias, Maria Odela Leite da Silva. 1984. *Quotidiano e Poder em São Paulo no Século XIX.* São Paulo: Brasiliense.

DIEESE. 1986–1994. Monthly bulletins from the Departamento Intersindical de Estatística e Estudos Sócio-Econômicos.

Dijk, Teun A. Van. 1985. "Structure of News in the Press." In *Discourse and Communication,* pp. 69–96. Berlin: de Gruyter.

Dilley, Roy. 1992. "A General Introduction to Market Ideology, Imagery, and Discourse." In *Contesting Markets: Analysis of Ideology, Discourse, and Practice,* ed. R. Dilley, pp. 1–36. Edinburgh: Edinburgh University Press.

DiMaggio, Paul. 1979. "Review Essay: On Pierre Bourdieu." *American Journal of Sociology* 84 (6): 1461–1474.

Dinsmoor, James. 1990. *Brazil: Responses to the Debt Crisis; Impact on Savings, Investment, and Growth.* Washington, DC: Inter-American Development Bank.

Dittmar, Helga. 1992. *The Social Psychology of Material Possessions.* New York: St. Martin's Press.

Dominguez, Virginia. 1990. "Representing Value and the Value of Representation: A Different Look at Money." *Cultural Anthropology* 5 (1): 16–44.

Douglas, Mary, and Baron Isherwood. 1979. *The World of Goods.* New York: Basic Books.

Dowmunt, Tony. 1993. *Channels of Resistance: Global Television and Local Empowerment.* London: BFI Publishing.

Earp, Fábio Sá. 1993. "Modernização, Conflito e Inflação: Notas sobre o Caso Brasileiro." In *Na Corda Bamba: Doze Estudos sobre a Cultura da Inflação,* ed. J. R. Vieira, L. Neves de Holanda Barbosa, L. C. Delorme Prado, M. A. P. Leopoldi, and M. C. D'Araujo, pp. 95–112. Rio de Janeiro: Relume Dumará.

Eder, Klaus. 1993. *The New Politics of Class: Social Movements and Cultural Dynamics in Advanced Societies.* London: Sage Publications.

Ehrenreich, Barbara. 1989. *Fear of Falling: The Inner Life of the Middle Class.* New York: Harper.

Eisenberg, Peter L. 1974. *The Sugar Industry in Pernambuco, 1840–1910: Modernization without Change.* Berkeley: University of California Press.

Elias, Norbert. 1978. *The Civilizing Process.* Vol. 1 of *The History of Manners.* New York: Urizen Books.

Epstein, David. 1973. *Brasília, Plan and Reality: A Study of Planned and Spontaneous Urban Development.* Berkeley: University of California Press.

Ewen, Stuart, and Elizabeth Ewen. 1982. *Channels of Desire: Mass Images and the Shaping of American Consciousness.* New York: McGraw Hill.

Fairclough, Norman. 1998. "Political Discourse in the Media: An Analytical Framework." In *Approaches to Media Discourse,* ed. A. Bell and P. Garrett, pp. 142–162. Oxford: Blackwell.

Faria, Vilmar E. 1983. "Desenvolvimento, Urbanização e Mudanças na Estrutura do Emprego: A Experiência Brasileira nos Ultimos Trinta Anos." In *Sociedade e Política no Brasil pós-64,* ed. B. Sorj and M. H. Tavares de Almeida, pp. 35–70. São Paulo: Brasiliense.

———. 1991. "Cinqüenta Anos de Urbanização no Brasil." *Novos Estudos do CEBRAP* 29:98–119.

Fausto Neto, Antônio. 1994. "Vozes do Impeachment." In *Mídia, Eleições e Democracia,* ed. H. Matos, pp. 159–190. São Paulo: Scritta.

Featherstone, Mike. 1991. *Consumer Culture and Postmodernism.* London: Sage Publications.

———. 1993. "Global and Local Cultures." In *Mapping the Futures: Local Cultures, Global Change,* ed. J. Bird, B. Curtis, T. Putnam, G. Robertson, and L. Tickner, pp. 169–187. New York: Routledge.

Fernandes, Rubem César. 1993. "Inflação e Desconfiança." In *Na Corda Bamba: Doze Estudos sobre a Cultura da Inflação,* ed. J. R. Vieira, L. Neves de Holanda Barbosa, L. C. Delorme Prado, M. A. P. Leopoldi, and M. C. D'Araujo, pp. 43–48. Rio de Janeiro: Relume Dumará.

Fine, Ben. 1995. "From Political Economy to Consumption." In *Acknowledging Consumption,* pp. 127–163. London: Routledge.

Fiske, John, and John Hartley. 1978. *Reading Television.* London: Methuen.

Fiuza, Sílvia. 1990. "Identidade Jovem em Camadas Médias Urbanas." *Comunicação* 18 (Universidade Federal do Rio de Janeiro): 47–82.

Fjellman, Stephen M. 1992. *Vinyl Leaves: Walt Disney World and America.* Boulder: Westview.

Flynn, Peter. 1993. "Collor, Corruption, and Crisis: Time for Reflection." *Journal of Latin American Studies* 25:351–371.

Font, Mauricio. 1990. *Coffee, Contention, and Change in the Making of Modern Brazil.* New York: Blackwell.

Fontaine, Pierre-Michel. 1985. *Race, Class, and Power in Brazil.* Los Angeles: Regents of the University of California, Center for Afro-American Studies.

Fowler, Roger. 1994. "Hysterical Style in the Press." In *Media Texts: Authors and Readers,* ed. D. Graddol and O. Boyd-Barrett, pp. 90–99. Clevedon, UK: Open University.

Frieden, Jeffry A. 1986. "The Brazilian Borrowing Experience: From Miracle to Debacle and Back." *Latin American Research Review* 22 (1): 95–131.

Friedman, Jonathon. 1989. "The Consumption of Modernity." *Culture and History* 4:117–130.

———. 1991. "Consuming Desires: Strategies of Selfhood and Appropriation." *Cultural Anthropology* 6 (2): 154–163.

———, ed. 1994. *Consumption and Identity.* Chur, Switzerland: Harwood Academic Publishers.

Frow, John. 1987. "Accounting for Tastes: Some Problems in Bourdieu's Sociology of Culture." *Cultural Studies* 1 (1): 59–73.

———. 1993. "Knowledge and Class." *Cultural Studies* 7 (2): 240–281.

Frykman, Jonas, and Orvar Lofgren. 1987. *Culture Builders: A Historical Anthropology of Middle Class Life.* New Brunswick: Rutgers University Press.

Furtado, Celso. 1963. *The Economic Growth of Brazil.* Berkeley: University of California Press.

———. 1977. "The Early Brazilian Sugar Economy." In *Haciendas and Plantations in Latin American History,* ed. R. Keith, pp. 63–84. New York: Holmes and Meier.

Garcia, Márcio. 1995. "Avoiding Some Costs of Inflation and Crawling toward Hyperinflation: The Case of the Brazilian Domestic Currency Substitute." Paper delivered at the Latin American Studies Association XIX International Congress, Washington, DC, Sept. 28–30.

García Canclini, Néstor. 1995a. *Consumidores y Ciudadanos: Conflictos Multiculturales de la Globalización.* Mexico: Grijalbo.

———. 1995b. *Hybrid Cultures: Strategies for Entering and Leaving Modernity.* Minneapolis: University of Minnesota Press.

Garnham, Nicholas. 1993a. "Bourdieu, the Cultural Arbitrary, and Television." In *Bourdieu: Critical Perspectives,* ed. C. Calhoun, E. LiPuma, and M. Postone, pp. 178–192. Chicago: University of Chicago Press.

———. 1993b. "The Mass Media, Cultural Identity, and the Public Sphere in the Modern World." *Public Culture* 5 (2): 251–265.

Gerbner, George. 1985. "Mass Media Discourse: Message System Analysis as a Component of Cultural Indicators." In *Discourse and Communication,* ed. T. A. Van Dijk, pp. 13–25. Berlin: de Gruyter.

Gerth, H. H., and C. Wright Mills. 1958. *From Max Weber: Essays in Sociology.* New York: Oxford University Press.

Glasser, Theodore L., and James S. Ettema. 1991. "Investigative Journalism and the Moral Order." In *Critical Perspectives on Media and Society,* ed. R. K. Avery and D. Eason, pp. 203–226. New York: Guilford Press.

Goldstein, Donna. 1999. " 'Interracial' Sex and Racial Democracy in Brazil: Twin Concepts?" *American Anthropologist* 101 (3): 563–578.

Grossberg, Lawrence. 1991. "Strategies of Marxist Cultural Interpretation." In *Critical Perspectives on Media and Society,* ed. R. K. Avery and D. Eason, pp. 126–162. New York: Guilford Press.

Grun, Roberto. 1992. "Sindicalismo e Anti-Sindicalismo e a Gênese das Novas Classes Médias Brasileiras." *DADOS* 35 (3): 435–471.

Guillermoprieto, Alma. 1994. *The Heart That Bleeds.* New York: Random House.

Guimarães, A. S. A. 1987. "Estrutura e Formação das Classes Sociais na Bahia." *Novos Estudos do CEBRAP* 19:57–69.

———. 1997. "Racismo e Restrição de Direitos Individuais: A Discriminação Racial Publicizada." *Estudos Afro-Asiáticos* 31:51–78.

Hall, Stuart. 1979. "Culture, the Media, and the Ideological Effect." In *Mass Communication in Society,* ed. J. Curran, M. Gurevitch, and J. Woollacott, pp. 315–348. Beverly Hills: Sage Publications.

———. 1980. "Encoding/Decoding." In *Culture, Media, Language: Working Papers in Cultural Studies, 1972–1979,* ed. S. Hall, D. Hobson, A. Lowe, and P. Willis, pp. 128–138. London: Hutchinson.

———. 1986. "The Relevance of Gramsci for the Study of Race and Ethnicity." *Journal of Communication Inquiries* 10:5–27.

———. 1991. "Signification, Representation, Ideology: Althusser and the Post-Structuralist Debate." In *Critical Perspectives on Media and Society,* ed. R. K. Avery and D. Eason, pp. 88–113. New York: Guilford Press.

Halle, David. 1993. *Inside Culture: Art and Class in the American Home.* Chicago: University of Chicago Press.

Hamburger, Esther Império. 1999. "Politics and Intimacy in Brazilian Telenovelas." Ph.D. diss., University of Chicago. Forthcoming: Universidade Federal do Rio de Janeiro.

Hannerz, Ulf. 1987. "The World in Creolization." *Africa* 57 (4): 546–559.

Hanchard, Michael, ed. 1999. *Racial Politics in Contemporary Brazil.* Durham: Duke University Press.

Hansen, Elizabeth R. 1976. "Santana: Middle Class Families in São Paulo, Brazil." Ph.D. diss., City University of New York.

Haraway, Donna. 1988. "Situated Knowledges: The Science Question in Feminism and the Privilege of Partial Perspective." *Feminist Studies* 14 (3): 575–599.

Hart, Keith. 1992. "Market and State after the Cold War: The Informal Economy Reconsidered." In *Contesting Markets: Analysis of Ideology, Discourse, and Practice,* ed. R. Dilley, pp. 214–230. Edinburgh: Edinburgh University Press.

Hartley, J., and M. Montgomery. 1985. "Representations and Relations: Ideology and Power in Press and TV News." In *Discourse and Communication,* ed. T. A. Van Dijk, pp. 233–269. Berlin: de Gruyter.

Hasenbalg, Carlos. 1979. *Discriminação e Desigualdades Raciais no Brasil.* Rio de Janeiro: Graal.

———. 1985. "Race and Socioeconomic Inequalities in Brazil." In *Race, Class, and Power in Brazil,* ed. P.-M. Fontaine, pp. 25–41. Los Angeles: Regents of the University of California, Center for Afro-American Studies.

Hasenbalg, Carlos, Nelson do Valle Silva, and Luiz Claudio Barcelos. 1989. "Notas sobre Miscegenação no Brasil." *Estudos Afro-Asiáticos* 16:188–197.

Haynes, Michaele T. 1998. *Dressing Up Debutantes: Pageantry and Glitz in Texas.* Oxford: Berg.

Hebdige, Dick. 1979. *Subculture: The Meaning of Style.* London: Methuen.

Heilborn, Maria Luiza. 1992. "Dois é Par: Conjugalidade, Gênero e Identidade Sexual em Contexto Igualitário." Ph.D. diss., Universidade Federal do Rio de Janeiro.

Heyman, Josiah. 1994. "The Organizational Logic of Capitalist Consumption on the Mexico–United States Border." *Research in Economic Anthropology* 15:175–238.

———. 1997. "Imports and Standards of Justice on the Mexico–United States Border." In *The Allure of the Foreign: Imported Goods in Post-Colonial Latin America,* ed. B. Orlove, pp. 151–184. Ann Arbor: University of Michigan Press.

Hirschman, Albert O. 1982. *Shifting Involvements: Private Interest and Public Action.* Princeton: Princeton University Press.

Holloway, Thomas. 1980. *Immigrants on the Land: Coffee and Society in São Paulo, 1886–1934.* Chapel Hill, NC: University of North Carolina Press.

Holy, Ladislav. 1992. "Culture, Market Ideology, and Economic Reform in Czechoslovakia." In *Contesting Markets: Analysis of Ideology, Discourse, and Practice,* ed. R. Dilley, pp. 231–243. Edinburgh: Edinburgh University Press.

Howes, David, ed. 1996. *Cross-Cultural Consumption: Global Markets, Local Realities.* London: Routledge.

Hutchinson, Isabella, William Cunningham, and Russell Moore. 1976. *Social Class and Consumer Behavior in São Paulo, Brazil.* Austin: University of Texas Press.

Instituto Brasileiro de Geografia e Estatística. 1994. *Anuário Estatístico do Brasil 1993.* Rio de Janeiro: IBGE.

Jackson, Kenneth T. 1985. *Crabgrass Frontier: The Suburbanization of the United States.* New York: Oxford University Press.

Jackson, Peter. 1993. "A Cultural Politics of Consumption." In *Mapping the Futures: Local Cultures, Global Change,* ed. J. Bird, B. Curtis, T. Putnam, G. Robertson, and L. Tickner, pp. 207–228. London: Routledge.

Jackson, Peter, and Nigel Thrift. 1995. "Geographies of Consumption." In *Acknowledging Consumption,* pp. 128–143. London: Routledge.

Jensen, Klaus B. 1992. "The Politics of Polysemy: Television News, Everyday Consciousness, and Political Action." In *Culture and Power: A Media, Culture, and Society Reader,* ed. P. Scannell, P. Schlesinger, and C. Sparks, pp. 218–238. London: Sage Publications.

Kaplan, Caren. 1996. *Questions of Travel: Postmodern Discourses of Displacement.* Durham: Duke University Press.

Klugman, Karen, Jane Kuenz, Sheldon Waldrep, and Susan Willis, eds. 1995. *Inside the Mouse: Work and Play at Disney World.* Durham: Duke University Press.

Kopytoff, Igor. 1986. "The Cultural Biography of Things: Commoditization as Process." In *The Social Life of Things: Commodities in Social Perspective,* ed. A. Appadurai, pp. 64–94. Cambridge: Cambridge University Press.

Kottak, Conrad Phillip. 1983. *Assault on Paradise.* New York: Random House.

———. 1990. *Prime-Time Society: An Anthropological Analysis of Television and Culture.* Belmont, CA: Wadsworth.

Kovarick, Lúcio. 1985. "The Pathways to Encounter: Reflections on the Social Struggle in São Paulo." In *New Social Movements and the State in Latin America,* ed. D. Slater, pp. 73–94. Amsterdam: CEDLA.

Kress, Gunther. 1986. "Language in the Media: The Construction of Domains of Public and Private." *Media, Culture, and Society* 8 (4): 315–419.

Kuenz, Jane. 1995. "It's a Small World After All." In *Inside the Mouse: Work and Play at Disney World,* ed. K. Klugman, J. Kuenz, S. Waldrep, and S. Willis, pp. 54–78. Durham: Duke University Press.

Lakha, Salim. 1999. "The State, Globalisation, and Indian Middle-Class Identity." In *Culture and Privilege in Capitalist Asia,* ed. M. Pinches, pp. 251–274. London: Routledge.

Lamont, Michèle, and Marcel Fournier. 1992. *Cultivating Differences: Symbolic Boundaries and the Making of Inequality.* Chicago: University of Chicago Press.

Langman, Lauren. 1992. "Neon Cages: Shopping for Subjectivity." In *Lifestyle Shopping: The Subject of Consumption,* ed. R. Shields, pp. 40–82. London: Routledge.

Larson, Brooke, and Rosário León. 1995. "Markets, Power, and the Politics of Exchange in Tapacarí, c. 1790 and 1980." In *Ethnicity, Markets, and Migration in the Andes,* ed. B. Larson and O. Harris, pp. 224–255. Durham: Duke University Press.

Lassalle, Yvonne. 1997. "The Limits of Memory: The Cultural Politics and Political Cultures of Three Generations of Andalucians." Ph.D. diss., City University of New York.

Lave, Jean. 1988. *Cognition in Practice: Mind, Mathematics, and Culture in Everyday Life.* Cambridge: Cambridge University Press.

Leal, Ondina F. 1986. *A Leitura Social da Novela das Oito.* Petrópolis: Vozes.

——. 1990. "Popular Taste and Erudite Repertoire: The Place and Space of Television in Brazil." *Cultural Studies* 1:19–29.

Lee, Martyn. 1993. *Consumer Culture Reborn: The Cultural Politics of Consumption.* London: Routledge.

Leeds, Anthony. 1964. "Brazilian Careers and Social Structure: A Case History and Model." *American Anthropology* 66:1321–1347.

Leff, Nathaniel H. 1972. "Economic Development and Regional Inequality: Origins of the Brazilian Case." *Quarterly Journal of Economics* 86: 243–262.

Lesser, Jeffrey. 1995. *Welcoming the Undesirables: Brazil and the Jewish Question.* Berkeley: University of California Press.

——. 1999. *Negotiating National Identity: Immigrants, Minorities, and the Struggle for Ethnicity in Brazil.* Durham: Duke University Press.

Levine, Robert M. 1978. *Pernambuco in the Brazilian Federation.* Stanford: Stanford University Press.

Lévi-Strauss, Claude. 1969. *Elementary Structures of Kinship.* Rev. ed. Boston: Beacon.

Lewin, Linda. 1979. "Some Historical Implications of Kinship Organization for Family-Based Politics in the Brazilian Northeast." *Comparative Studies in Society and History* 21:262–292.

Lima, Márcia. 1995. "Trajetória Educacional e Realização Socio-Econômica das Mulheres Negras." *Estudos Feministas* 3 (2): 489–505.

Lima, Venicio A. de. 1993. "Brazilian Television in the 1989 Election." In *Television, Politics, and the Transition to Democracy in Latin America,* ed. T. Skidmore, pp. 97–117. Baltimore: Johns Hopkins University Press.

Lins da Silva, Carlos Eduardo. 1985. *Muito Além do Jardim Botânico: Um Estudo sobre a Audiência do Jornal Nacional da Globo entre Trabalhadores.* São Paulo: Summus.

Loaeza, Guadalupe. 1992. *Compro, Luego Existo.* Mexico: Editora Patria.

Lockhart, James, and Stuart B. Schwartz. 1983. *Early Latin America*. Cambridge: Cambridge University Press.

Lofgren, Orvar. 1994. "Consuming Interests." In *Consumption and Identity*, ed. J. Friedman, pp. 47–70. Harwood Academic Publishers.

Lomnitz, Larissa, and Ana Melnick. 1991. *Chile's Middle Class: A Struggle for Survival in the Face of Neoliberalism*. Boulder: Lynne Rienner.

Lopes, Marciano. 1989. *Divinas Damas*. Fortaleza: Tipoprogresso.

Love, Joseph. 1980. *São Paulo in the Brazilian Federation*. Stanford: Stanford University Press.

Luckman, Thomas, and Peter Berger. 1964. "Social Mobility and Personal Identity." *Archives Européennes Sociologiques* 5:331–343.

Lunt, Peter, and Sonia Livingstone. 1992. *Mass Consumption and Personal Identity*. Buckingham, UK: Open University Press.

Mafra, Clara. 1993. "Autoridade e Preconceito: Estudos de Caso sobre Grupos Ocupacionais das Classes Médias em Campinas." Master's thesis, Universidade Estadual de Campinas.

Markoff, John, and Silvio R. Duncan Baretta. 1990. "Economic Crisis and Regime Change in Brazil: The 1960s and the 1980s." *Comparative Politics* 22:421–444.

Marsden, T., and N. Wrigley. 1995. "Regulation, Retailing, and Consumption." *Environment and Planning* 27:1899–1912.

Martinez-Alier, Verena. 1974. *Marriage, Class, and Colour in Nineteenth-Century Cuba*. Cambridge: Cambridge University Press.

Matos, Heloíza, ed. 1994. *Mídia, Eleições e Democracia*. São Paulo: Scritta.

Mattelart, Armand, and Michèle Mattelart. 1992. *Rethinking Media Theory*. Minneapolis: University of Minnesota Press.

Mauss, Marcel. 1967. *The Gift*. 1925. Reprint, New York: Norton.

McCracken, Grant. 1990. *Culture and Consumption: New Approaches to the Symbolic Character of Consumer Goods and Activities*. Bloomington: Indiana University Press.

McDonough, Peter. 1981. *Power and Ideology in Brazil*. Princeton: Princeton University Press.

McKendrick, Neil, John Brewer, and J. H. Plumb. 1982. *The Birth of a Consumer Society: The Commercialization of Eighteenth-Century England*. Bloomington: Indiana University Press.

Meade, Teresa A. 1997. *"Civilizing" Rio: Reform and Resistance in a Brazilian City, 1889–1930*. University Park: Pennsylvania State University.

Miceli, Sérgio. 1972. *A Noite da Madrinha*. São Paulo: Perspectiva.

Mies, Maria. 1982. *The Lace Makers of Narsapur: Indian Housewives Produce for the World Market.* London: Zed Press.

Miles, Alice Catherine. 1992. *Every Girl's Duty: The Diary of a Victorian Debutante.* London: Andre Deutsch.

Miller, Daniel. 1987. *Material Culture and Consumption.* Oxford: Blackwell.

———. 1994. *Modernity: An Ethnographic Approach.* London: Routledge.

———, ed. 1995a. *Acknowledging Consumption.* London: Routledge.

———. 1995b. "Consumption and Commodities." *Annual Review of Anthropology* 24:141–161.

———. 1997. *Capitalism: An Ethnographic Approach.* Washington, DC: Berg.

———. 1998. *A Theory of Shopping.* Ithaca: Cornell University Press.

Mills, C. Wright. 1969. *White Collar.* 1951. Reprint, New York: Oxford University Press.

Moog, C. Vianna. 1954. *Bandeirantes e Pioneiros: Paralelo entre Duas Culturas.* Rio de Janeiro: Civilização Brasileira.

Moore, Alexander. 1980. "Walt Disney World: Bounded Ritual Space and the Playful Pilgrimage Center." *Anthropological Quarterly* 53 (4): 207–218.

Morley, David. 1980. *The "Nationwide" Audience: Structure and Decoding.* London: British Film Institute Television Monograph.

———. 1986. *Family Television: Cultural Power and Domestic Leisure.* London: Comedia.

———. 1991. "Where the Global Meets the Local: Notes from the Sitting Room." *Screen* 32 (1): 1–16.

Morris, Meaghan. 1988. "Things to Do with Shopping Centres." In *Grafts: Feminist Cultural Criticism,* ed. Susan Sheridan, pp. 193–225. New York: Verso.

Mukerji, Chandra. 1983. *From Graven Images: Patterns of Modern Materialism.* New York: Columbia University Press.

Mukerji, Chandra, and Michael Schudson, eds. 1991. *Rethinking Popular Culture: Contemporary Perspectives in Cultural Studies.* Berkeley: University of California Press.

Nader, Laura. 1969. " 'Up the Anthropologist'—Perspectives Gained from Studying Up." In *Reinventing Anthropology,* ed. D. Hymes, pp. 284–311. New York: Random House.

Nash, June. 1994. "Global Integration and Subsistence Insecurity." *American Anthropologist* 96 (1): 6–30.

Nazzari, Muriel. 1991. *Disappearance of the Dowry: Women, Families, and Social Change in São Paulo, Brazil, 1600–1900.* Stanford: Stanford University Press.

Needell, Jeffrey. 1987. *A Tropical "Belle Epoque": Elite Culture and Society in Turn-of-the-Century Rio de Janeiro.* Cambridge: Cambridge University Press.

——. 1988. "A Ascensão do Fetishismo Consumista." *Revista Brasileira de Ciências Sociais* 8 (3): 39–58.

Newcomb, Horace. 1991. "On the Dialogic Aspects of Mass Communication." In *Critical Perspectives on Media and Society,* ed. R. K. Avery and D. Eason, pp. 69–87. New York: Guilford Press.

Newman, Katherine S. 1986. "Symbolic Dialects and Generations of Women: Variation in the Meaning of Post-Divorce Downward Mobility." *American Ethnologist* 13 (2): 230–252.

——. 1988. *Falling from Grace: The Experience of Downward Mobility in the American Middle Class.* New York: Random House.

——. 1993. *Declining Fortunes: The Withering of the American Dream.* New York: Basic Books.

Nizza da Silva, Beatriz. 1984. *Sistema de Casamento no Brasil Colonial.* São Paulo: Queiroz.

Norvell, John. 1997. "Sex and Color in Copacabana." Ph.D. diss., Cornell University.

O'Connor, Flannery. 1949. *Wise Blood.* New York: Farrar, Straus, and Giroux.

Oliveira, Francisco de. 1988. "Medusa ou as Classes Médias e a Consolidação Democrática." In *A Democracia no Brasil: Dilemas e Perspectivas,* ed. F. W. Reis and G. O'Donnell, pp. 210–231. São Paulo: Vértice.

Ortiz, Renato. 1991. *A Moderna Tradição Brasileira.* São Paulo: Brasiliense.

Ortner, Sherry. 1991. "Reading America: Preliminary Notes on Class and Culture." In *Recapturing Anthropology: Working in the Present,* ed. Richard Fox, pp. 163–187. Santa Fe: School of American Research Press.

Osterberg, Dag. 1988. "Two Notes on Consumption." In *The Sociology of Consumption,* ed. Per Otnes, pp. 310–321. Oslo: Solum Forlag.

Owensby, Brian. 1999. *Intimate Ironies: Modernity and the Making of Middle-Class Lives in Brazil.* Stanford: Stanford University Press.

Pastoré, José. 1979. *Desigualdade e Mobilidade Social no Brasil.* São Paulo: Queiroz.

——. 1986. "Desigualdade e Mobilidade Social: Dez Anos Depois." In *A Transição Incompleta: Brasil desde 1945,* vol. 20, ed. Edmar Bacha and H. Klein, pp. 31–60. Rio de Janeiro: Paz e Terra.

Patillo-McCoy, Mary. 1999. *Black Picket Fences: Privilege and Peril among the Black Middle Class.* Chicago: University of Chicago Press.

Perlmutter, Amos. 1970. "The Myth of the Myth of the New Middle Class." *Critical Studies in Society and History* 12 (1): 14–26.

Perrone, Charles. 1989. *Masters of Contemporary Brazilian Song: MPB, 1965–1985.* Austin: University of Texas Press.

Philibert, Jean-Marc. 1989. "Consuming Culture: A Study of Simple Commodity Consumption." In *The Social Economy of Consumption,* ed. H. J. Rutz and B. Orlove, pp. 59–84. Lanham: University Press of America.

Pierson, Donald. 1972. *O Homem no Vale do São Francisco.* Vol. 3. Rio de Janeiro: Suvale.

Pierucci, Antônio Flávio. 1987. "As Bases da Nova Direita." *Novos Estudos do CEBRAP* 10:26–45.

Pierucci, Antônio Flávio, and Marcelo Coutinho de Lima. 1991. "A Direita que Flutua." *Novos Estudos do CEBRAP* 29:10–27.

——. 1993. "São Paulo 92, A Vitória da Direita." *Novos Estudos do CEBRAP* 35:94–99.

Pinches, Michael. 1996. "The Philippines' New Rich: Capitalist Transformation amidst Economic Gloom." In *The New Rich in Asia: Mobile Phones, McDonalds, and Middle Class Revolution,* ed. R. Robison and D. Goodman, pp. 105–133. London: Routledge.

——. 1999. "Entrepreneurship, Consumption, Ethnicity, and National Identity in the Making of the Philippines' New Rich." In *Culture and Privilege in Capitalist Asia,* pp. 275–301. London: Routledge.

Pinheiro, Paulo Sérgio de M. S. 1975. "Classes Médias Urbanas: Formação, Natureza, Intervenção na Vida Política." *Revista Mexicana de Sociología* 37 (2): 445–474.

Pinho, Wanderley. 1970. *Salões e Damas do Segundo Reinado.* São Paulo: Livraria Martins Editora.

Pintaudi, Maria Silvana, e Heitor Frúgoli, Jr. 1992. *Shopping Centers: Espaço, Cultura e Modernidade nas Cidades Brasileiras.* São Paulo: UNESP.

Plank, David N. 1996. *The Means of Our Salvation: Public Education in Brazil, 1930–1995.* Boulder: Westview Press.

Polanyi, Karl. 1944. *The Great Transformation.* New York: Farrar & Rinehart.

Portes, Alejandro. 1985. "Latin American Class Structure: Their Composition and Change during the Last Decades." *Latin American Research Review* 20 (3): 7–39.

Quadros, Waldir José de. 1991. "O "Milagre Brasileiro" e a Expansão da Nova Classe Média." Ph.D. diss., Universidade Estadual de Campinas.

Raboy, Marc, and Bernard Dagenais, eds. 1992. *Media, Crisis, and Democracy:*

Mass Communication and the Disruption of Social Order. Newbury Park, CA: Sage Publications.

Rapp, Rayna. 1978. "Family and Class in Contemporary America: Notes toward an Understanding of Ideology." *Science and Society* 42:278–301.

Reichmann, Rebecca. 1999. *Race in Contemporary Brazil: From Indifference to Inequality.* University Park, PA: Pennsylvania State University Press.

Rezende, Claudia Barcellos. 1990. "Diversidade e Identidade: Discutindo Jovens de Camadas Médias Urbanas." *Communicação* (Universidade Federal do Rio de Janeiro) 18:5–25.

Rodrigues, Arakcy M. 1989. "Práticas e Representações de Pequenos Funcionários Públicos de São Paulo." *Revista Brasileira de Ciências Sociais* 11 (4): 85–103.

Rolnik, Raquel, L. Kowarik, and N. Somekh, eds. 1991. *São Paulo: Crise e Mudança.* São Paulo: Brasiliense.

Romanelli, Geraldo. 1986. "Famílias de Camadas Médias: A Trajetória da Modernidade." Ph.D. diss., Universidade de São Paulo.

Rosemberg, Fúlvia, R. Pinto, and E. Negrão. 1982. *A Educação da Mulher no Brasil.* São Paulo: Global.

Rouse, Roger. 1995. "Thinking through Transnationalism: Notes on the Cultural Politics of Class Relations in the Contemporary United States." *Public Culture* 7 (2): 353–402.

Rubim, Antônio Albino Canelas. 1993. "Política em Tempos de 'Media': Impressões de Crises." In *Comunicação e Cultura Contemporâneas,* ed. C. A. Messeder Pereira and A. Fausto Neto, pp. 149–168. Rio de Janeiro: Notrya Editora.

Rutz, H. J., and B. Orlove, eds. 1989. *The Social Economy of Consumption.* Lanham, MD: University Press of America.

Sachs, Jeffrey, and Alvaro Zini Jr. 1995. "Brazilian Inflation and the 'Plano Real.' " Paper delivered at the Latin American Studies Association XIX International Congress, Washington, DC, Sept. 28–30.

Saes, Décio. 1985. *Classes Médias e Sistema Política no Brasil.* São Paulo: Queiroz.

Saffioti, Heleith. 1978. *Women in Class Society.* New York: Monthly Review Press.

Saito, Hiroshi. 1980. *A Presença Japonesa no Brasil.* São Paulo: Universidade de São Paulo.

Salem, Tânia. 1985a. "Família em Camadas Médias: Uma Revisão da Literatura Recente." *Boletim do Museu Nacional* 54:25–39.

——. 1985b. "A Trajetória do Casal Grávido: De Sua Constituição à

Revisão de Seu Projeto." In *Cultura da Psicanálise,* ed. S. Figueira, pp. 36–61. São Paulo: Brasiliense.

Scheper-Hughes, Nancy. 1992. *Death without Weeping: The Violence of Everyday Life in Brazil.* Berkeley: University of California Press.

Schmink, Marianne. 1984. "Household Economic Strategies: Review and Research Agenda." *Latin American Research Review* 19 (3): 87–101.

Schneider, Jane. 1971. "Of Vigilance and Virgins." *Ethnology* 10 (1): 1–24.

———. 1988. "European Expansion and Hand Crafted Cloth: A Critique of Oppositional Use-Value vs. Exchange Value Models." *Journal of Historical Sociology* 1 (4): 431–437.

Scott, James. 1976. *The Moral Economy of the Peasant: Rebellion and Subsistence in Southeast Asia.* New Haven: Yale University Press.

Seaton, Jean. 1981. "The Sociology of the Mass Media." In *Power without Responsibility: The Press and Broadcasting in Britain,* pp. 264–286. London: Routledge.

Selby, Henry A. 1991. "The Oaxacan Urban Household and the Crisis." *Urban Anthropology* 20 (1): 87–98.

Selby, Henry A., A. Murphy, and S. Lorenzen. 1990. *The Mexican Urban Household: Organizing for Self-Defense.* Austin: University of Texas Press.

Sheriff, Robin. 1997. " 'Negro' Is a Nickname That the Whites Give to the Blacks: Discourses on Color, Race, and Racism in Rio de Janeiro." Ph.D. diss., City University of New York.

———. 2000. "Exposing Silence as Cultural Censorship: A Brazilian Case." *American Anthropologist* 102 (1): 114–132.

Shields, Rob, ed. 1992. *Lifestyle Shopping: The Subject of Consumption.* London: Routledge.

Silverstone, Roger, and Eric Hirsch. 1992. *Consuming Technologies: Media and Information in Domestic Spaces.* London: Routledge.

Simmel, Georg. 1978. *The Philosophy of Money.* 2d ed. London: Routledge.

Simões, Solange de Deus. 1992. "Classe Média Profissional no Brasil: Teoria e Organização Política e Sindical." In *Ciências Sociais Hoje,* pp. 160–199. Rio Fundo Editora / ANPOCS.

Singer, Paul. 1988. "Refleções sobre a Inflação, Conflito Distributivo e Democracia." In *A Democracia no Brasil: Dilemas e Perspectivas,* ed. F. W. Reis and G. O'Donnell, pp. 60–84. São Paulo: Vértice.

Skidmore, Thomas. 1993. *Television, Politics, and the Transition to Democracy in Latin America.* Baltimore: Johns Hopkins University Press.

Slater, D. 1997. "Consumer Culture and the Politics of Need." In *Buy This*

Book: Studies in Advertising and Consumption, ed. M. Nava, A. Blake, I. MacRury, and B. Richards, pp. 51–63. London: Routledge.

Smart, Alan. 1993. "Gifts, Bribes, and Guanxi: A Reconsideration of Bourdieu's Social Capital." *Cultural Anthropology* 8 (3): 388–408.

Sola, Lourdes, Christopher Garman, and Moises Marques. 1998. "Central Banking, Democratic Governance, and Political Authority: The Case of Brazil in Comparative Perspective." *Revista de Economia Política* 18 (2): 106–131.

Souza, Julia Filet-Abreu de. 1980. "Paid Domestic Service in Brazil." *Latin American Perspectives* 7 (1): 35–61.

Spitulnik, Debra. 1993. "Anthropology and Mass Media." *Annual Review of Anthropology* 22:293–315.

Stein, Stanley, and Barbara Stein. 1970. *The Colonial Heritage of Latin America.* New York: Oxford University Press.

Stepan, Alfred. 2000. "Brazil's Decentralized Federalism: Bringing Government Closer to People?" *Daedalus* 12 (2): 145–169.

Stolcke, Verena. 1988. *Coffee Planters, Workers, and Wives: Class Conflict and Gender Relations on São Paulo Plantations, 1850–1980.* New York: St. Martin's Press.

Straubhaar, Joseph, Organ Olsen, and Maria Cavaliari Nunes. 1993. "The Brazilian Case: Influencing the Voter." In *Television, Politics, and the Transition to Democracy in Latin America,* ed. T. Skidmore, pp. 118–136. Baltimore: Johns Hopkins University Press.

Tannenbaum, Frank. 1960. *Ten Keys to Latin America.* New York: Vintage.

Thomas, Nicholas. 1991. *Entangled Objects: Exchange, Material Culture, and Colonialism in the Pacific.* Cambridge: Harvard University Press.

Thompson, E. P. 1971. "The Moral Economy of the English Crowd in the Nineteenth Century." *Past and Present* 59 (1): 76–136.

———. 1976. "The Grid of Inheritance." In *Family and Inheritance: Rural Society in Western Europe, 1200–1800,* ed. J. Goody, J. Thirsk, E. P. Thompson, pp. 328–361. Cambridge: Cambridge University Press.

———. 1993. *Customs in Common: Studies in Traditional Popular Culture.* New York: New Press.

Thompson, John. 1984. *Studies in the Theory of Ideology.* Berkeley: University of California Press.

Tomlinson, Alan. 1990. Introduction to *Consumption, Identity, and Style: Marketing, Meanings, and the Packaging of Pleasure,* pp. 13–33. London: Routledge.

Tomlinson, John. 1991. *Cultural Imperialism, A Critical Introduction*. Baltimore: Johns Hopkins University Press.

Topik, Steven. 1978. "Middle-Class Brazilian Nationalism, 1889–1930: From Radicalism to Reaction." *Social Science Quarterly* 59 (1): 93–104.

Trigo, Maria Helena Bueno. 1993. "Educação e Reprodução Social no Grupo Cafeicultor Paulista." In *Família, Mulher, Sexualidade e Igreja na História do Brasil,* ed. Maria Luiza Marcílio, pp. 197–203. São Paulo: Loyola.

Turner, Frederick Jackson. 1986. *The Frontier in American History*. Tucson: University of Arizona Press.

Urry, John. 1988. "Cultural Change and Contemporary Holiday-Making." *Theory, Culture, and Society* 5:35–55.

——. 1990. "The Consumption of Tourism." *Sociology* 24 (1): 22–35.

van Gennep, Arnold. 1960. *The Rites of Passage*. Chicago: University of Chicago Press.

Vanneman, Reeve, and Lynn Weber Cannon. 1987. *The American Perception of Class*. Philadelphia: Temple University Press.

Veblen, Thorstein. 1953. *The Theory of the Leisure Class*. 1899. Reprint, New York: New American Library Mentor Edition.

Velho, Gilberto. 1980. *A Utopia Urbana*. Rio de Janeiro: Zahar.

——. 1981. *Individualismo e Cultura: Notas para uma Antropologia da Sociedade Contemporânea*. Rio de Janeiro: Zahar.

Velho, Otávio. 1979. "The State and the Frontier." In *Structure of Brazilian Development,* ed. N. Aguiar, pp. 17–35. New Brunswick, NJ: Transaction Books.

Vieira, José Ribas, L. Neves de Holanda Barbosa, L. C. Delorme Prado, M. A. P. Leopoldi, and M. C. D'Araujo, eds. 1993. *Na Corda Bamba: Doze Estudos sobre a Cultura da Inflação*. Rio de Janeiro: Relume Dumará.

Viotti da Costa, Emília. 1966. *Da Senzala à Colônia*. São Paulo: Difusão Européia do Livro.

Wallerstein, Immanuel. 1991. "The Bourgeois(ie) as Concept and Reality." In *Race, Nation, Class: Ambiguous Identities,* ed. E. Balibar and I. Wallerstein, pp. 135–152. London: Verso.

Warde, Alan. 1992. "Notes on the Relationship between Production and Consumption." In *Consumption and Class,* ed. R. Burrows and C. Marsh, pp. 15–31. New York: St. Martin's Press.

Weffort, Francisco C. 1965. "Política de Massas." In *Política e Revolução no Brasil,* ed. O. Ianni, P. Singer, G. Cohn, and F. Weffort, pp. 161–198. Rio de Janeiro: Civilização Brasileira.

Weinstein, Barbara. 1982. "Brazilian Regionalism." *Latin American Research Review* 17 (2): 262–276.

———. 1996. *For Social Peace in Brazil: Industrialists and the Remaking of the Working Class in São Paulo, 1920–1964.* Durham: Duke University Press.

Wells, John. 1977. "The Diffusion of Durables in Brazil and Its Implications for Recent Controversies Concerning Brazilian Development." *Cambridge Journal of Economics* 1:259–279.

Wharton, Edith. 1913. *The Custom of the Country.* New York: Charles Scribner's Sons.

Wilk, Richard. 1989. "Houses as Consumer Goods: Social Processes and Allocation Decisions." In *The Social Economy of Consumption,* ed. H. J. Rutz and B. Orlove, pp. 297–322. Lanham, MD: University Press of America.

———. 1994. "Consumer Goods as Dialogue about Development: Colonial Time and Television Time in Belize." In *Consumption and Identity,* ed. J. Friedman, pp. 97–118. Harwood Academic Publishers.

———. 1996. *Economies and Cultures: Foundations of Economic Anthropology.* Boulder: Westview Press.

Williams, Brackette. 1989. "A Class Act: Anthropology and the Race to Nation across Ethnic Terrain." *Annual Review of Anthropology* 18:401–444.

Williams, Rosalind. 1982. *Dream Worlds: Mass Consumption in Late Nineteenth-Century France.* Berkeley: University of California Press.

Willis, Susan. 1995. "The Family Vacation." In *Inside the Mouse: Work and Play at Disney World,* ed. K. Klugman, J. Kuenz, S. Waldrep, and S. Willis, pp. 34–53. Durham: Duke University Press.

Winddance-Twine, Frances. 1998. *Racism in a Racial Democracy: The Maintenance of White Supremacy in Brazil.* New Brunswick: Rutgers University Press.

Winter, Mary. 1991. "Interhousehold Exchange of Goods and Services in the City of Oaxaca." *Urban Anthropology* 20 (1): 67–84.

Wood, Charles H., and José Alberto Magno de Carvalho. 1988. *The Demography of Inequality in Brazil.* New York: Cambridge University Press.

Woollacott, Janet. 1982. "Messages and Meanings." In *Culture, Society, and the Media,* ed. M. Gurevitch, T. Bennett, and J. Curran, pp. 91–111. London: Methuen.

Worsley, Peter. 1981. "Social Class and Development." In *Social Inequality: Comparative and Developmental Approaches,* ed. G. Berreman, pp. 221–255. New York: Academic.

Wright, Eric Olin, ed. 1989. *The Debate on Classes.* London: Verso.

Wuthnow, Robert. 1987. *Meaning and Moral Order: Explorations in Cultural Analysis.* Berkeley: University of California Press.

Xavier, Ismail. 1998. "From the Religious Moral Sense to the Post-Freudian Common Sense: Images of National History in Brazilian Tele-Fiction." *Studies in Latin American Popular Culture* 17:180–195.

Young, Ken. 1999. "Consumption, Social Differentiation, and Self-Definition of the New Rich in Industrializing Southeast Asia." In *Culture and Privilege in Capitalist Asia,* ed. M. Pinches, pp. 56–85. London: Routledge.

Zukin, Sharon. 1990. "Socio-Spacial Prototypes of a New Organization of Consumption: The Role of Real Cultural Capital." *Sociology* 24 (1): 37–56.

——. 1991. *Landscapes of Power: From Detroit to Disney World.* Berkeley: University of California Press.

PERIODICALS

The Brazilians

Estado de São Paulo

Folha de São Paulo

O Globo

Istoé

Jornal do Brasil

Jornal da Tarde

New York Times

Veja

Veja São Paulo

Vejinha

Vejinha Rio

World Press Review

INDEX

Maureen O'Dougherty is a research fellow
at the Institute on Race and Poverty at the University
of Minnesota.

Library of Congress Cataloging-in-Publication Data

O'Dougherty, Maureen.
Consumption intensified : the politics of middle-class
daily life in Brazil / Maureen O'Dougherty.
p. cm.
Includes bibliographical references and index.
ISBN 0-8223-2879-8 (cloth : alk. paper)
ISBN 0-8223-2894-1 (pbk. : alk. paper)
1. Middle class—Brazil—Economic conditions—20th
century. 2. Middle class—Brazil—Political activity.
3. Consumption (Economics)—Brazil. 4. Brazil—
Economic conditions—1985— I. Title.
HT690.B7 O36 2002
305.5″5′0981—dc21   2001054304